J.B. Graham.

Christ Church

HIS
(British)
£3.50

THE DEFEAT OF JOHN HAWKINS

Portrait, without provenance, of John Hawkins as a young man

THE DEFEAT OF
JOHN HAWKINS

A Biography of His
Third Slaving Voyage

by

RAYNER UNWIN

Ruskin House

GEORGE ALLEN & UNWIN LTD
MUSEUM STREET LONDON

FIRST PUBLISHED IN 1960

PRINTED IN GREAT BRITAIN
in 12 on 13 point Centaur type
BY SIMSON SHAND LTD
LONDON, HERTFORD AND HARLOW

For Merlin

PREFACE

GEOGRAPHY, as E. C. Bentley defines it, is about maps, but Biography is about chaps. To write the biography of a voyage implies an amalgam of both subjects. Although Sir John Hawkins is the central figure in the actions recounted in this book, it is in no way intended to be a full-length portrait of the man. Indeed Hawkins' third slaving voyage by itself can give only a limited insight into the character of the most original, patient and self-effacing seaman of Elizabethan times.

It is intended that, by telling the story of this particular voyage, a double purpose may be served. In an historical perspective we can now appreciate that Hawkins' third expedition to the Slave Coast and the Spanish Main marked a turning-point in naval strategy, and established between England and Spain the future pattern of their political destiny. But equally, by telling as faithfully and circumstantially as the facts permit the story of a single expedition, and by gathering together the many fragmentary accounts into a unified narrative, a picture emerges typical in its generality of all such voyages.

Through the pages of Hakluyt a pageant of hardships cheerfully endured, of hazardous undertakings and painfully-acquired knowledge, dazzles the reader. The diligent researchers of recent years have quarried from the archives of Mexico and Spain, and the records and State Papers of this country, a wealth of additional material. Our background knowledge of Elizabethan voyages is confusing in its abundance, vivid but often unsustained, and all too frequently enmeshed in a web of political motives that almost obscures the lustre and elemental simplicity of a sea-borne enterprise.

Considerations of state-craft cannot be ignored, but Hawkins' expedition of 1567-8 has been documented from so many points of view that an attempt can be made to present it as an integrated human narrative of events. Not only the captain but the cabin boy has left his recollections, and these can be compared against the reports of the Admirals and Inquisitors of Spain. It is surprising how little they differ on points of fact.

But stated facts give the reader very little insight into the conditions, so common or well-established as to deserve no comment, under which Elizabethan sailors lived and worked on shipboard and on shore. Just as Hawkins carried with him the accumulated wisdom of the pilots and navigators of previous voyages, so his chronicler has gleaned from the records of his contemporaries incidents of routine, observation or common experience that usefully supplement the existing narratives. Thus far, and no further, has imagination been allowed to intrude.

The history of ships and voyages is, in essence, the story of men. As Hawkins is the dominating figure in this particular adventure, it is fitting that a debt of gratitude should be acknowledged to the scholarship and well-reasoned judgments of his biographer, Dr J. A. Williamson. Although he has had to wait many centuries for his achievements to be fairly assessed, Hawkins has at last been fortunate. Dr Williamson's books are worthy of the man he memorializes.

One further word about Hawkins is needful for those who are not already familiar, through Dr Williamson's biography, with the total span of his long and well-occupied life. Thirty-five must strike the reader as an incredibly young age at which to be entrusted with the command of a royal fleet. So it was, but by Elizabethan reckoning this was no strange thing. It was an age when men matured early and, as often as not, died early too. Boys destined for a life at sea were experienced sailors in their teens, and Hawkins would almost certainly have had twenty years of seagoing behind him before he took command in the *Jesus* for the first time.

When first we encounter him in this book he was an experienced, but not yet famous, captain. He was well known in Plymouth for the name he bore and for the profitable trading-fleet that he and his brother operated. In London, amongst those concerned with maritime affairs, his previous two excursions to the Indies with cargoes of slaves had singled him out as an imaginative and resourceful merchant-adventurer. But the position he was destined to hold as a national figure stemmed from his ill-chance at San Juan de Ulua, and flowered when, as rear-admiral of the fleet that harried the Great Armada to its doom, he received the accolade at sea.

His work as an administrator, and as an innovator in ship-building, was still confined to his own vessels. The years when he exercised these skills over the royal fleet were yet to come—a period of achievement less spectacular than a command at sea, but to his country probably the most valuable service he gave.

None of these events concern us here, except in placing the third slaving voyage in the context of the life of its commander.

This book came to be written by a strange chance. Some years ago Mr George Steiner drew my attention to an account of David Ingram's travels in Herbert Wendt's interesting book *Ich Suchte Adam*.* In searching for further information I became absorbed in the intricate chain of circumstance that terminated in Ingram's journey. Apart from the orderly account in Dr Williamson's biography, no attempt seems to have been made to correlate the plentiful material and present the voyage as a unified and organic whole. This has been my endeavour.

In general terms, and on particular points I have received valuable assistance from several sources, for which I am most grateful. Dr J. A. Williamson, Dr Alvin Whitley and my brother David Unwin have offered many thoughtful comments and deserve particular thanks; in addition I have solicited information from many sources and invariably received the most helpful response. Professor Michael Lewis, Dr H. Wendt, Mrs M. J. Simpson, the City Librarian of Plymouth, Mr R. W. Sims of the British Museum of Natural History, and the officials of the National Maritime Museum, the University Library, Cambridge, the British Museum and the London Library have all been most generous with their time and knowledge.

The illustrations with which I have been able to furnish the book need a special word of acknowledgment and thanks. The

---

* Since translated under the title *I Looked for Adam* (vide Bibliography).

pictures of the *Jesus* and the *Minion* come, by permission of the Masters and Fellows of Magdalene College, Cambridge, from the Anthony Roll held in the Pepysian Library of that college. For the portrait of Don Martin Enriquez I am indebted (through Miss D. M. K. Ledger) to the Museo Nacional de Historia, Chapultepec Castle, Mexico. The picture of San Juan harbour has kindly been provided by the Director of the Archivo de Indias, Seville. The illustrations of the Inquisition—the penitent and the *auto de fe*—come from P. van Limborch, *Historia Inquisitionis* (Amsterdam, 1692), the engravings of Hawkins and Drake from H. Holland, *Herωologia Anglica* (London, 1620), Michael Lok's map of the North Atlantic from R. Hakluyt, *Divers Voyages touching the discoverie of America* (London, 1582), and the map of Plymouth harbour forms part of Cotton MSS., Aug, I, i, 41: all these are reproduced with permission from the British Museum. Lastly, the alleged picture of Hawkins—the Hope Portrait—is reproduced by permission of the Trustees of the National Maritime Museum, Greenwich. If, as seems possible, this attribution is correct, Hawkins is depicted, as in no other known likeness, at about the age he would have attained when the events in this book took place.

RAYNER UNWIN
Bloomsbury
Summer 1959

CONTENTS

		page
PREFACE		9
1	*The Birth of the Venture*	17
2	*The Sailing*	35
3	*The Mutiny*	53
4	*The Slave Coast*	71
5	*The Walls of Conga*	91
6	*The Middle Passage*	110
7	*The Islands and the Main*	119
8	*The Treasurer*	139
9	*The Desperate Choice*	153
10	*The Second Fleet*	170
11	*The Fight at San Juan*	189
12	*The Homecoming of the Minion*	212
13	*The Overlanders*	231
14	*The Prisoners in Spain*	251
15	*The Prisoners in Mexico*	263
16	*The Improbable Walk*	293
SELECT BIBLIOGRAPHY		313
INDEX		315

ILLUSTRATIONS AND MAPS

Portrait, without provenance, of John Hawkins
as a young man   *frontispiece*

Plymouth in mid-Elizabethan times   *facing page* 32

The *Jesus of Lubeck*   33

Map of the West African coast   *page*   72

Map of Mexico and the Spanish Main   120

The moorings at San Juan de Ulua in 1590   *facing page* 176

Don Martin Enriquez, Viceroy of Mexico   177

John Hawkins and Francis Drake   *page* 208

The *Minion*   *facing page* 224

A Spanish *auto de fe*   225

A penitent wearing the sanbenito   *page* 270

Michael Lok's map of the North Atlantic in 1582   298

CHAPTER 1

The Birth of the Venture

ON the afternoon of September 16, 1567, John Hawkins, alone in his cabin in the *Jesus of Lubeck*, sat down to write to the Queen. It was a difficult letter to compose, for he had much at stake, and the whole of a long-planned undertaking depended upon its reception. Queen Elizabeth, he knew, was intolerant of actions that savoured of trickery, and although she and his friends and backers at Court seemed hitherto to have had confidence in him, he had betrayed to none of them his own devious and conflicting plans. 'My sovereign good Lady and Mistress,' he commenced, 'Your Highness may be advertized that this day the Portingals who should have directed us this pretended enterprise have fled.'

These two Portuguese, Antonio Luis and André Homem—sometimes known as Gaspar Caldeira—were in themselves the whole reason why, as he wrote, his ships and two of the Queen's, laden and armed and fully manned, lay at anchor in the harbour of Plymouth, waiting for a favourable wind. Without these two men, renegades from their own country, one of the largest and most minutely planned expeditions ever to leave England on a distant voyage was baffled and purposeless.

Such was the news that Hawkins composed himself to break; and yet, as leader and commander of this squadron, Hawkins seemed curiously unmoved by the defection of his guides. It was not entirely that he was by nature taciturn, and reserved displays of emotion for occasions when they could produce an acknowledged effect; those who had observed him closely that day—his personal servants and the supercargoes in whose charge the two renegades had been placed and whose duty it had been to report their flight—must have noticed an excitement and tension in their captain's face that could not wholly be attributed to frustration. Some men, later, declared that Hawkins had connived with or even aided the Portuguese to escape, smuggling them aboard a small craft bound for Brittany. Equally unsubstantiated was the report that, on arrival in France, Luis and Homem were arrested and hung, drawn and quartered on account of the many cynical deceptions they had practised. Such were rumours, and Hawkins himself kept secrets well.

Little was known of the character and past deeds of the two renegades. They had been merchants in their own country, but their reasons for leaving it were never satisfactorily established. They had traded, they claimed, up and down the Guinea coast, exercising the privileges of commerce that the papal Bull of Alexander VI had granted exclusively to those under the Portuguese crown.

Good returns rewarded those who undertook the hazards of this trade under a royal licence. Beyond the Cape Verde islands the unprofitable desert shore gave place to an inhabited coast, where malaguette pepper could be bartered for trifles and later sold in European markets where spices were prized and scarce. There was traffic also in slaves to surplant the almost-exterminated West Indian tribes that worked for Spanish masters. Further still along the coast there was gold dust in the rivers, washed down from unknown hills that might, who knew, rival the fabulous riches of Caravaya in Peru; and ivory too was to be had abundantly.

Against such lures were set the perils of the voyage in small ships through treacherous and badly-charted waters, the prevalence of sickness and the treachery of the blacks. There were plenty of men in Portugal prepared to take the risk, and not in Portugal alone. The French, some of whom may have had scruples about slaving, had no such regard for the sanctity of a Portuguese trading monopoly. Their ships ranged the coast of Senegal and Guinea in defiance of all proscription, and, increasingly in recent years, the English had followed suit.

It was the French that Luis and Homem had first approached

after leaving their own country, and the story they told so inflamed their hearers that an expedition was fitted out with the utmost speed and secrecy. In 1566, under the command of Peyrot de Monluc, a group of adventurers sailed for the Guinea coast bearing with them the two renegades. Their objective, it was said, was an unexploited and virtually unlimited source of gold not many leagues inland from the coast, the whereabouts of which the two Portuguese claimed to have discovered. On reaching the island of Madeira, de Monluc, in need of water and fresh provisions, made to enter the port of Funchal. The Portuguese batteries fired on him, and, in order to achieve his ends, he changed his entry into an assault. In this he was successful, capturing both harbour and town; but he himself was killed in the battle, and the victory proved disastrous to the expedition. Leaderless and disorganized, the survivors, having sacked the town, scattered and took their ships home.

Luis and Homem were undiscouraged. They offered their services to Spain and attempted to persuade Philip II to equip a venture, but found him distrustful. Then it was to the English Court that they turned with their secret. The Queen herself offered no state support. She had no love for the Portuguese monopoly of West African trade and was prepared, when occasion offered, to encourage her subjects to infringe it. But the indirect impertinence of privateering was one thing, a direct royal challenge to Portugal was another. Not for a moment would the Queen have considered such a gamble, even had she believed all the circumstantial stories that the two renegades told.

There were at the Court, however, merchants and peers who, individually or as syndicates, would eagerly finance a trading voyage that was ably led and promised good returns. Indeed the Queen herself would at times allow a royal ship to be chartered for such an expedition, and stood to gain or lose together with the private backers. To gain the support of a group of such merchant-adventurers was the next task to which Luis and Homem addressed themselves, and here they were more successful. Several men of influence and substance seemed prepared to believe the greater part of their story. Even Sir William Cecil, the Queen's

Secretary and wisest counsellor, a man more prone to caution and disbelief than enthusiasm, was interested in the venture.

Thus it came about that a syndicate was formed to plan the best way of exploiting Luis and Homem's discovery. Men with money to invest like Sir William Garrard and Sir Lionel Ducket lent their names to the project, experienced seamen such as William Winter added counsel, and Benjamin Gonson, the Treasurer of the Navy, gave authority to the group. There were other backers too, illustrious in Court circles, whose names were not made public. They met together privately, gauging the support they could raise and interrogating the two Portuguese minutely. In principle they approved the idea of an expedition and started to negotiate for the royal sanction to undertake it.

It was natural that, at an early stage, the sponsors should choose a captain to direct the operations they were planning by sea and land. There were many brave men and fine sailors in the country, but one who was pre-eminently suitable. John Hawkins, a comparatively young man in his middle thirties, combined the shrewdness of an experienced administrator with a grasp of policy uncommon among the skilled seamen of his day. He came from a Plymouth family, and since his boyhood had been accustomed to merchant adventuring and the handling of ships and men.

When the syndicate called him to join them in their counsels, they were faced by a man of a sad and reserved manner with an uneasy mouth fringed by a thin, closely-clipped auburn beard, scarcely betraying his stubborn and careful disposition. But his close-set grey eyes and broad brow indicated a man of assurance and command.

In dress he was unostentatious but not niggardly. Usually he appeared before them in a black doublet, trimmed in the finest cambric at the neck and wrist, with breeches of the same colour, padded with bumbast, and stockings of silk. His buttons and buckles were of gold and pearl, carefully wrought; and the short sword that he always carried at his side was of damasked steel, and sheathed in a velvet scabbard. At Court he was inconspicuous, and from the gravity of his bearing seemed old amongst his contemporaries.

He was, nonetheless, quite a newcomer to such circles. Before he set out on his previous voyage, in command of a royal ship for the first time—the same *Jesus of Lubeck* in which he now sat and wrote—he had been granted an audience with the Queen. She found, it may be judged, that this blunt, confident young commander was worthy of her trust; and when he returned a year later with his ships intact, and laden with pepper and ivory from Guinea and gold, silver, hides, sugar and pearls from the Indies, her interest in him was confirmed.

As he wrote his letter Hawkins thought back to that first interview, and to more recent meetings, trying in his phrases to catch the Queen's sympathy by plain speaking, which he knew she admired, yet concealing his drift until he had hinted at the benefits she might reap. It is a difficult thing to cajole a Queen, and dangerous too, when, like Elizabeth, the disposition is moody and likely to veer with gusts of suspicion from enthusiasm into anger. He had heard of the terrifying change of manner that could overtake her when an unwary phrase or action gave offence. Even Cecil had hinted that he was not immune from the Queen's wrath. So far, for the most part, Hawkins had been kindlily received, but he was careful in her presence to forget that she was a young woman of his own age who might be tempted by flatteries and vanities of address. He talked to her, as he had learnt best, frankly, as man to man.

Hawkins, when he had heard from the syndicate at Court the proposals of the two Portuguese renegades, was thoroughly sceptical. He had met such stories and such men before, and placed little trust in them. But the tide of enthusiasm was too strong for him to stem, and, indeed, he had no great wish to back down. He had no faith in the quest, but he knew that such an expedition, if it was to be attempted, would need ambitious planning—a great fleet, well equipped and amply endowed. The object of the voyage was the Guinea coast, which he had twice before explored. But on each previous occasion Africa had been only the first step. Laden with slaves seized from the river villages along the shore, he had followed the trade winds to the Indies and sold his cargoes to the Spaniards before returning home. If, on this occasion, the renegades proved as false as he suspected, neither he nor his promoters would be disappointed if he repeated yet again, but on a grander scale, the lucrative exchange of negroes for Spanish gold.

He may not have explained his reasoning at the council table, but he gave an honest declaration of his doubts and a pledge, on behalf of his brother William and himself, of £2,000 towards the risks and in anticipation of the rewards. His fellow backers were no less confident, and the Queen herself was prevailed upon to lend two of her great ships to form the spearhead and majesty of the enterprise.

At their anchorage in the Medway the *Jesus of Lubeck* and the *Minion* were prepared for sea; their canvas and rigging were overhauled and renewed, the shipwrights had busied themselves replacing faulty timbers and caulking the seams, officers were selected and crews mustered. Hawkins supervised the loading of stores, and when the ships moved up the Thames to the Tower he argued with William Winter about the appropriate armament. A charter-party was drafted; and Hawkins took post-horses to Plymouth to arrange with his brother which of their own ships should accompany the expedition, and to see to their equipment.

Throughout the summer of 1567 the preparations were pressed forward with speed, partly because an autumn sailing was necessary to avoid bad weather in home waters and to achieve the longest period of endurable weather on the coast, partly because no one could predict whether considerations of policy or parsimony might cause Elizabeth to change her mind. Late in August the *Jesus* and *Minion* sailed from London to join the rest of the fleet at Plymouth, and a few days later the merchants and supercargoes who were to accompany the adventurers left by road for the same destination, bringing with them the two Portuguese.

It was on the eve of departure, therefore, that Hawkins was faced with the escape of his guides; too late to retract from the venture without loss, but too soon to sail without receiving fresh instructions. In a mood of anxious anticipation he set himself to ask formal permission to undertake a voyage of his own devising. 'And although this enterprise cannot take effect,' he wrote, and added with a touch of satisfaction, '(which I think God hath provided for the best) I do ascertain Your Highness that I have provision sufficient and an able army to defend our charge and to bring home (with God's help) forty thousand marks gains without the offence of the least of any of Your Highness' allies or friends.' Lightly he sketched his long-pondered plans and sealed the letter. He entrusted it to George Fitzwilliam, his intended companion on this voyage as of old, and the only man, perhaps, to whom Hawkins cared to unburden his mind.

With the utmost speed, so that rumour did not precede him, Fitzwilliam took the letter and rode to London to deliver it to the Queen.

More than a week would elapse before Hawkins could hope to receive the Queen's verdict; but meanwhile he was determined to press on with his preparations, and thanks to his foresight very little rearrangement would be necessary to convert the expedition to a new purpose. A certain amount of equipment for constructing a fort on the Guinea coast, as a base camp and a shield to protect the route to the gold-fields, would need to be unloaded, and the space cleared to accommodate a cargo of slaves. But Hawkins had already, with devious excuses, taken on board a lading of linen and bales of cloth of a quality too fine to be squandered on trade in Africa, yet entirely suitable for the Spanish settlers in the Indies. He had also shipped, deep in the hold of the *Jesus*, innumerable sacks of dried beans, the customary food for negroes who endured the trials of the middle passage.

The beans, in fact, had almost betrayed him, for while he was engaged in persuading old Edward Baeshe, the Surveyor of Victuals to the Queen's fleet, that such a quantity was a necessary part of his stores, the Spanish ambassador, Don Guzman de Silva, had learnt of the matter, and his suspicions were aroused. Both the Queen and Cecil had already declared to him that Hawkins' preparations were in no way connected with another expedition to the Indies. De Silva had been satisfied, especially after Hawkins, whom he invited to dine from time to time in an atmosphere of wary cordiality, had emphatically volunteered a similar assurance. But a lading of beans could not be ignored. Beans meant slaves, and slaves were saleable only in the Indies. Once again de Silva approached the Queen with his doubts, and once again, with some trouble, he had been reassured.

It had been, Hawkins reflected, a tiresome, difficult business to plan and prepare the expedition so far. He was as impatient as any sea-captain to take a fair wind and sail out beyond the snares of the shore; but he was methodical and orderly by nature, and, unlike many of his fellow captains, preferred to sail with the full backing of legality and official approval. He was willing to negotiate his way slowly and abide the outcome. But he could have wished for better fortune on this occasion. The affair of the beans had been only the beginning, and he doubted if the defection of the Portuguese would mark the end, of his trials.

Even when the *Jesus* and *Minion*, fully armed and stored, were preparing to move from the Thames to join the rest of the fleet at Plymouth, a misfortune had occurred. The upper deck had been crowded with the kinsmen and friends of the crew saying their farewells before a year's absence, when, without warning, a badly-secured piece of heavy gear fell to the deck, killing instantly a girl who was standing underneath. By a curious chance a similar accident had occurred on the *Jesus* when Hawkins set sail on his previous voyage in 1564. On that occasion, just as they were hoisting sail and clearing the harbour, an officer was killed by a block falling from aloft. In each case it was an inauspicious beginning: some of the crew, indeed, took it as an omen of the ill-success of the voyage.

But a fair wind gave the two ships an uneventful trip to Plymouth, and when they had come to anchor in the Catwater, and seen the preparations that were afoot to complete the enterprise, most men forgot the augury of death.

While John Hawkins was occupied in London his elder brother, William, a merchant and citizen of note in Plymouth, had been busy preparing several of their own craft for sea. The largest vessel that the brothers contributed to the squadron was the *William and John*, a ship of 150 tons and named after them. They appointed Thomas Bolton to command her, and James Raunce as her master, or executive officer.

Raunce was not long back from an earlier expedition that the Hawkins brothers had dispatched under Captain John Lovell to the Slave Coast and the Caribbean. Like most professional sailors Raunce was eager to be afloat again, and with many of his shipmates had signed on for this new ambitious venture. Amongst these enthusiasts was a young kinsman of Hawkins, Francis Drake. The trip under Lovell had been his first experience of voyaging in distant waters, and had sharpened his appetite to return.

One of Lovell's squadron, the *Swallow*, had returned early from the African coast, and been refitted during the summer. Like the shrewd merchant he was Hawkins hated to see a good ship lie idle. The ravages of the previous voyage had been carefully repaired, and the *Swallow* was considered suitable to take her place in the new expedition. She was a trim, new ship of 100 tons, but she lacked powerful armament. Before he sailed Hawkins caused a modern brass gun, a saker, to be transferred from his flagship to reinforce her battery of eight less-powerful pieces.

The *Judith* and the *Angel*, small craft of fifty and thirty-three tons, completed the squadron, together with a pinnace, towed astern, and designed for general duties and for reinforcing the ships' boats at landings. It is possible that one of these vessels, none of which was well-armed, was contributed not by Hawkins but by a gentleman-member of the syndicate.

The two great ships in Hawkins' fleet were the Queen's: the *Jesus of Lubeck* and the *Minion*. The *Jesus*, a 700-ton-ship of impressive power, had been built in the Baltic for the merchants of the Hanseatic League and sold in 1545 to Henry VIII together with three other vessels. She was constructed, after the fashion of those days, with towering forecastle and aftercastle, housing battery over battery of guns. She was squat in shape, but noble to look upon when running before a light breeze—the sails at her four masts full-bellied, and her prow seeming to tip down as she forged ahead. At her yard-arms were fitted curved sickles, designed to tear an opponent's rigging and sails when grappling at close quarters, and from her cubbridge heads—the lateral bulwarks that rose fore and aft of her low waist—guns pointed inwards to destroy those who boarded her at her lowest point. She was a great ship of a past age, for, already, experienced sea-fighters were learning to avoid a hand-to-hand struggle with such floating fortresses and relied rather on shooting from a distance with more powerful guns.

The *Jesus* nonetheless suited Hawkins admirably as a flagship, for he desired trade more than battle, and despite her years she was an impressive and commodious vessel. He made sure, however, that she was adequately armed with modern weapons of war. The guns he relied on most, his culverins, sakers and the heavier, short-range cannon, were already mounted. But not wishing to strain his ship with too much top-hamper, he relegated most of the antiquated fowlers and bases, with which he had been issued, to the hold as ballast.

Seen from a distance the *Jesus* inspired awe, but those who had sailed in her spoke more of her faults. The fact that she was highly-charged caused her to be top-heavy. She pitched horribly in a moderate sea and was difficult to steer at all close to the wind. She leaked too, despite all the caulking that could be given her. Hawkins had installed the new chain pumps for his previous trip, but there had been few days when they were not in use. It could be said that a leaky ship caused fewer fevers to breed from stagnant water in the bilges, but despite such reassurances her crew knew that she had been condemned as unseaworthy early in Elizabeth's reign and only reprieved and patched up because of the cost of replacing her. Because of these defects Hawkins had obtained the use of an imposing flagship on most favourable terms: he had sailed in her before, and knowing her qualities was glad to accept her perils.

As master, Hawkins chose Robert Barrett, a young man of twenty-four on whom he had learned to rely. Barrett was born and had grown up in Saltash, but, like his cousin Drake, had spent little of his time ashore since achieving manhood. One particular advantage he brought with him, beyond his uncommon skill with men and ships, was a fluent knowledge of the Portuguese and Spanish languages. In appearance, according to the recollection of Miguel Ribero, a Portuguese who had met him off the Guinea coast, he was 'a well-built man of graceful person, his beard which is scanty being red, his eye light of colour . . . and the face pitted with the marks of smallpox'.

The merchants and gentlemen who were to accompany the expedition were also accommodated in the *Jesus*; and Drake, though longing for an independent command, was kept under his commander and kinsman's eye for the start at any rate. Hawkins never liked or put much trust in land soldiers, but a detachment had been deemed necessary for operations ashore, and in charge of these men was Captain Edward Dudley, a choleric and impetuous officer, but of a simple courage.

Of the *Minion* no sailor cared to speak much. She was an unlucky ship, famous for saving herself and killing her crew. Older even than the *Jesus*, she had been constructed more than thirty years before from the timbers of a ship bearing the same name. Her burthen was 300 tons, and like the *Jesus* she was four-masted and highly-charged fore and aft, but her main battery was carried on two decks. Of recent years her voyages to the Guinea coast had been so frequent that her crew declared she knew her way there, and added, wryly, that she could find her way back alone.

Within the last decade her history had been tragic and triumphant. In 1558 the *Minion* and two other ships sailed in company to Africa: only two returned, their crews so ravaged by sickness that scarcely a dozen men were left on deck to see them home. Three years later she set forth again only to collide in mid-Channel with a companion ship. Two months of dockyard work saw her at sea once more, but the season was so advanced that she was forced to turn back, half-sinking from a storm, her upperworks rotten and her crew drenched. Next year she returned to the coast of Guinea with one other ship. They traded and skirmished with Portuguese caravels and galleys as they went. At one point the *Minion* was almost destroyed when a barrel of powder exploded below decks; but both vessels returned to England with a score of dead and a score of fit men between them. The treasure she had gained was more precious than the lives she had lost, and in 1564 she was yet again chartered from the Queen on a Guinea venture. With her went two other ships. One, the *Merlin*, blew up before they had left English waters. The commander of the remaining ships was captured by the Portuguese ashore and the second vessel, the *John Baptist*, was taken with all her crew near Elmina, the fort built by the Portuguese to protect their Gold Coast trade. No news was heard of the *Minion* whose loss was considered certain. But nine months after setting forth she was heard of at the Azores, the remnant of her crew gaunt with hunger and disease; and when, a month later, she entered the Thames, her sails patched and the bright paintwork chipped and scarred from her upperworks, there was found in her capacious hold a fabulous wealth of ivory and gold.

It was such a ship that John Hampton commanded under Hawkins' direction, and he and John Garret, the master, must have worked hard to dispel the anxieties of their fearful and superstitious crew. Indeed the men's trepidation was not wholly unwarranted.

These were the six ships that had come together at Plymouth late in August, equipped to establish the first permanent English foothold on the African coast, and defend it, as would surely be necessary if the fabled gold proved real. Hawkins had himself shown his guides, the two renegades, all the preparations that had been made, and they appeared delighted with what they saw. There were still a few bales of trading goods to be stored away in the holds of the small ships, fine taffetas and lengths of coarse kersey cloth. Several tons of manacles also needed to be brought on board without arousing suspicion, and there were several last-minute vacancies on the muster-roll, which could be filled by newly-returned Plymouth seamen. A week at the outside and, weather permitting, they would be able to sail.

But the wind had risen from the south-west, driving briskly, bringing grey skies and a hint of rain; while it remained in that quarter there was no hope of leaving harbour. Some of the newer ships could sail as close as six points to the wind, but most of the older square-rigged vessels like the *Jesus* were less weatherly and could not easily beat their way clear of the harbour against such a wind. But at the mouth of the Catwater they were well sheltered, for the surrounding hills and the deep recesses of the sea provided Plymouth, then as now, with a splendid natural anchorage. They let go their second anchors and set a watch lest squalls came and the ships dragged.

Thanks to the watch Hawkins had some warning of the approach of seven unexpected and unwelcome visitors. They were warships, fully rigged and powerfully armed. The leading ship was still to seaward of St Nicholas' island and almost concealed behind the promontory of How Start when Hawkins, summoned urgently from his cabin, arrived on deck. Even at a distance he recognized them as vessels from the Spanish Netherlands fleet, and although the two nations were at peace, he knew enough of the ways of the sea and the chances of treachery to be thoroughly alarmed. All hands were piped to action stations, the anchor cables were shortened and men sent aloft, climbing up the ratlins to the fighting-tops and yards so that the two ships could be got under way before they were surprised.

Hawkins had taken the precaution of mounting his batteries before he left the Thames, but he knew that many commanders, whilst in safe waters, preferred to keep their heavy guns below on the ballast where they added less to the top-weight of their ships. It did not seem improbable that this confident and unheralded Flemish fleet was bent on mischief, if it could be easily achieved. But Hawkins was not a man to be caught sleeping: he ordered the magazines to be opened and all guns loaded.

Meanwhile the Flemish squadron, the following wind swelling its sails, was approaching swiftly. The leader, bedecked with flags and penants, had taken the customary channel and left St Nicholas' island to port. This little island in the middle of the Sound had long been uninhabited except for a small chapel, but recently it had been fortified, and even from the *Jesus* they could see the flag flying above the breastworks. Hawkins watched the leading ship pass the island without pause, her topsails still set and her ensign undipped. His fears were confirmed, and he immediately dispatched a pinnace to alert the town.

The custom of the sea dictated that all friendly ships entering a foreign port should pay tokens of respect. The Flemish squadron had failed to do so, and it required no words to interpret the challenge. Hawkins could see them clearly now. They were making straight for the Hoe, and he anticipated that they would turn away from him and come to anchor at a discreet distance. In this he was mistaken: no sooner had they cleared How Start than they turned towards him and made for the entrance to the inner harbour. It was an audacious manoeuvre, for if there was a trap the Flemish admiral was sailing into it. But obviously he was relying upon the surprise that his sudden appearance would cause. Hawkins watched the distance between the ships narrow. The insolent flag was still undipped, and the leader had come within range of his culverins. He ordered them to open fire, aiming high at the ensign.

A ragged burst of fire from those guns on the *Jesus* and *Minion* that could be brought to bear was followed by a moment of silence. On the gundecks the culverins were dragged clear of the ports. In the haze of acrid smoke that enveloped them their crews rammed home fresh charges and hauled them back on their carriages to the firing position.

Without deviating from its course the Flemish squadron sailed on. They fired no answering shot, neither did they dip their flag. Once again Hawkins gave the command to open fire, but this time to aim lower. The gunlayers on the *Jesus* aimed well, and from his high vantage on the poop Hawkins could see several hits scored on the hulls of the advancing vessels. It was evident that such accurate fire could only be answered or avoided. The Flemish admiral chose the latter course. A signal-flag fluttered, and the whole squadron luffed, their sails slack at the yard; then, regaining the wind, prepared to retreat to the west.

As they turned they furled their topsails and lowered their flags in a belated salute.

Hawkins watched the retreat of the seven ships and saw them anchor out of range under the lee of St Nicholas' island. One of the two tenders that sailed with them was seen to come along-side their flagship, and before many minutes had passed hasten to the inner harbour, punctilliously observing all courtesies as it passed the ancient fort that guarded the narrows.

Hawkins was puzzled, but not displeased, by the sudden and

unexpected turn that events had taken. He was, perhaps, a little proud of the success of his brief action, and had had no time to reflect upon its repercussions. But he realized that he had not seen the end of the affair, so, charging the watch to report to him on the slightest suspicion, he went below to dress.

The Mayor of Plymouth was the first to receive the Flemish officer who had been sent ashore to lodge a protest against the unfriendly welcome his squadron had received. John Ilcombe was not particularly abashed by the complaint. He already knew of, and approved, Hawkins' action, but was disinclined to argue the matter himself. The officer reported that his commander's fleet had been fired on by two ships, unknown to them, in the Sound. The mayor affected surprise that they had noticed neither the standard flown by the *Jesus*, nor the distinctive green and white paintwork that marked her as a royal ship. The complaint, he declared, should be answered by the guardian of the Queen's peace in the port, the captain of the *Jesus*, a Mr John Hawkins.

Immediately the Flemish boat was sighted leaving the inner harbour, Hawkins, realizing that his ship would be the next place of call, set the stage for a formal reception on board the *Jesus*. In the waist of the ship he arranged his personal guard of footsoldiers, armed with partisans, in two ranks. All sailors with duties on deck wore tunics of the royal colours, and a group of officers and gentlemen dressed and armed in the fashion of the day stood by the rails. He himself, attired in his finest clothes, paced between his guard, his hand on the pommel of his sword, closely followed by Jean Turren, his personal trumpeter, in a brilliant tabard. The upper deck presented a scene of contrived splendour which Hawkins fully intended should impress and awe his visitor.

While the Flemish emissary was boarding the *Jesus* Hawkins did not cease pacing the deck, his face set and his lips thin with suppressed anger. For a moment he ignored the officer who waited, hat in hand. Then, turning to him before he could voice his grievance, Hawkins vehemently demanded to know what ships these were that had insulted the English flag and provoked a disturbance of the Queen's peace? Why had they insolently disregarded the courtesies of the sea? Who was their commander, and what was his intention? Did he come in war or peace?

The envoy, who had come aboard with the confident assurance of one who was prepared to justify himself by blustering, was reduced first to answering his accuser. His admiral, he said, was Alphonse de Bourgogne, Baron de Wachen, who commanded this armed squadron from the Spanish Netherlands fleet, and was preparing to meet his sovereign, Philip II, at sea. The King, he said, was even now on his way from Spain to the Low Countries, and required an escort to protect him. It had been bad weather that had driven his ships to seek sanctuary in Plymouth Sound, and they had been shocked to receive such a discourteous and provocative reception from a nation with whom they were at peace.

Hawkins was little disposed to accept such an unconvincing explanation. He knew the Flemish admiral de Wachen of old, and it was not the first time he had entered an English port. A seaman of his experience knew the established conduct of the sea, and had no need to seek shelter from such weather as they had been having. He suspected too—rightly as it turned out—that King Philip's voyage was another fabrication. The Spanish Ambassador was at the bottom of this plot, he felt sure. De Silva's suspicions had certainly been aroused, and what more effective way of allaying them than causing the whole of Hawkins' enterprise to be destroyed before it sailed? It was easy to provoke a quarrel—the neglected salute would have been enough—and at worst an apology and some offer of recompense would assuage the Queen. De Wachen had been relying on a surprise raid catching the English unprepared. He had failed, and was now trying to extricate himself.

These thoughts Hawkins did not pass on to the Flemish officer. But he did not relax from the anger he had assumed. His reply was brief and he allowed no argument. The ships he commanded, he declared, were the Queen's, and although amity existed between their two sovereigns the Admiral would do well to recognize that no discourtesy or stubbornness on the part

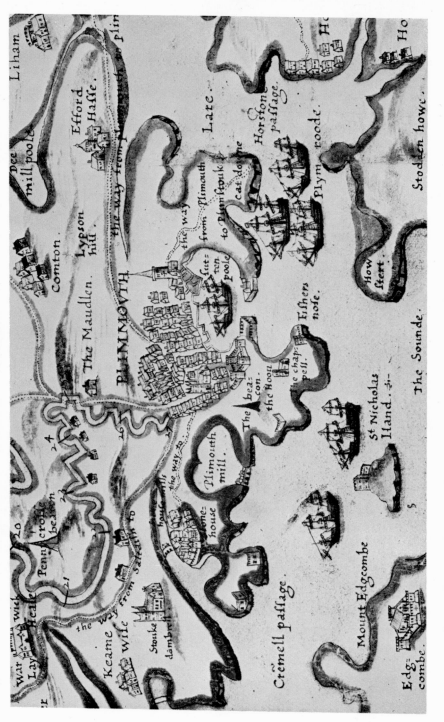

Plymouth in mid-Elizabethan times. The three ships on the right are lying in the Catwater

The *Jesus of Lubeck*

of a visiting ship to an English port would be tolerated by him. With such words Hawkins turned away and resumed his walk.

Sternness, Hawkins knew from his experience as a trader, could often be doubly effective if it was followed by a generous gesture. Not an hour elapsed after the departure of de Wachen's messenger before a boat from the *Jesus* made its way to the Flemish squadron bearing a gift of fresh provisions—always a welcome addition to the diet of men who had been long at sea. The carcasses of a dozen sheep, a barrel or two of London beer and a number of chickens and other delicacies would, Hawkins hoped, soothe the smart which de Wachen must surely feel. He received thanks enough, but, unknown to him, the Flemish admiral sent messengers to London to report his reception to de Silva, and de Silva was quick to complain about Hawkins' aggressiveness to Cecil and the Queen. These reports prejudiced the reception of Hawkins' own account of the incident which arrived later, and caused Cecil to write, on the Queen's authority, a rebuke to her subject, forbidding him to take such presumptuous action in her name again.

By an irony of fate it was not many months before Hawkins needed most desperately a confirmation of those powers he had been chided for wielding, when once again he sighted a Spanish fleet from his desolate moorings at San Juan de Ulua.

Hawkins' sojourn at Plymouth was proving uncomfortably eventful, and before his preparations for sailing were complete a further incident added to his cares. A Spanish ship taking a cargo of Flemish prisoners captured in the Duke of Alva's wars in the Low Countries and destined for the galleys, touched at Plymouth to break her voyage. One afternoon as she was lying at anchor in the Sound, her crew drowsy after their midday meal and her human cargo safely shackled below hatches, a boat-load of adventurers from the shore, with masked faces and brandishing their weapons, crept on board and with little difficulty seized the ship. Having secured the crew they busied themselves in releasing the prisoners, with whom they departed ashore before an alarm could be raised.

Not unnaturally the Spanish captain was furious and immedi-

c

ately suspected Hawkins, whom he knew to be unfavourably disposed towards his country, of having perpetrated the outrage. Besides, Hawkins had boasted to de Wachen that he maintained the Queen's peace in Plymouth. It was to Hawkins, therefore, that the enraged Spaniard addressed himself as soon as he had been freed. He accused him of having instigated the raid and demanded satisfaction. Hawkins tried to be conciliatory. He commiserated with the captain, and proved, as best he could, his own innocence and ignorance of what had taken place. He suggested, as was indeed probable, that some of the numerous refugees from Flanders, men who had fled to England on account of their faith in increasing numbers in recent years, Calvinists or the proscribed Anabaptists, had organized the liberation of their compatriots. He promised to do what he could to persuade the authorities ashore to track them down.

But for all he said he could not appease the Spaniard. Once again conflicting reports from Hawkins and from an apparently injured Spanish national chased each other to the English court. Even at a distance Hawkins could imagine Cecil's mounting exasperation at what he would consider, however unjustly, to be irresponsible conduct; and he feared greatly lest the Queen, so preoccupied with Scottish cares, should take a sudden dislike of these petty distractions and forbid the enterprise.

It was some consolation that de Wachen had removed his squadron from the port after lingering many days. The damage he had done was not apparent, but the reproof he had occasioned rankled with Hawkins, and now that the flight of the Portuguese renegades had added a third misfortune to his three weeks' stay in Plymouth, he feared lest his good name at Court might have suffered irremediably. Only George Fitzwilliam, bearing the reply to his latest letter, could resolve that fear; and he awaited his return impatiently, yet outwardly with the deliberate and unflurried calm that was habitual to him. A calm that many mistook for craftiness because he betrayed to no man the incomplete directions of his thought.

CHAPTER 2

The Sailing

TEN days after setting out, George Fitzwilliam returned to Plymouth, bearing the reply that the Queen had caused Cecil to write to Hawkins' proposals. Immediately he arrived on board he was shown down to the Admiral's cabin where Hawkins received him.

It was, we know, a spacious but low-ceilinged room, elegantly furnished under Hawkins' own direction; the bulkheads panelled, and hung with tapestries of intricate design. The details of its equipment we must infer. Ranged within reach were the books and instruments of the sea that Hawkins never tired of studying. Two bronze globes, probably of German workmanship, were conspicuous; one, engraved with the zodiac, recorded the pattern of the stars, the other the known world. An astrolabe of brass hung down from a hook on the wall, the engraved dial worn faint from daily use in determining the ship's latitude. There were other instruments, no less precious: a set of hour-glasses, a compass so that he should never be ignorant of the ship's course, and an arbalist—a long cross-staff—easier to use than an astrolabe in a heavy sea. There was also a mass of his own notes in one corner of the cabin: information on pilotage in strange waters, and observations of his own and of his father's before him of the signs and portents of the sea.

Dominating the cabin, in all likelihood, there would have been a long wooden council table, immovably bolted to the deck, and a piece of heavy ordnance, mounted on its carriage, pointing outward through a gunport in the overhanging stern. The *Jesus* was a fighting ship, and when the call came for action no part of the vessel was less involved than another. A brazen gun intruding in his private cabin would be a constant reminder to Hawkins that trading and fighting were often indistinguishable occupations.

The sight of his friend's confident entry told Hawkins that the news was good. Taking the folded paper that Fitzwilliam produced from his wallet, the Admiral broke the seal. He recognized Sir William Cecil's writing and read hastily through the preliminary sentences until he reached the kernel of the message. He had expected the preamble of reproach and querulous indignation, but this was quickly forgotten in his deep joy on learning that the Queen had accepted his proposals. The voyage would take place.

With the letter came fresh articles wherein the Queen confirmed her consent to a voyage to those parts of Africa not under the dominion of the King of Portugal nor paying tribute to him, for the purpose of loading slaves for sale in the Spanish Indies as had been done on previous occasions. It is not difficult to imagine that, on laying down the paper, Hawkins broke into one of his rare smiles.

Fitzwilliam would then have been questioned minutely about his reception at Court, and have told his captain of the divided counsel and conflicting reports that were circulating; of how he had used his skill to persuade the doubtful syndicate that Hawkins' proposal was the best solution, and how he had been able to petition the Queen on their behalf. Even then he felt he might not have succeeded, for it was widely believed that Hawkins had ill-used the renegades and forced their flight; but by a lucky chance some letters that they had written before their departure were discovered, and it was apparent that in their own opinion the treatment they had received had been exemplary. Small as it was this discovery may have swung the balance. At all events he had secured the necessary sailing orders, and he urged Hawkins not to delay lest cold winds blew once more from Court.

Hawkins needed no such warning. Immediately he summoned his officers, received their reports on the state of preparation in the various ships, and told them that they sailed with the next favourable wind. When they were dismissed, and he was alone once more in his cabin, we may imagine him turning to the bronze

globe of the earth, spinning it slightly until the indented cirque
of West Africa was foremost. Towards those far shores he bent his
thoughts.

For more than a century Portuguese navigators had explored
and exploited the African coast. Some had never come back, but
those who succeeded them always pushed a little further into the
unknown and marked where another great river swept through
some silted estuary to the sea, or forced their way upstream in
small boats through sluggish channels fringed by mangrove
swamps. Beyond these seaborne explorations lay fabulous lands,
terrifying yet desirable. The markets and mines of Timbuktu
were richer, some said, than Cibola itself where the streets were
paved with gold, and further still lay the broad frontiers of the
Empire of Prester John: a land where the fantastic and unimagin-
able was true, ruled over by a Christian Emperor-priest of un-
counted wealth.

But little progress was made inland: there was enough to be had
on the shore, and for many years only Portuguese ships sailed
there. They established a fort on the coast they had named
'the mine of gold', and hopefully called it *São Jorge da Mina* or,
for short, *El Mina*. But there were no mines, only the filtered
dust of gold from the rivers. A few other settlements and strong-
points sprang up over the years, and some traders and go-betweens
set themselves up in creek villages, producing a half-caste brood
only recognizable as Portuguese by a sword, or a shirt or a few
words of their fathers' speech. There were priests too, but never
enough to drive out paganism.

At first the caravels brought back gold and ivory from Guinea
and pepper from Senegal, together with such curious rarities as
civet and the medicinal horns of unicorns. A few slaves were
taken, and the practice received the sanction of Pope and King;
but there was small need for their labour until the Spaniards,
whose sphere of influence and exploration lay to the west, discovered that the African negro was a hardy and tractable labourer,
suitable for their plantations and mines. A trade sprang up, controlled at 10,000 slaves a year, and centred on the island of São

Thomé. Selling prices were established, and both the kingdoms of Spain and Portugal profited by the commission they received from the exercise of the monopoly they had established.

There was no difficulty in providing the yearly quota. The negro tribes and settlements along the coast were disunited and ravaged by strife. An unaccountable, explosive migration from the centre of the continent was taking place, and groups of the Sumba tribe, moving behind the littoral of Guinea and Senegal, brought with them waves of war and disruption, the ripples of which, reaching the Portuguese on the coast, made the bartering of slaves an easy undertaking.

The first half of the sixteenth century saw the establishment and regularization of the Portuguese slave-trade from Guinea. There were few nations who were equipped to interfere, much as they might envy so lucrative an opportunity. A very few voyages were made in defiance of the monopoly—some of the earliest were undertaken by John Hawkins' father, William, in his little ship the *Paul*, trading with Guinea and Brazil in the 1530s. But the English were less prepared for such forays than the French— Huguenots for the most part, unconstricted by statecraft at home, and amongst the finest sailors afloat. French pirates and French privateers swarmed down the coast; they lurked amongst the islands and scoured the coastlines of Senegal. Some traded in their own right, others plundered the Portuguese. They found the local defences, except around Elmina, insufficient and ineffective. No threats would deter them, and the Portuguese, confident but over-extended, became seriously alarmed.

Half-way through the century the English joined the French, and hunted alone or in packs between the Cape Verde Islands and São Thomé. In the year that John Hawkins prepared to sail from Plymouth, 200 sail of Frenchmen had passed the Canary Islands on their various plundering missions, despite Portuguese threats to sink all ships that ventured past the Azores. There is little doubt that the accession of a Protestant Queen in England gave encouragement to the English privateers and traders, but even in Mary's reign, and despite the disapproval of her Spanish husband, adventurers had left English ports for Guinea, and others laid plans to go.

Early in her reign Portuguese emissaries had tried to persuade Elizabeth to forbid encroachments by her subjects into African waters, but she and Cecil had refused to recognize that the unknown world should be arbitrarily divided between Spain and Portugal by the decree of a Pope, whose authority she, like her father before her, did not recognize. It was poor comfort to the Portuguese ambassadors to be assured that territories occupied by Portugal would be respected: to both parties it was common knowledge that there were no permanent forts or settlements in all the length of Senegal, and few in Guinea. Yet no more would Elizabeth promise, and the ambassadors knew that behind their backs the Queen aided and encouraged many an English enterprise to those debatable shores.

A distant voyage undertaken in Hawkins' day was seldom a placid occupation. The boundaries of war and peace were less clearly defined than now. A squadron of ships several weeks' sailing from port could exercise the authority of a petty kingdom on the high seas, making alliances or conquests as it thought fit in the reasonable assumption that once home a little bribery and a ready tongue could placate most past quarrels. Piracy, to be sure, was never countenanced, but pirates did not carry the authority of any nation. Occasionally they were tolerated, but never defended. They worked for their own gain and suffered death if they failed, unprotected by any man. They were brutal and unscrupulous for the most part and prospered where treasure was great and authority weak, notably in the Spanish West Indies and off the African coast.

Many of the actions, recounted of English seamen in the pages of Hakluyt, that seem most piratical were, however, legal and tolerated. They fall into that curious limbo between peace and war known as privateering—the rough justice of the sea. If the ship of an English merchant was seized or sunk, or her cargo confiscated, there was, often enough, little redress to be had through official means. But the Queen was empowered to issue letters of marque that authorized her subject to take reprisals against the nation that had ill-treated him, and enter into a private war until his loss had been recovered. Letters of marque were recognized amongst nations as excluding their holders from the stigma and punishment of pirates, though their actions might in all other respects be indistinguishable. The high seas were perilous to the unwary. Any sail that was sighted was a potential enemy, and in distant waters particularly, where flight might be impossible, few ships ventured unless they were armed for defence. Merchantmen were equipped for war, and fighting ships were ballasted with cargo. The two functions of trade and defence were united in a single vessel.

In the year 1567, England was at peace with both Portugal and Spain. Yet at sea it was a hostile truce. Privateering had bred its own increase, and in waters that the two great Catholic kingdoms looked upon as exclusively their own, ships fought at sight. But neither side could afford to declare war openly. England was careful, too, under its Tudor sovereigns, never to goad both Spain and Portugal into rash action at the same time. Under Queen Mary some amity was established with Spain, and in the early years of Queen Elizabeth's reign the same self-interested diplomacy persisted. Portugal was the most vulnerable of the two Catholic powers, and her hold on Africa was discovered to be weak. Against her, therefore, were directed the depredations of Lok and Winter, Carlet and Towerson, Fenner and Lovell. Meanwhile Spain, with her more inaccessible colonies across the Atlantic suffered little from English intrusions, though sadly plagued by pirates and freebooters from France. She was watchful, realizing perhaps that her own means of defence were little stronger than those of the Portuguese in Africa, but she had few causes for complaint.

It was unfortunate that Hawkins, unblessed by an historical perspective, could not appreciate that England was growing strong enough at sea to make a challenge to Spain inevitable. He had conceived a quite different role for himself as the first English seaman to lead his ships into Spanish-controlled waters. On his first and second voyages to the Indies he had seen for himself the inadequacy of the local defences. He had watched the garrison and population of many small settlements flee inland at the sight of his sails entering harbour, and he had heard stories of the terror and disorganization that the haphazard assaults of pirates caused. Warships from Spain were never at the right place at the right time to afford help. The wealth of the islands and the main lay open to assault. He determined to defend it. Not so many years ago England and Spain had been allied by a royal marriage. No public act had revoked that friendship. The appearance of his squadrons in forbidden waters had provoked fear, not because of their actions but because of their strength. Why, he reasoned, should not this presence be welcomed as an upholder of law and order, as an ally of Spain and an enemy of pirates. His trading had certainly been profitable, but it had been scrupulously honest. It seemed no unreasonable bargain.

He did not hope that the idea would find official favour. It was an admission of Spanish weakness to allow a proud and successful poacher to turn gamekeeper. Even if they had trusted Hawkins' integrity (which they did not) it would have been an impossible precedent for the Spaniards to allow. But what in Spain would seem a diplomatic humiliation might be seen to have advantages amongst the Spanish colonists in the Indies themselves. Hawkins was determined to try. He was not afraid of fighting, but his most successful trade had always been conducted peacefully and he was hungry for quick returns.

What Hawkins did not realize was that, even as he was preparing his third slaving voyage, the Spaniards were themselves shaking off the indolent and careless direction of their overseas territories that had so dangerously weakened their hold on the Indies. They had dispatched an ably-led fleet to re-establish their authority throughout the islands, and in addition sent a warning to all governors that no illicit trading was to be conducted with such unlicensed adventurers as 'Juan Aquines'. Hawkins' dream of protective trade was snuffed out by the Spaniards themselves.

The brazen globe in Hawkins' cabin showed the limits of the known world, between which the unmarked stretches of the sea seemed innocent highways linking together islands and continents. A serene plain in which engraved dolphins and spouting whales played between the network of lines that established the geometry of latitude and longitude. But the airs that blew and buffeted the seas from above, and the tides and currents that tugged them from below, had no place in the miniature world of maps. Experience, and knowledge of the ways of the sea, were just as important to the sea-captain as the instruments of navigation that he carried. Particularly on a trading voyage no captain would be so foolhardy as to venture willingly into waters he had not sailed before, unless he had on board a trustworthy pilot. Hawkins was lucky in this respect. Even though he had lost his guides he knew the coast to which he proposed to sail and could plot his course accordingly.

On the globe the way from Plymouth to Sierra Leone in the middle of the slaving grounds seemed reasonably straightforward; but a sailing ship was at the mercy of winds and currents and could not make a direct passage. At the start a westerly course was necessary to gain an offing, otherwise a changing wind might trap his ships in the Bay of Biscay and many days be profitlessly employed beating to windward against the current. When enough sea-room had been achieved, Hawkins hoped to run free before the prevailing wind, weather Cape Finisterre and touch the Canary Islands to water his ships and transact certain private business of his own. Thence a clear run should take him between the Cape Verde islands and the coast of Senegal, where the best slaves could be taken. Four thousand miles would have been traversed and the new year be upon them before the slave-decks were full and a westerly course could be shaped to the Indies.

From the Senegal River, where the desert shores of Barbary gave way to more fertile and inhabited lands, Hawkins could follow the coast with assurance. He and many of his crew had ranged these waters in past years. But beyond the River Sestos he had never sailed. Here, in the Bight of Benin, was the heart and strength of the Portuguese empire, and the greatest source of gold. But, like the Bay of Biscay, it was a trap for sailing ships. Once past Cape Palmas the coast bends eastwards, and the current follows the coast. The prevailing winds blow from the sea, and few ships were able either to beat back up the coast, or sail westwards to the Indies, until they had reached so low a latitude that the middle passage was made unendurable by great heat and fitful breezes. The little caravels from Portugal, their triangular sails adorned with the Cross of Christ, that each year ferried the wealth of Elmina back to Lisbon, had arduous and prolonged return voyages. Some privateers, it is true, rounded the Cape of Palms, but they sought treasure rather than slaves, and the Portuguese for their part preferred to keep the peace round their settlements and collect their licensed quota of slaves further afield. It became customary, therefore, amongst privateers and pirates, to regard the Gold Coast as a dangerous but profitable area for trading and robbing, whereas the Senegal coastline was the preserve of slavers and those who were content with a modest but safe return.

Hawkins' expeditions had always had slaves as their primary objective and had had no wish to challenge the galleys of Elmina or the fleets that Portugal seasonally sent to Guinea. Such encounters had been frequent in recent years, and both sides could claim honours; but no interloper could add that they had helped his trading activities.

Hawkins for his part desired nothing better than a quick lading and a peaceful departure. He had no wish to linger long enough to draw the enemy's fire. But the Portuguese, whose spies had been as active as those of Spain in watching the preparation of Hawkins' fleet, were convinced that an assault on Elmina itself was intended. No lesser objective would justify such an extensive expedition. They were thoroughly alarmed, and prepared an armed squadron to intercept him. Too late as it turned out, for their quarry had done his business in Africa before the hunters arrived.

As he pondered on his course and weighed the hazards he would need to overcome, Hawkins could not have been unmindful of the unexpected dangers that an encounter with Portuguese warships might provide. Only three months before, George Fenner, whom he knew as a brave and skilful captain, had brought his ship, the *Castle of Comfort*, into Portsmouth after an ominously unsuccessful cruise in African waters. From him Hawkins would have learnt how hard it had become to cajole or force trade, and of the very real danger presented by roving squadrons of Portuguese warships now engaged in patrolling the debatable waters south of the Azores. The English ship had lived up to its name, for it had proved itself a redoubtable fighter against great odds. Fenner may have boasted of the tactics he had adopted to avoid boarding and to maintain the weather gauge, shooting with his modern and well-mounted guns at a range that preserved his own lighter craft from being crippled. Hawkins, commanding a fleet far more powerful but less manoeuvrable, had much to learn from Fenner's experiences of Portuguese fighting technique and the ordering of battle, and may have enacted many an imaginary engagement to himself, until he was satisfied that even with old ships he could maintain an ascendancy under most conditions.

Very evidently conditions on the coast were becoming more difficult to exploit each season. But Hawkins found it hard to believe that within two years, since his last trip, he would encounter serious trouble. He had laid his plans well and good luck had never yet deserted him. Besides, his intelligence service was as reliable as any in the country.

The Hawkins brothers collected information from many sources. Their own ships gleaned the gossip of foreign ports, and they had friends and contacts on whom they could rely in all the merchant centres of the western world. News from the sea or from far off places travelled slowly and often unreliably, but nonetheless few events of maritime interest failed to reach Hawkins at least as quickly as they came to the ears of government. The channels by which news reached him was a secret no merchant as cautious and self-interested as Hawkins would confess. He had long learned the art of silence when he suspected rivals in trade of attempting to pick his brains. We may judge, however, that Fenner's sad story did not greatly cast him down.

Any lingering doubts Hawkins may have had regarding the adequacy of his expedition were dispelled when, on one of the last days of September, his private fleet left Sutton Pool and dropped anchor in the Catwater near the *Jesus* and *Minion*. Seen all together they formed an imposing fleet, versatile and well-

armed. On board were just over 400 men, chosen with more dis-
crimination than was usually possible for such a voyage. Hawkins'
fame and the legend of his invariable success were responsible for
more volunteers coming forward than he had need of, and he
scarcely needed the services of the impress. He himself had chosen
his officers, few of whom were untried in his service, and they in
turn had helped select the crew.

Against over-manning his ships Hawkins seems to have taken a
strong stand. Many gentlemen, especially those who were more
land-soldiers than seamen, declared that he jeopardized the success
of his ventures by taking so few men on board. Young Drake for
one repeatedly argued with him on this question. There would be
casualties during the course of the voyage, he urged; if not by
fighting then at least by disease. Whoever heard of a major
expedition that was not dogged by fevers, scurvies and fluxes
on the lower deck? If they left England with a crew barely
sufficient for their needs, where could they hope to find replace-
ments thousands of miles from home? But Hawkins was always
adamant, refusing to discuss the matter of complement with
Drake, or listen to soldiers' arguments. He had seen such expeditions set off before, the lower decks packed with men. The rations
of a four-man mess had been stretched to feed six or even eight,
and at the start there was scarcely room below decks for even the
watch off to stretch out and sleep. Not many weeks at sea and a very
different picture presented itself. Food and drink, never plentiful,
became pinched, and the men, weakened by malnutrition, were
an easy prey for the dysentery and fever that spread like wildfire
in the dark, confined messdecks. Not a day would pass without a
burial, and those who survived were too weak and demoralized to
make an effective fighting force.

Hawkins had watched many such ships return to Plymouth with
an empty hold and scarcely enough fit men to lower the sails.
Sometimes he had pointed them out scornfully to be the result of
letting soldiers take command at sea. He had proved to his own
satisfaction that overcrowding was the root of the trouble.
Whenever the ordering of an expedition had been in his hands he
had seen that no more than sufficient crew was carried to work

and fight the ships. Fewer men meant more room for rations; and Hawkins knew that the sailor who got his gallon of beer and pound of biscuit daily was a contented instrument for his purposes. In addition the lack of crowding below decks seemed to reduce epidemics. To such an extent had he found this true in his own experience that his record of human casualties was unusually low, and in part may have accounted for the veneration in which he was held by his crew. A veneration that Hawkins liked to encourage through personal contacts, and an air of sharing the burden of responsibility with the lowliest of his seamen. Some officers— but seldom those who had served under him—declared that he would disclose to a common seaman more than he told his own lieutenants. To such critics, accustomed to a more obviously authoritarian commander, he would answer that the weakness of the fleets of Portugal and Spain was the ignorance and lack of purpose of the fighting men. The English seaman could be relied upon to use his wits, and well repaid any trust that was given him.

But Hawkins' birth and upbringing made it natural that he should turn to professional sailors for the little companionship he needed. There was nothing of the aristocrat in his breeding. His family had risen from the people through commercial acumen. The counting-house and the sea were considered to be more important aspects of education than book-learning. Although he was not old he could not remember his first sea voyage, but he guessed that then as always he had worked his passage, probably in one of his father's ships. He had never been allowed to play the gentleman, and when, on his father's death, he and his brother inherited a merchant fleet and a small fortune, he had lost the desire. Power and authority grew from experience. The incisive command that he wielded from the *Jesus* was founded on no inbred pre-eminence, but on agility of mind, self-confidence and a technical mastery of the craft to which his life had been dedicated.

Now that the fleet was assembled and only the west wind delayed its departure, Hawkins considered it safe to write one final letter to Cecil, not in the expectation of a reply, but to justify once again his conduct during his month's vigil in Plymouth Sound. It rankled with him that he had been misunderstood and his

actions misinterpreted. During his absence the seeds of suspicion
that he feared still lurked at Court might grow into open distrust,
and his return might not be as welcoming as he could desire.
Once at sea no defence could be maintained against slanders at
home. After a little time details would be forgotten, and accusations be based on prejudice. Hawkins was jealous of his good name
and planned more anxiously for the future than most of his fellow
sea-captains would have troubled to do. His friends might call
it stubbornness; indeed Hawkins was never willing to shrug his
shoulders and let events take their course unargued. But motives
and character are intertwined. They seldom allow a simple explanation. As a trader Hawkins loved efficiency and finality.
A clear-cut decision pleased him, no matter how much detailed
work was involved. It irked him, therefore, to leave behind an
obscure picture of his public actions. 'That I have always desired
the name of an orderly person and have always hated folly, my
doings before this have been witness and now are.' In such words
he addressed the Queen's Secretary, and proceeded to recapitulate
at length the events of the past month, tidying up loose ends.
Having sealed his letter and delivered it ashore he dismissed land
thoughts from his mind and became a seaman once again, impatiently waiting for a wind.

On Sunday, October 1st, Hawkins and those of his company
that could be spared would doubtless have attended divine service
in St Andrew's, the mother church of Plymouth. It would be,
they all realized, the last time that they would tread on English
soil for a year, and some of them, in all probability, would never
return at all. To undertake an ocean voyage was itself something
of a sacrament, and for Hawkins the solemnity of the Sunday
service must have been deepened by prayers offered for the prosperity and well-being of the enterprise that was about to set
forth. To each officer these prayers were a memorial of his responsibility, to each seaman a recollection of his helplessness, before
God. He alone would accompany their ships across the waters,
and to Him they dedicated the success of their undertaking.

As they filed out of the church any who cast an eye upward at the weathercock on the tower would have seen that the wind had changed and was blowing gently off the land. It was not fitting that they should sail on a Sunday, but in the morning they knew they would depart. The narrow cobbled streets from St Andrews to Sutton Pool, where the ships' boats lay waiting to receive them, resounded for a time with the music of drum and trumpet and the tramp of feet as the men marched past, shouting farewell to the onlookers. The noise died down, the seamen were ferried out to their ships in the Sound, and a Sunday tranquillity returned to the town.

Hawkins himself, we may presume, had two last calls to pay. First he went to his brother William, who, a few days before, had been elected mayor of Plymouth, and took his leave. Thence he turned to his own house in Kinterbury Street where Katherine, his wife, and their only son, Richard—a boy of seven, still too young to undertake a year-long voyage—awaited him. Farewells were swiftly said, and soon afterwards Hawkins left them and embarked.

Early on Monday morning there was a bustle of activity on board all seven ships. The gilded and brightly-coloured upperworks were further decorated by painted wooden shields and canvas screens. Conspicuous amongst the heraldic devices displayed were Tudor dragons, and Hawkins' own, recently-awarded crest, a negro bound by a cord. Banners of embroidered silk fluttered from short poles both fore and aft. From the fighting tops coloured cloths were draped, and from each masthead slender pennants, long enough had there been no wind to touch the sea, writhed in the breeze. All the smaller boats had been taken aboard and stowed in the waist. The *Swallow* had taken the pinnace in tow, and the three other large ships each had a longboat astern. Booms and gangways were shipped and the ships rode to a single anchor. The open gunports displayed the brazen muzzles of their weapons. Seamen in canvas jackets could be seen climbing the ratlins and thronging the tops.

There was an air of expectation amongst the crowd that had assembled on the Hoe to watch the departure. Many of the onlookers had husbands or sons on board the ships, and although the distance was too great to make a personal farewell it was a brave sight to watch a great fleet set forth, and an encouragement to shout a last Godspeed to the adventurers.

The hour of departure came at last. Hawkins—a tiny figure, scarcely recognizable from the shore—emerged from his cabin and took his stance high on the aftercastle of the *Jesus*. Behind him stood his trumpeters, and to the sound of music unseen men strained against the capstan bars and slowly the dripping anchor cable was hauled in. As the anchor hove in sight, and the knot of men on the forecastle sluiced the mud from the flukes and fixed the catting tackles to secure it outboard, the trumpets sounded again; the Royal Standard was broken at the maintop and the red cross of St George at the foretop. Immediately afterwards, like a bud bursting into flower, the sails were set. First the foresail crumpled for an instant then, catching the wind, leaped forward. Each yard and each mast contributed its petal of sail. The ships grew in size as each fresh canvas tautened and held the breeze. Slowly the hulls themselves, that had rested so inertly upon the water, stirred with new life. Bowsprits dipped towards the sea; ripples whitened and curled back on either side of narrow prows. An uncertain wake showed that the ships were under way. The spirit of life had touched them. Within minutes they were possessed of a proud and elegant power.

The *Jesus* led, and as they gained steerage-way the five other vessels followed her in line astern. She did not make directly for the open sea, but came due west in order to pass close inshore and acknowledge the cheers of the watchers on the Hoe. A gusty land-breeze helped their voices to carry across the water, and there were few sailors who did not line the starboard side, straining to identify some familiar figure amongst the multitude grouped upon the green turf. Even men who by choice spent most of the year afloat were moved by the parting, and many of the younger seamen wept at the poignancy of this last farewell, praying privately for a safe return.

As the *Jesus* came abreast the Chapel of St Catherine—a squat little building, walled around and dominating the seaward approaches to the harbour—she fired her guns in salute. A con-

D

fused roar of voices answered her from the shore, and from the church-tower came a clamour of pealing bells. Usually such a sound was a warning of alarm to the citizens of Plymouth, but not now. Mingling with the bells and shouting could be heard the strains of martial music from the trumpeters and drummers on the ships. Last minute messages were screamed out, and the wind lost them. Gradually the ships drew away from the assembled crowd. Children ran along the cliff to keep abreast a few minutes longer before they too were left behind. The noises ashore ceased to reach the ships, and the sailors themselves became silent. Abruptly the musicians were dismissed and the order was given to luff and steer for the mouth of the Sound.

Amongst the dejected ships' companies the boatswains and corporals moved briskly. A sudden flood of duties allowed no time for brooding or regret. More sails needed to be set and trimmed, and ropes flaked down for running. The anchors were lashed in position and the gay trimmings that had ornamented each vessel were stowed away in the carpenter's store below the orlop. Only the boats' crews, towed astern by the bigger ships and bobbing in their wake, noticed St Nicholas' Island and the town of Plymouth gather the autumn haze about them, and fade first into a toneless outline, then merge imperceptibly into the hills behind. It was not long before the substance had been drained out of the land, and as the realities of the shore receded so, equally quickly, did any desire not to depart from it ebb. The sailors felt under their feet the long slow swell bearing in from the west, and listened with delight to the grumbling undersong of the ship, the creaking of timbers, the moan of wind in the shrouds and the slapping of water against the bows. These noises encompassed their lives, and no deep-water sailor ever regretted hearing them again.

There was no pause in the fleet's progress as it cleared Plymouth Sound. Hawkins was his own pilot and knew the approaches to his home port as well as any man alive. He spoke his instructions to Robert Barrett, the master, who stood on the poop beside him. Outwardly he was unmoved by the pageantry and sadness of departure. All his feelings were concentrated on the work in hand. The sea and the sky, benign under a weak autumnal sun, occupied his thoughts. The two elements held many messages for one skilled to interpret them, and Hawkins read them as a musician will read a page of score. He stood with legs astride to balance himself against the roll of the ship, with his back to the wind and to the other ships of his fleet. Occasionally he turned to see that they were keeping station behind him. Above him and before towered the scooped hollows of the *Jesus'* sails, as white almost as the flock of gulls that flew alongside, gliding easily on the same following wind that urged them forward.

The Mewstone and Rame Head were cleared and the breeze freshened. On the port bow a disturbance in the pattern of the sea betrayed the treacherous, half-concealed Eddystone rock. Taking a bearing on it Hawkins ordered the helm to be put up and a more westerly course shaped. This done he handed over to Barrett and went below.

Now that they were in open water and had established their course the master piped all hands to muster in the waist. From every corner of the ship the men assembled. Those who had worn Hawkins' colours on leaving harbour had already discarded them and slipped into their own tarred canvas jackets and breeches of coarse cloth. Many of them had no other clothes, and most were barefoot. A rough, piratical crew they seemed, unshaven and uncouth. But Elizabethan sailors travelled light and lived in hopes of plunder. They were no less staunch or obedient for lack of uniform, and expected neither comfort nor ease from their profession.

As the men gathered in the waist of the *Jesus* the boatswain and his mates pushed them into some order. When all those not actually on duty had arrived Robert Barrett descended from the poop, and the division of the ship's company into two watches began. Barrett, as chief of the starboard watch, had first choice, and the sailor he picked fell out to starboard. The chief of the port watch chose second, and his man went to the port side. Thus by alternate choice the two watches were assembled. Each man then joined with a friend from the opposite watch to share a mattress (if either possessed such a luxury) or at least bedding-space in the nooks and corners beside the guns or behind the stanchions on the orlop. There was little enough room in the dark, confined quarters below decks for even the watch off to lie down and rest undisturbed.

As soon as these personal arrangements had been made the assembly was dismissed, some to their duties on the upper deck, others, who had the watch below, to draw their first rations of hard biscuit and beer. The unalterable routine of a sea-voyage began to occupy them; a rhythmical alternation of watchfulness and rest by day and night. The sounding of the hourly bell when the quartermaster turned the glass of filtered sand to mark the progress of the watch, the morning and evening prayers, the scrupulous issue of food and drink, the exactly timed interludes of sleep, all these artifices of routine brought order and a feeling of security to men who had cast themselves on the undisciplined ocean wastes. The sea is lonely and hostile, and men who entrust themselves to her vast fecklessness will always band together and create a fellowship stronger and harsher than any on land. They will impose a form—a pattern of action and behaviour—to bind that fellowship together, and try to lose their individual fears in the purpose and order of the group.

So established and accepted was this discipline of the sea that many sailors found it admirable for its own sake. They experienced less pleasure in their freedom ashore than they anticipated, and were ever eager for the strict rhythm of ship life. The old hands on Hawkins' ships only needed to be allotted their watch, their messmates and their rations, before slipping willingly into the anonymity of a member of the ship's company. They scarcely knew where they were going or why. They were not even curious. The further that the horizons of the world opened before them, the more willingly they applied themselves to their daily cares.

CHAPTER 3

The Mutiny

O N the third day after leaving Plymouth the wind, that had carried the fleet in good order on a south-westerly course, dropped. A change in the weather seemed imminent. Hitherto each ship had followed Hawkins blindly for he had not disclosed, even to his captains, the sailing instructions that were to govern the voyage. Now, however, an opportunity offered itself. A banner was hung out at the mizzen yard of the *Jesus* summoning a council. Immediately sails were furled and the coxswains brought alongside the pinnace and longboats that had been towed astern. From each ship the captain and master was rowed across the still waters to where the *Jesus* lay with bare poles, almost becalmed. They were greeted with ceremony as they clambered aboard, and taken aft to the Admiral's cabin.

When all had assembled Hawkins told them formally of the purpose of the voyage, and handed to the captain of each ship a copy of the Articles on which the conduct of the fleet was to be based. Those who had sailed with him before found the same scrupulous attention to detail and anticipation of all eventualities that had characterized his earlier instructions. He touched on matters of discipline, signalling and station-keeping; he laid down the times of worship and the division of spoils. Nothing was left to chance. In order that no man could plead ignorance he commanded that the Articles be read to the ships' companies at service time twice a week. On his previous voyage when he disclosed his sailing orders in the harbour of Ferrol, whence he had been driven by a contrary wind, he had added a summary to his instructions. George Fitzwilliam, who had been present in the cabin of the *Jesus* on that occasion, recalled the impression that his words had made, and how applicable they were to the present voyage. 'Serve God daily', he had commanded them, 'love one another, preserve your victuals, beware of fire, and keep good company.'

In addition to the Articles Hawkins gave each of his captains a rendezvous, to which they were to sail independently if by chance they lost touch with the main fleet. At Santa Cruz on the island of Tenerife in the Spanish-owned Canary Islands there was a good harbour, and Hawkins had friends among the merchants ashore with whom he intended to discuss business. It was here that he chose to reassemble his fleet if it should be scattered. But if some units touched first at the less public island of Gomera it was considered wise for them to fill their water-barrels there, in case a lengthy visit by a depleted fleet at the main port provoked hostility or encouraged a chance attack. The Spaniards in the Canaries were usually friendly, but it was never wise to tempt them by a display of weakness.

The day after the conference on the *Jesus* a full gale blew up. The ships opened out from the close station they had been keeping, and rode before the storm with only a heavily-reefed foresail set. There had been little warning at the onset, and it had been hard work to lower the sails. At the same time all gunports and hatches needed to be closed, and loose gear secured. The ships were bucketing and dipping into confused seas whipped up by the wind, and the decks were slippery with water and at moments awash. The wind shrieked in the rigging, died moaning, then gathered force again and hurled itself at the rigid little slips of sail and plucked at the shrouds that barred its passage. The sky closed in and seemed to join the water, with sheets of driven rain blotting out the lunging ships from their companions. No longer could a course be steered. The helmsman felt the rudder at one moment knocked sideways by a sliding mass of water, the next it scarcely gripped in the trough of an enormous wave. On the open deck lifelines were rigged, for it became well-nigh impossible to cross from the poop to the forecastle without support. Below decks the guns were double-lashed; it was fearful to imagine the effect of a gun breaking loose and uncontrollably rolling and smashing all that lay in its path.

Worst of all was the fate of the two men who crouched, isolated and defenceless, in each of the three boats that the larger vessels towed astern. The storm had come upon them suddenly, before there was a chance to bring them back aboard. They could do little to help themselves. The great ships sped headlong before the gale, blindly and unmanageably plunging into the waves. Their towering poops loomed darkly through the blown spindrift, perilously close at times when the seas threatened to fling the half-swamped boats against their gilded sides, then suddenly receding until with a jerk the towing-lines tautened in a shower of spray and wrenched them forward again, scending into green water.

No boat could endure such a wild run for long. The *Swallow* lost her pinnace and the *Minion* her longboat, together with their helpless crews, when the seas overwhelmed them and the towing-lines snapped. The *Jesus*, however, succeeded in saving her men before conditions became impossible. Through Hawkins' seamanship she was able to turn a little towards the wind and her great upperworks afforded some shelter on the lee side. The stern towing-lines were passed forward, and slowly they were able to haul the boat alongside into less troubled waters. Lifelines were lowered, and the boat's coxswain and his mate, half-drowned and exhausted from exposure, were dragged on board. The longboat had to be abandoned, and the ship, no longer held against the wind, swung back into the course of the gale and fled with it across the sea.

At first they occasionally caught glimpses of their companions running free on a parallel course at the mercy of the wind. But they could pay little regard to them. Each ship fought its own battle with the elements, alone. Although she was the largest vessel the *Jesus* laboured hardest under the stresses of the storm. Her enormous top-hamper caught each gust and drove her drunkenly from side to side. She was slow to right herself, and many times it seemed likely that she might capsize. On this score Hawkins was less worried than by the water she was shipping.

He knew the *Jesus* to be both crank and leaky. The first fault was uncomfortable, but the second might be deadly. Since the very beginning of the storm he had had the carpenter report to him at intervals on the depth of water in the well of the ship, and he had set men to work on the chain pumps. Relays of ten men were working the long-handled brakes at each pump, and for a while they seemed able to keep the water-level in the bilges under control. But from all over the ship water was seeping down into the well. Despite the care with which Hawkins had supervised the caulking of the seams, the hatches and gunports had chinks through which the sea could penetrate; the strained timbers worked themselves free from their seal of oakum, and sea water spurted through the cracks. On each deck a film of dark water slid to and fro with the motion of the ship, saturating everything in its course.

Sailors whose duties took them below, and the carpenter's mates who worked deep down upon the ballast, carried candles in horn lanterns to give them a dull glimmer of light by which they could grope their way. Day and night had no distinction in the dark caverns of the ship. No light came from outside, and although they had some respite from the wind that howled and battered at them on deck, even that noise was preferable to the eerie wrenching and grinding of great timbers, and the resonant blows of the sea, that surrounded them in the dank, flickering gloom of the abandoned messdeck.

There was little sleep to be had that night, or in the two nights following. All hands were on the alert, and work at the pumps became increasingly desperate. During the pauses between their spells of duty groups of men clustered together wherever they could find some protection from the wind and the driving rain, watching the masts and standing rigging with unspoken apprehension. They were too exhausted to talk against the continual shriek of the wind. Not one of them had a dry garment, and they were chilled to the bone. From time to time there was an issue of thin, cold beer and biscuit—but no hot food, as the galley fire had been doused at the beginning of the storm.

Four days the gale continued with unabated fury. The grey

morning light disclosed the same angry seas with confused white crests, and there was no break in the lowering scud that hemmed them in. Hawkins himself had scarcely left the poop by day or night. He seemed almost dazed with fatigue, his eyes bloodshot from the wind. But he was still alert to the reports that came to him of conditions below the waterline. Here the situation was grave indeed. Many seams had opened and the pumps were helpless to cope with the intake of water. The carpenter's mates groped in the semi-darkness to staunch the wounds of the ship; working by touch for the most part, for the candle-light could not penetrate beneath the black swirl of water that rose inch by inch around their legs. They used thinly-beaten sheets of lead as patches, and rammed oakum into the seams; but for the larger gashes, where the timbers were sprung and the treenails broken, they used strips of coarse baize-cloth. Right aft the damage was greatest, where following seas had pounded the *Jesus* most severely. At one point fifteen pieces of baize were needed before the influx of the sea could be stopped.

Work at the pumps never ceased. Only if they clogged was there a moment's interruption, and even then the men who rested, panting on the brakes, were impatient to continue their mechanical task. They worked until they were exhausted, and then another group took over. All of them realized that the *Jesus* was not a ship that could easily weather an Atlantic gale. Many of the sailors had met similar weather before, but none of them had heard such ominous sounds of rending and groaning, nor experienced such uncontrollable leaks. It was as though the old ship was crying out from the agony of dissolution. Yet, withal, the sight of Hawkins on the aftercastle, and the magic of his reputation, gave confidence to many. So long as he was with them, they felt, his craft would rescue them.

A captain has no one, unless it be God, in whom to place such confident trust. The third day of the gale, therefore, found Hawkins even more concerned than his crew for the safety of the ship. He knew how fast the water-level was rising in the hold, and he knew from experience how unseaworthy his once-condemned vessel really was. If the wind had let him he would have cut his losses and returned to England to refit. Indeed he began to doubt that, even if the storm abated, the *Jesus* would be in any condition to continue on the voyage. But the gale drove him farther and farther away from home, and as he watched the hourly disintegration of his flagship, he became convinced that only an act of God could save them in their present distress.

On the morning of the fourth day Hawkins decided that he could no longer conceal from his crew the hopelessness of their situation. He caused all those who could be spared from the pumps, and from other urgent duties, to assemble. The usual place of muster—the waist of the ship—was unusable. It was too slippery, and scoured by the waves. The meeting was held below decks by candle-light. There was no attempt at order. The seamen, bedraggled and exhausted, squatted and crouched wherever they could find support. Hawkins came amongst them and talked in an even, unemotional voice of the danger that they were in. He spoke with the flat detachment of a man worn out in body, yet his face retained its usual composure. Some words were lost through the pounding of the sea, but he made it clear to all that the ship could not endure long under the present conditions. 'You are no better than dead men', he told them.

There had never been optimism, but there had been faith, amongst those on board the *Jesus*. It was difficult to understand that even Hawkins had lost hope. A low, incredulous murmur greeted his announcement; there was not a sailor who was not cast down, and some wept openly. Hawkins paused for a moment to consider his next words. It was not his intention to abandon his men to grief while any chance of life remained. He had told them the truth, for he believed it to be his duty to give each man the opportunity to compose himself to meet his Maker. He had used up what skill he possessed in vain efforts to keep his ship sea-worthy: what happened in the next few hours he could not in-fluence. Only God could help, and with this in mind he had summoned his crew together while there was yet time.

Looking about him he saw the men swayed by a tired and hopeless sorrow. Once again he started to talk, exhorting them to join him in prayer, and telling them to put their faith in God who would not desert them. Together they knelt and Hawkins led them in prayer, encouraging them to substitute faith in a higher Power for faith in him. No man prays so fervently as when he is at the point of death, and many a recusant seaman found comfort of mind in the united prayers of intercession that were raised that morning to God.

All day the struggle to keep the ship afloat continued, and when night fell, although the gale continued to blow, their condition was no worse than it had been at daybreak. At any time they expected to founder, but the dreaded moment never came. Some men even managed to sleep, weary beyond fear. The monotonous clanking of the pumps droned on into the night. The noise, heard against the wild onslaught of wind and sea, was orderly and reassuring. The battle was still being fought: the *Jesus* had not yet capitulated.

By midnight those on deck noticed an easing of the wind. At first they were afraid to voice their hopes, but soon it became apparent that the storm had blown itself out. The rain squalls lifted, and through the torn rack of cloud a star or two appeared for a moment and was smothered. The ship still pitched heavily, but the waves that opened and closed around her were no longer feathered and confused. They rolled forward smoothly in a deep undulating swell, carrying the ship with them and battering her less. There was no doubt about it, the *Jesus* had ridden the storm and survived.

Within minutes every man was aware of the change of fortune, and for the first time in days they smiled to themselves and to their messmates, talking with nervous animation and forgetting their weariness.

By morning the wind had backed to the north and blew gently, allowing the sails to be set and a course to be steered. The sun rose on the port beam, dazzling in the clarity and pureness of its light. The decks glistened with moisture, streaking the wooden planks with salt-smears as it dried. On all sides the line of the horizon was revealed, as sharp and clean as a knife-cut. Up aloft in the fighting-tops the look-outs strained their eyes to catch sight of the five companion ships that had separated from them during the storm. There was not a sail in sight. The *Jesus* might, for all they knew, be the sole survivor of the fleet. Only at their meeting place in the Canary Islands would they know the full extent of the damage that had been suffered. Until then they sailed alone, wallowing through the ground-swell in the wake of the gale with a fair breeze behind them, cheerful to be alive.

Hawkins' first act that day was to summon all hands to join in a service of thanksgiving. Usually the quartermaster needed to chase the laggards from the messdecks to morning prayers with a rope's end, but on this occasion there was no need. God had interceded on their behalf and saved them from drowning. There was not a man unwilling to show his gratitude. Hawkins himself led his crew in worship, his back to the mainmast, and the words of the Lord's Prayer, the Psalm of David and the Creed rose in a murmur from the waist. Around them, like a new Convenant, wisps of steam sprang from the drying decks, rising with their prayers into the clear sky.

After they had given thanks Hawkins addressed the company. He told them that during the storm he had resolved, if he was able, to turn about and return home to refit. This morning, however, he had changed his mind and was resolved to pursue his original purpose. The carpenters had the leaks well under control, a fair wind was blowing them south, and from his calculations at sunrise they were not far off course. If they encountered no more bad weather the *Jesus* would carry them forward in safety.

Scarcely had he finished speaking when the look-outs cried that they could see a sail in the distance. The course was altered to intercept, and before long they identified it as the *Angel*. The *Jesus* closed to within hailing distance, and the crews greeted each other tumultuously. Thus they sailed southward in company, the largest and the smallest ships of the fleet. Of the other vessels they knew nothing, but they felt confident now that they would meet again sooner or later. Each evening the *Jesus* carried a lantern high up on her poop, and the little *Angel*, following astern, took its light as a guide. Each morning the look-outs clambered up the ratlins and scoured the horizon afresh, but until they neared Tenerife they sighted nothing.

Then, suddenly, they were joined by the *Judith*. The storm had flung her apart from the rest, and having survived without damage, she was shaping a solitary course for the rendezvous in the Canaries. During the night her tracks converged with those of the *Jesus* and *Angel*, and the light of dawn found them sailing almost in company together.

The three ships left the Portuguese island of Madeira unsighted to the east. The wind remained northerly, but the extreme visibility that followed in the wake of the storm softened to a haze at the horizon. It was not until they were within twenty miles of the island, therefore, that they saw the snow-capped Pike of Tenerife, looming like a pale shadow above the sea. *Pico de Teyde* the Spaniards called it—Hell Peak; a fang of volcanic rock rising out of the water twelve thousand feet high. To sailors it was a landmark and a symbol, for it stood on the boundary of the civilized world.

The roadstead of Santa Cruz was a busy meeting-ground for ships of all nations coming and going on trading ventures to all parts of the globe. On either side of the open, sandy bay which contained the port rocky promontories formed natural sites for defensive works, and the anchorage, although it shelved steeply, gave excellent protection from the weather, allowing ships to come close inshore with safety.

When Hawkins led his two small consorts into the roads he immediately saw that no other ships of his fleet had preceded him. There was only a large Spanish vessel, bound for the Indies, and a number of smaller craft. As he came within range he dipped his ensign and exchanged gun-salutes with the shore forts and the Spaniard. He anchored without apparent concern, but he chose his position carefully so that his ships were masked by those already at anchor from the batteries ashore. Hawkins, some people considered, was hypersensitive about taking risks with foreigners.

Even if he was distrustful by nature, Hawkins was nonetheless punctilious in observing the customary ceremonial and courtesies of his profession. In part it was self-interest, for he had built up valuable friendships over the years with the merchants and administrators of Santa Cruz; he had no wish to endanger these through a simple lack of civility. But there was another reason. Hawkins held a royal trust. He was, in effect, an ambassador at large, and acted with the Queen's authority. He took his responsibility seriously and displayed limitless patience and craft and tact to encompass his ends, at times when firier souls would have lost all patience and used the Queen's authority to further their own purposes. In the Queen's name, therefore, Hawkins made haste to send a friendly letter ashore to the Governor of Santa Cruz, informing him of his intentions—to collect his scattered fleet, take on water and buy provisions against payment. With the letter he sent suitable gifts. He wrote other letters too, inviting his friends among the merchants of the town aboard for dinner that evening; in particular he asked Pedro and Nicolas de Ponte, who had often in the past aided and advised him.

The Spaniards had never closed the Canary Islands to traders from other lands. Long before Hawkins conceived the idea of selling slaves in the Indies he and his fellow-countrymen had done business with this metropolitan outpost of Spain. Indeed it is probable that his friends the de Pontes, father and son, encouraged him to undertake his first voyage into the forbidden waters of America. Certainly they provided him with a pilot and letters of introduction to the merchants of the Indies. On his second slaving voyage too Hawkins had had conference with Pedro de Ponte on his way out and had received the latest intelligence from the west.

The Governor replied as courteously as Hawkins had written. The merchants and dignitaries of Santa Cruz thronged aboard to welcome an old friend and enjoy his hospitality. But someone, probably de Ponte, warned Hawkins that all was not well. His two previous voyages had been too successful for the Spanish authorities to ignore, and instructions had been given that he was to be prevented from undertaking another. When, therefore, the Spaniards in their turn invited Hawkins to a reception ashore he had an excuse prepared. The Queen, he declared, had expressly forbidden him to leave her ship.

Outwardly Hawkins gave no sign of his mistrust. Boats plied to and fro with water-casks all day, and some of the ravages of the storm were patched up in the still water of the harbour. Small craft rowed out from the shore piled high with oranges for sale. There was fresh fish and goat's meat to be bought and other welcome additions to their diet. For a while the steep-tubs in the chains remained unbroached. Everyone ate well.

The only complaint that reached him from the shore Hawkins dealt with promptly. It concerned the ship's baker, a member of one of the watering parties, who in an excess of Protestant zeal had seen fit to overturn a cross outside a hermitage. For his pains Hawkins had the man triced up to the mainmast for a couple of hours.

A careful watch was set by day and night, but trouble ~~when~~ when it came on the second day of their sojourn did not occur in the way that Hawkins was expecting. So intent had he been to anticipate the machinations of the Spaniards ashore that he was unaware of a bitter quarrel that had sprung up between two of the officers of his own ship. Hawkin's confidant, George Fitzwilliam, and Edward Dudley, the captain of the land soldiers, were the parties to the dispute, the original cause of which can only be guessed. Both men lost their tempers and harsh words were exchanged. With difficulty they refrained from blows, but agreed to meet ashore and fight it out. Dudley had already left the ship when Hawkins got wind of what was afoot. To settle private feuds by duelling was an intolerable breach of the discipline he had laid down—a subversion of his authority, and, besides, an unnecessary embarrassment in an already dangerous situation if the Spanish authorities became aware of the event, as they surely would.

In an explosion of anger, before which Fitzwilliam was wise enough to bend, Hawkins forbade his friend to keep his appointment, and sent a boat to the spot where Dudley was waiting with orders for him to return aboard immediately.

The interview that took place in Hawkins' cabin after Dudley had been brought back, angry and unappeased, was witnessed by no one. Hawkins had on the surface hidden his wrath that so insubordinate an act should have been attempted under his command. He spoke sharply to Dudley, reminding him of his responsibilities and the allegiance that was due to the commander of the expedition. In particular he stressed the folly of pursuing a private quarrel under the guns of their enemy the Spaniards. Now was no time for disunity; later, if necessary, he himself would supervise an affair of honour in some less perilous place.

But Dudley was beyond reason. He was ever intemperate: now he was almost incoherent with suspicion and rage. It is probable that he and Hawkins never had much love for each other. To an experienced, well-born soldier like Dudley it was galling to be put under the command of an upstart young provincial sailor. He fretted under his enforced inaction on board ship, and the slights to which he thought himself subjected. Angrily he dismissed his captain's suggestion and demanded immediate satisfaction; then, when Hawkins again refused, taunted him with the suggestion that he was protecting his friend Fitzwilliam.

A hasty temper was not one of Hawkins' usual characteristics, but Dudley's insinuation riled him intolerably. Stepping forward he struck at Dudley with his clenched fist. If he had calculated on sobering his opponent's hysterical anger by the blow, Hawkins misjudged his man. More probably he acted, for once, without reflection. Unhesitatingly Dudley drew the short sword that, like any Elizabethan gentleman, he carried at his side, and lunged at his commander.

In a flash Hawkins realized that Dudley's words, already insubordinate, had now, transformed into deeds, become an act of mutiny. His anger vanished. The affair had become far too serious for such an indulgence. No sooner had Dudley drawn his sword than Hawkins, jumping back, drew his own and cried out for assistance. The two men were alone in the cabin, but at the door were his servants, and the officers' quarters were within hail. Hawkins had no need to defend himself long. Dudley's first stroke had drawn blood, but once he was prepared for the attack Hawkins parried the blows and pressed forward against his adversary, wounding him in the arm. It was all over in a few seconds. The door of the cabin burst open, revealing to those who entered the terrifying sight of their commander, one eye closed by a gash of blood, with drawn sword, locked in close combat with the captain of land forces.

Without hesitation they seized Dudley from behind and held him pinioned. Their duty lay towards Hawkins. There was a moment's silence when only the panting breath of the two combatants could be heard. Then Hawkins dropped his guard and walked a few paces away. In a surprisingly even voice he commanded them to take Dudley to his cabin and place him under guard and in irons. By this time a crowd of officers and men had assembled at the cabin door, and as the news of the assault upon their captain spread a cry went up demanding that Dudley be put to death. There was a surge of men towards him, and a tumult rose amongst the crowd in which voice after voice demanded that he be summarily punished. Hawkins stepped between his angry seamen and the arrested man. Blood was running down his face from the wound over his right eye, matting his beard and staining his already dishevelled clothes. He spoke with authority, assuring them that he was not gravely hurt but forbidding them to harm the prisoner. At the same time he promised a quick and public hearing into the assault upon his person. Thanking them for their intervention, he dismissed all but the surgeon from his cabin to allow his wound to be dressed.

Later that day the decks were cleared and all hands piped to muster in the waist of the *Jesus* to witness the arraignment of Edward Dudley on a charge of mutiny. In the intervening hours tempers had calmed, and men were less inclined to be stirred by the emotions of the moment. They had had time to reflect upon the awful seriousness of the charge and were uneasily conscious of the retribution that would surely follow Dudley's court martial. They were about to witness an act of justice. The prospect distressed them, not because they doubted that it was just, but because they felt the shadow of the disgrace upon themselves. A ship's company has a unity of its own. A happy ship, like a healthy body, reflects the harmony of its members. If a gunner shoots well, the deck hands take a rightful share of the glory: if he shoots badly, the captain and the cabin boy share equally in the disgrace. Triumphs or tragedies are accepted in the name of the ship, not of the individual. Dudley's mutiny, therefore, struck deeply at the crew through their feeling of collective responsibility. They were abashed by an assault that challenged the very fabric of good order. Dudley himself had time in the confinement of his cabin to reflect upon the folly of his conduct. Now that the blood had cooled, his blind, pugnacious rage seemed almost incredible. His differences with Fitzwilliam had been trivial, and with Hawkins he had had no quarrel at all. It was scarcely possible to recreate the spirit that had moved him to such senseless actions. Yet the aching wound in his arm, and the fetters on his legs, were memorials of his rashness. His heart sank under the pity of it. He had been trained to arms, and knew very well the punishment he could expect. He had meted out sentences of death for lesser offences himself, and never considered them undeserved. He saw no reason why his own crime should be mitigated. The summons to his trial, when it came, found him despondent at his disgrace, but resigned and devoid of rancour. He could not appear dignified as he was led, between armed men, to the place on the thronged deck where he would face his accuser. He still wore the clothes in which he had fought, torn and stained with blood. His sword had been taken from him; he was hatless and in chains. He was a figure of pathos, and those who had cried out against him a few hours before when they saw him armed and angry in Hawkin's cabin now took pains to avoid his glance.

Not until the muster had been taken and the prisoner had stood for some minutes surrounded by the silent ranks of those who were once his companions did Hawkins make his appearance. He had changed into fresh clothes, but bore the marks of Dudley's wound with a bandage covering his right eye.

The accused man was commanded to stand forward, and the charge against him was read out. When he had finished Hawkins addressed himself to Dudley, asking him if he considered that he could justify his actions. Impetuously Dudley threw himself down before his captain, acknowledging on his knees that he had indeed committed an offence, of which, now, he was utterly ashamed. His remorse was visible in his eyes, and his voice choked as he continued to speak, not in defence of himself, but of the proceedings that were being taken against him. If he had had command of men, he said, and one among them had attempted a similar act against himself, he would have had him hanged for his crime. He could not defend his deed, but only pleaded for mercy.

In reply Hawkins declared that for his part he could easily forgive Dudley for his assault, but there were weightier factors to be considered. The mutiny had imperilled the Queen's ship, and the men in her who had been placed in his charge. It had been doubly dangerous in being perpetrated in a possibly hostile port. Not on his own account, therefore, but as the Queen's legate, he found it necessary to administer punishment.

To drive home the reasons for his decision Hawkins took an historical analogy, and recounted the story at some length. The crew, who were largely unlettered men, listened intently to the parable and quickly understood the inference he intended. Even Dudley acknowledged that the comparison was just, and told Hawkins that he was resigned to whatever fate was considered fitting.

When he had finished speaking Hawkins turned to the boatswain, whose office by custom was also that of executioner, and in a solemn yet decisive voice ordered him to load an arquebus with two bullets. The boatswain ran to fetch the weapon, and Hawkins once again addressed Dudley, telling him to make his peace with God for he was about to die.

Although he had nerved himself to accept his punishment, the final verdict overwhelmed the unfortunate prisoner. He sobbed openly, and his distress infected those around him. Within a few minutes many of the ship's company were themselves kneeling and imploring their captain to show mercy. But Hawkins remained inflexible, scarcely seeming aware of their supplications.

The gun was loaded, primed, and handed to Hawkins. He motioned to one side those who stood in the line of fire, then demanded of Dudley if he was ready.

'I have done with the world,' the condemned man replied, 'and I am ready to receive the punishment that you have appointed for me.'

In the midst of outspoken grief Hawkins placed the foot of the supporting rest upon the deck, and swung the barrel of the gun against Dudley's temple. He paused for a moment; then, in a loud voice ordered the irons to be struck from the prisoner's legs. At the same time he laid aside the fatal weapon and took Dudley by the hand.

An act of grace is ever popular, and Hawkins in a superbly-acted scene both punished and preserved. Dudley had experienced all the terror of execution and would emerge from the anguish of his ordeal purged of all treason and confirmed in loyalty. The witnesses to the drama had also experienced a catharsis. Their wills had been turned from anger towards mercy. A mutiny had been transformed into a voluntary act of unity; forgiveness had usurped hate. No outward act of justice could achieve these things. Hawkins had played a part at the trial not of a judge but of an interpreter, translating his seamen's inarticulate and unformed desires into the language of humanity.

Even Hawkins who had planned the denouement was surprised and moved by the wild wave of enthusiasm and emotion that greeted his actions. There was a tumult of voices. Men cheered and cried out in a spontaneous burst of loyalty and love. The carpenter sprang forward to release Dudley from his fetters, but before he could reach him the reprieved soldier had fallen to his knees before Hawkins, begging that he should not be released unless he received his captain's willing forgiveness. He had done a deed, he cried, for which he wished to die unless Hawkins could help him to erase its memory. Hawkins raised Dudley to his feet and spoke gently to him; he assured him that the episode was now closed and he would willingly see that all record of it was expunged. Taking his arm, he walked aft with him, leaving the assembled crew to discuss the painless justice of the trial in the waist.

On the evening of the fourth day of their sojourn at Santa Cruz the watchman on the *Jesus* noticed that the vessels to landward were shifting their berths. Silently, almost invisibly, black shadows glided across the starlight, and the lights along the shore were obscured for a moment as ship after ship crept out of the anchorage. As soon as Hawkins was aware of the manoeuvre he knew what to expect. The screen between his fleet and the shore batteries was being withdrawn, and at first light the Spaniards could open fire on him without warning.

With equal secrecy, therefore, he caused his own ships to set their sails and take up new berths out of the range of the shore forts. The morning found them once more at anchor, but further along the coast, several miles from the port. His boats still plied peacefully to and fro with water-barrels, and gave no outward sign of suspicion. But the Governor and those with him, who were engineering the destruction of Hawkins' fleet, realized very well that their plot had been discovered.

The Governor sent a message out to Hawkins professing surprise that he should have moved. Hawkins replied with a courteous reiteration of the friendship that existed between their two countries. But it was obvious that he could no longer stay in the neighbourhood of Santa Cruz as an honoured guest. The barriers of courtesy were almost down, and Hawkins had no wish to provoke a skirmish so early on his voyage. He ordered his boats to return and had them hoisted on board. All his business ashore had been completed, and the last barrels could be filled with water at some less-frequented place. Anchors were weighed, and the three vessels set sail once more, leaving the town of Santa Cruz just out of range. As they passed, the guns ashore fired six times in salute, and Hawkins punctiliously replied.

A little further along the coast of Tenerife the *Jesus* and the *Angel* paused in the bay of Adessia, but Hawkins sent the *Judith* on ahead to the island of Gomera in order to link up, if possible, with the remaining three ships of his scattered fleet. A day later Hawkins had news of them—a coasting vessel had seen them at anchor off Gomera. Without further delay the two ships followed the same course that the *Judith* had steered the day before. They skirted the high, forbidding cliffs that fall hundreds of feet into deep water, searching the anchorages for their companions.

At last they came upon them; four ships (for the *Judith* had joined them) peacefully anchored in a small bay. Three weeks had passed since the storm flung them apart; now at last they were together again. Across the water each ship fired a joyous round of salutes. The rumble of gunfire echoed in the rocky crags that surrounded their anchorage, and white smoke drifted gently across the bay.

The fleet had suffered no great damage, and was now amply provisioned. A few last ladings of fresh food had been purchased, and the Governor of the island came on board himself to welcome Hawkins and encourage him to stay. But to remain was a luxury. Valuable time on the slaving grounds had already been lost. Two days was all that Hawkins would allow to complete the preparations. On November 4th he departed, leading his reunited squadron on a southerly course towards Cape Blanco on the African coast, aided by a mild following wind.

CHAPTER 4

The Slave Coast

THE first ship to sight the African coast hoisted a banner at her maintop. A low, unbroken line of grey land gradually came into view on the port hand; as featureless as a bank of mist, but harder in outline. The *Jesus* altered course in order to sail closer inshore and identify some landmark. Before long the sonorous murmur of the surf could be heard, a majestic uninterrupted rumble as wave after wave arched and broke against the barrier of land.

The deep pulses of the sea are unaffected by calms or storms. They gather their power in unplumbed waters and traverse the ocean spaces almost unnoticed by the ships that sail over them. The shelving of the land constricts their flow, forcing the swell upwards until it topples forward in a confusion of white breakers. The endless battle between earth and water is fought far out from the beach, but the thunder of the combat, after the moon's champion has been tripped and falls, reverberates on the sounding-board of the shore, and can be heard, on exposed coasts, miles out at sea.

At night, or in bad weather, it is often the luminous line of surf and the mutter of rollers pounding on the beach that warns the sailor of the approach of land. Such a coast, on however calm a day, is inviolable. Often it is well-nigh impossible to take a small boat through the enormous surf, and a ship needs to find an anchorage well-protected from the landward tug of the waves before it can pause.

There are few harbours on the Barbary coast. The beaches and low cliffs of russet and white sand present an unblemished

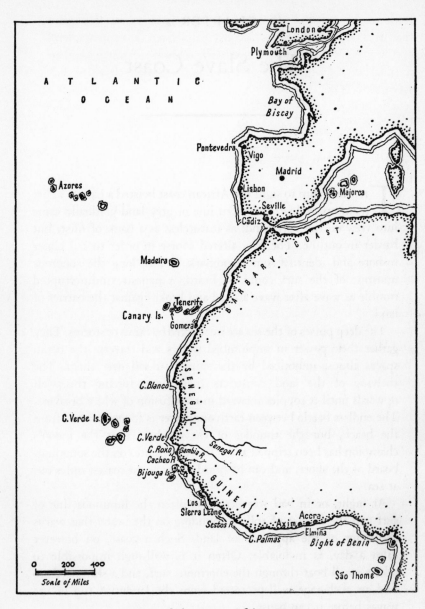

Map of the West African coast

front to the Atlantic. To Hawkins, therefore, it was important that he should not oversail the convenient haven that the headland of Cape Blanco afforded. Its appearance from seaward was unmistakable: a flat, desolate plateau edged by cliffs of white rock seventy feet high with a single conical hill, in shape like a sentry box. Hawkins remembered it well from his previous voyages.

It was not Cape Blanco, however, that first halted the fleet. Directly in their path they sighted three small Portuguese fishing-craft with no sails set, seemingly at anchor about a mile off-shore. The water through which the English ships were now sailing was famous as a fishing ground. Mullet and sea-bream abounded, and fleets of small craft plied to and from Portugal, bringing the catch, none too fresh after the long voyage, home to market. The sight of three such caravels was familiar enough, and only curiosity, or desire to buy fish, would have caused Hawkins to pause. At first he hailed them, but, receiving no reply, he sent a boat across and boarded them. There was not a man on board. Evidently they had been abandoned by their crews and left to the mercy of the first strong wind that might blow. But first they had been ransacked, or perhaps looted, for every sail and all movable gear had been taken away, and only their cargoes of half-rotten fish remained in the holds. Hawkins himself inspected each of the caravels, and remembering the pinnace he had lost, determined to take the newest of them with him.

He was fully entitled to seize a vessel in this manner, as he had discovered her abandoned on the high seas. Legally his right was incontestable. But he was sailing without letters of marque, and he realized that an unwitnessed act of appropriation would almost certainly be misinterpreted by the Portuguese authorities as soon as they learnt of it. A policy of caution demanded witnesses, and Hawkins, in his anxiety that no failure in the letter of the law should cloud his actions, determined to obtain some. Far out at sea he had sighted the square sails of two other fishing boats, obviously engaged in their trade. To them he dispatched the *Judith* and the *Angel* with instructions to bring them along after him to the anchorage at Cape Blanco. Even if they could not explain the mystery, they could at least vouch publicly for the legality of his action. The larger ships of his squadron took the three abandoned caravels in tow and resumed their southerly course.

Cape Blanco, it transpired, was close at hand. Before many hours the *Jesus* led the way into the protection of the west bay and dropped her anchor. A few Portuguese fishing boats were already there, for the fishing season was at its height, but little else. There was talk of establishing a fort, but the trade was too poor to be worth either plundering or protecting. The desert swept down into the sea, and fresh water was scarce. No crops would grow, and only nomads and traffickers in salt frequented the coastal lands. To sailors fresh from England there were strange sights to be seen. Men in white cloaks and turbans led strings of camels over the dunes, bound for distant trading centres; and groups of Touregs, their faces veiled from sight, watched the ships from a distance. There was little contact between the two races. The desert dwellers were suspicious and treacherous, and their numbers few; for these reasons they were not sought after as slaves, even if it had been possible to take them by surprise. Hawkins knew it was a waste of time to try. He had chosen this quiet anchorage to complete the refitting of his ships, and to make ready the lower decks to receive their black cargo.

The day after his arrival the *Judith* and the *Angel* rejoined him, bringing with them one of the two fishing-boats. Hawkins summoned the master aboard and questioned him about the ownership of the three ships that he had found. He was told that three weeks before, a squadron of French ships had sailed past. They had plundered and ransacked the three tiny caravels, and used the crews so roughly that after their departure they had abandoned their craft in terror and fled ashore to seek protection from the nearby base that the Portuguese maintained under license from the Berber Chiefs. Since then they had shown no willingness to return to their ships.

Hawkins explained the circumstances under which he had

appropriated the three caravels, and told the Portuguese captain that it was his intention to retain one of the boats, and fire the others before he left harbour, in order to prevent them from falling into the hands of the natives. The Portuguese seaman agreed that he was entitled to take such action, but suggested that, given a little time, he might be able to get into touch with the men from the abandoned craft, and bring them back with him to Cape Blanco. With Hawkins' approval he set out, and two days later returned accompanied by the masters of two of them.

Once again Hawkins stated his intentions, and his case was ruefully acknowledged to be just. Finding Hawkins of a milder disposition than they had feared, they plucked up courage to suggest that as the English fleet could only use one of the abandoned caravels it was a needless waste to burn the other two. Hawkins agreed, and offered to sell the boats back to their original owners. But the two Portuguese captains who stood before him were obviously poor men and incapable of raising money. Indeed Hawkins had only to look at them to realize they spoke the truth when they declared their inability to pay. Nonetheless he persisted, offering them the two boats at the ludicrously low price of forty ducats, payable if they wished in a year or two's time.

Obviously Hawkins was not concerned with the money he might or might not receive. It was the documentation of a legal and generous transaction that he desired. Not unnaturally the Portuguese were delighted to accept his terms. The fittings of the two ships alone were worth more than the price Hawkins asked. They had expected to lose everything, and were astonished by the leniency of their treatment. Without argument the necessary papers were signed and sealed, and when Hawkins left the harbour, after a sojourn of fifteen days, two of the caravels remained behind. The third, flying the English flag, added a seventh sail to his fleet.

Passing from Cape Blanco to the Senegal River Hawkins kept his fleet well out to sea. The wavering line of sand dunes with occasional patches of grey scrub concealed no stir of life. It was a needless risk to bring his ship closer inshore. He waited until the discoloration of the sea showed that he had reached the river's mouth before he checked his course. Near the banks of the River Senegal were the villages of the most northerly negro tribe, the Jalofs. They were a tall and hardy race, accustomed to poverty and therefore excellent as slaves. Their straw huts were unprotected from assault, but they had experienced too many depredations from the sea to be caught except by guile. Unless they were surprised at the first attempt it was useless to pursue them.

Sailing as close inshore as he dared, and sounding his way with lead and line, Hawkins worked his way down the coast to the vicinity of Cape Verde, the westernmost point of Africa. The smaller craft were given the task of finding a beach where it would be safe to land. Towards evening they reported a suitable place, sheltered to seaward by a small island. The fleet then withdrew for the night and anchored offshore, hoping that no suspicion had been aroused.

Two hours before dawn nearly two hundred men, led by Hawkins himself, were silently ferried ashore at the chosen landing place. They had muffled their oars, and the drummer who, by custom, sounded the beat for the rowers from the leading boat was silent. From Hawkins' row-barge a white flag fluttered to prevent, if possible, any of the other craft from overtaking him by mistake. A strict silence was enjoined, for it was hoped that they might surprise a village that Hawkins believed to exist some miles up-country, and capture the inhabitants at daybreak before they had risen from sleep. Hawkins was the first to leap ashore, and Dudley followed him. Whispered commands were passed, a guard was left behind to defend the beach, and the main party, shouldering their weapons, disappeared into the darkness. Daylight was upon them when they stumbled upon a large cluster of huts, ranged close together in a circle with a few palm trees around them, and some patches of cultivated ground where millet had been grown. The silence seemed to indicate that surprise had been achieved. With a shout of encouragement Hawkins and Dudley led their men in a charge.

But the huts were empty, and the sailors who had raced so confidently forward were checked, and paused in bewilderment. The hot ashes of a fire showed that their ambush had not long been anticipated, and a few minutes later there was shouting from the fringes of the encampment. A party of sailors had surprised a group of women and children hiding in the bushes, and one or two were captured. Before they could pursue the remainder, however, a fierce, barbaric howling broke out, and the Englishmen found themselves subjected to attack from all sides.

Six hundred negroes, the sailors reckoned, must have been concealed amongst the scrub and behind the dunes around the village. Once they had revealed themselves they advanced without fear, undeterred by the arquebus fire that was directed at them. For the most part they were armed with short throwing-spears and bows, but the rain of arrows that opened their assault did little damage. The English party were helmeted and wore buff jerkins that repelled the light shafts. Some of the sailors received glancing wounds on their unprotected limbs, and Hawkins himself was struck by an arrow in the left arm, but they paid little regard to such annoyances. Their own crossbows and the ~~deadly~~ fire from the arquebuses were already taking their toll. When the first wave of attackers had failed to dislodge them, the Englishmen in their turn moved forward. The first shock of surprise had vanished, and much of their terror with it. The almost naked savages could not stand at close quarters against a resolute body of well-armed men. Hawkins and Dudley, with drawn swords, led the counter-attack, but their opponents did not wait to receive them. Swiftly they withdrew; but whenever the Englishmen halted for breath they found themselves once again surrounded and plagued with missiles thrown from a distance. Only occasionally could they match their swords and partisans against the hide shields and curved moorish scimitars that some of the negroes carried.

During such scuffles Hawkins cried out to his men, urging them to capture rather than kill. In this manner a few slaves were taken. But for every prisoner captured one of his fighting-men was needed as a guard. Very quickly Hawkins realized that to continue to attack would be profitless, and might indeed become dangerous if his forces weakened or were divided. There was no alternative but to call a retreat. With nine captives in their midst the English party closed their ranks and fought their way back to the beach. Not a man had been lost, and no one seemed badly wounded. They congratulated each other on a lucky escape.

They joked about the affair when they were safely back on board, and showed their scratches to those who had stayed behind with the pride of old campaigners. A score of them had arrow wounds, but most of them were too trivial to take seriously. Two days later they regretted their levity. Many of the arrows had been poisoned, and those whose wounds had not been cleansed by bleeding or washing were seized with a convulsion not unlike lockjaw. The force of the spasms almost choked them, and their terrified comrades forced their mouths open with wedges of wood until the fit had passed. Between the attacks they talked lucidly, but gradually their powers failed them and after a week of agony eight of the afflicted sailors died. Anxiously they watched for the fatal symptoms to appear in Hawkins or Dudley, both of whom had received similar wounds, but mercifully both men escaped unharmed. On the lower deck it was rumoured that one of the captive negroes, with whom Hawkins had been closeted in an attempt at interrogation, had taught their captain to draw the poison from his wound with a clove of garlic. If it was so Hawkins did not choose to extend the application of the remedy. *Most unlike him.*

The aftermath of death had terrified the crew, and although Hawkins thought to remain in the neighbourhood of Cape Verde in the hope of discovering and attacking some other native settlement, it was obvious that he would not willingly be supported by his men. It also seemed likely that the whole district was alarmed. At night, when the wind was still, drums could be heard from the shore, beating out a message of warning, and many eyes would watch his movements if he attempted to land again. Reluctantly, therefore, he summoned back on board the scouting parties he had sent out and set sail once more down the coast.

The fleet rounded Cape Verde and kept station behind the *Jesus* throughout the night. It would have been an uneventful stage on their journey had they not lost a man overboard. By the time they discovered that he was missing it was useless to turn back and search for him. If he had not been drowned he would certainly have been seized by the sharks that had joined their convoy: unwelcome companions whose grey fins glided lazily through the water in the very shadow of the ships.

First light found them off the wide estuary of the Gambia. The river was navigable and a good slaving ground, for there were many settlements along its banks. In all probability Hawkins intended to take his ships up the river, but to his chagrin he found that he had been preceded. Six small vessels were at anchor off the bar, and before daylight revealed them he had crept to within four miles without their being aware of his presence. Hastily they weighed and made for the open sea, but Hawkins easily cut them off and halted them with a shot across the bows.

As he approached he saw from their colours that they were French ships, outlaws like himself in these forbidden waters. Their commander was summoned aboard the *Jesus*, and Hawkins learned, as he had guessed, that trade rather than slaves was their object.

Exactly what passed between Hawkins and Captain Planes—or, as the sailors anglicized it, Bland—is not entirely clear. According to the most likely accounts all but one ship in the French squadron were found to possess letters of marque which Hawkins respected. The largest and most desirable vessel, both in equipment and seaworthiness, had been captured from the Portuguese and possessed no such credentials. It was a useful ship of 150 tons, armed with eight guns, and Hawkins coveted it. Some reports indicate that he tortured several Frenchmen and seized it forcibly, but such behaviour seems out of character and would hardly have earned him the loyalty that Bland and his men later displayed. More probably he struck a bargain with the French captain, offering to incorporate the Portuguese vessel in his own fleet and let her sail with her own crew on his more ambitious project under the English flag. The prospect of far more substantial returns than he could have hoped to gather by plundering the coast seems to have persuaded Captain Bland; and he was assured that if he shared equal risks he could expect equal rewards.

The rest of the French squadron prepared to return home. Their holds were already full of hides and other goods that had been seized or received in trade. But Hawkins was glad to obtain a few luxuries from them such as cider, almonds and figs in exchange for linen and pewterware. He was also able to confirm that these were the ships that had terrorized the Portuguese fishermen off Cape Blanco and caused them to abandon their ransacked boats. To have been preceded down the coast by such a disruptive band of privateers was undoubtedly bad for serious trade. Hawkins must have been relieved to have caught up with them, and doubtless their most recent depredations caused him to abandon any plans for raiding the river-villages of the Gambia.

All day the thirteen ships lay close together under the cloudless blue sky. Bland reorganized his squadron, and at Hawkins' instruction they renamed the Portuguese bark the *Grace of God*. In charge of this new addition to their fleet he placed his young kinsman, Francis Drake. He was only twenty-two years old, and it was his first command, but Hawkins had found him trustworthy in handling both ships and men. He knew that Drake could be relied upon to detect any deceit of which the Frenchmen might be guilty.

By nightfall the reorganization had been accomplished. A breeze sprang up that struck cool against the skin after the intense, brooding heat of the day. At intervals along the flat coastline the glimmer of bush fires could be seen where the dry scrub and grass savannahs were being cleared before the sowing of crops. Above the glow of the fires, and arching overhead in crystalline splendour lay the scattered stars, casting the bloom of their cold light over the decks and standing rigging of the anchored ships. When the moon rose the men on watch retired into the shadows. They feared the pernicious influence of that planet and would not expose themselves unnecessarily to her beams. Intolerable burning pains, they said, variably struck down those careless enough to fall asleep with the moon's radiance on their faces.

Seamen are early risers, and Hawkins' fleet was astir at the first glimmerings of light in the east. As the eight ships were preparing to depart a message came across to the *Jesus* from one of the small French vessels that were being left behind, asking if it might be allowed to join the English squadron. Hawkins told them that he was agreeable, and a ninth sail was hoisted and turned on a southerly course towards Cape Roxo.

The wind was mild and fitful. Before they had gone far the sails were hanging limp at the yards, and with every stitch of canvas set they could scarcely maintain steerage-way. The vessels with shallow draught kept inshore, sounding as they went for there were treacherous shoals in places. All the time the look-outs scanned the coast in the hope of detecting good landing-beaches and signs of habitation. It was a monotonous task. Rivers leaked sluggishly into the sea, sometimes through thickets of stalk-rooted mangrove, sometimes through sandbars tufted with coarse grass. There were no distinctive landmarks against which they could plot their progress. Occasional groups of palm or baobab caught the eye, but for the most part low grey smudges of sand alternated with equally low patches of olive-green vegetation. It was impossible to tell what lay beyond.

At length, as they loitered down the coast, the look-outs spied a group of natives watching their progress from a sandy beach. Signalling their intention to the rest of the fleet, the nearest vessel lowered its boats which rowed towards the shore. Beneath their clothes the crews concealed their weapons, but as they approached they waved coloured cloths and trinkets in a show of friendliness. They landed without difficulty, and as they jumped out on to the beach thousands of tiny ghost-like crabs scuttled from beneath their feet. The negroes had neither moved towards them nor fled at their approach, but stood eyeing them curiously from the fringes of the bordering forest. The sailors attempted to talk with them, displaying their trifles and pointing to some empty water-barrels to prove the innocence of their mission. But they were neither welcomed nor repulsed, and when they advanced towards the natives, hoping at the last moment to rush forward and seize them, they found themselves alone upon the beach; for the blacks, mistrusting them, had slipped away.

Disconsolately the landing party rowed back to their ship and reported their ill-success to Hawkins. Until the wind freshened there was little that they could do, and they fretted at the delay. Already they had spent nearly a month on the coast and had only nine slaves to show for it. It was a frustrating start for their trading prospects.

It was not far to Cape Roxo, a sandy spit of land, beyond which the coast takes a south-easterly turn and breaks up into a complex and scarcely-charted network of estuaries and islands. It is an indistinguishable maze today, so it is little wonder that in Hawkins' time the navigators who sounded their way through inlets edged with mangrove swamp, striving to find the true channel up rivers whose waters percolated into the sea through a hundred separate creeks, were unsure of their exact position. Often, indeed, they did not know for certain which river it was that they were penetrating. The air was always humid and heavy in these confined waters, and there was no wind to stir a sail.

The larger vessels could not approach the coast because of the shifting sandbanks that clogged the river mouths. The pinnaces and open boats shared the work between them, their crews rowing arduously against the stream, unprotected from the heat of the sun. The oily, steel-coloured water reflected the glare, and whenever the sailors approached the banks, in search of shade or a landing place, they were assailed by clouds of insects. Amongst these half-clogged waterways crocodiles and hippos were to be seen—fabulous and terrifying monsters whose size and malevolence grew with the telling. But worst of all was the oppressiveness of the swamp, that grew into a dread and hatred of the sage-green, featureless prison that was neither open water nor dry land.

The larger vessels being too precious to risk close inshore, Hawkins dispatched the *Judith*, the *Angel* and the small craft on several exploratory trips amongst the islands and sandbanks that lay to the south of Cape Roxo. In charge of these forays went Robert Barrett, the master of the *Jesus*, a man with experience of the coast. Dudley often accompanied him with a company of foot-soldiers to assist in any landing operations. But for the most part they rowed and sailed in vain. Even to sit still, out of the sunlight, was a clammy and exhausting experience, Yet as often as not they were forced to row from point to point, sounding constantly as they went, for neither chart nor memory could master the intricate web of reef and shoal. The tides, too, swept in a disorderly flood through the channels, and the drag of unexpected currents brought them perilously near to foundering.

It would have been a less dispiriting job if the results had been more triumphant. But soon even the crews who were left on board the great ships, and rode at anchor in deep water off the coast, became accustomed to the despondent return of the small craft, and learnt, after their turn of duty at the rowing-benches had come round, not to deride their empty-handed comrades. There was little that Hawkins himself could do to help. His knowledge of the coast was general; but within the crumbling estuaries guarded by the Bijouga Islands he knew only that several great rivers disembogued, and that the Portuguese had trading stations. With neither luck nor a pilot he realized that he would be fortunate to stumble upon them.

It was November 24th when he first took up station off Cape Roxo, and although he eagerly sent forth and received back his scouting parties, he doubted if by themselves they could unravel the topographical difficulties that beset them. He had placed his main fleet carefully, and waited with it in patience. Sooner or later he knew that some Portuguese trading craft, familiar with the devious waterways that lay ahead, would have to pass close to his anchorage, either rounding the Cape on its way south, or beating its way back to Portugal. He was not mistaken. Before very long a caravel was sighted threading its way north towards Cape Verde, from whence it came. Immediately Hawkins pounced on it. First he ascertained the cargo the vessel was carrying and started to bargain—in the friendliest fashion—for certain goods that it carried, offering in exchange wares from his own lading. After business came questioning, and Hawkins, using means that he never divulged, but which accorded at least with the appearance of legitimacy, extracted all the information he desired. The Portuguese authorities, when later they filed their complaints against Hawkins, asserted that he used torture against the seamen who fell into his hands. It is highly unlikely that he acted so clumsily. Such accusations were easy to make, and Hawkins was well aware of their danger. He did his best, by documentary proof, to vindicate his reputation at every turn, and, as a skilled negotiator, force was seldom the easiest way to achieve his ends.

In the river San Domingo—now known as the Cacheo River— some fifteen miles south-east of his anchorage, Hawkins learnt, lay several Portuguese caravels, employed under royal contract to ship the yearly quota of slaves to the Spaniards in the Indies. Their presence near the main Portuguese trading station at Cacheo was ample reason for the scarcity and timidity of negroes in the neighbourhood. All the tribes would have been thoroughly alarmed, and those who were most exposed to capture on the outlying islands had retired to the mainland and hidden themselves away from marauding sails.

Clearly the caravels themselves, if they were already laden with slaves, were worth investigating. But to force a passage up the river, even with detailed instructions, was too hazardous for Hawkins to undertake alone. The vessel that he had intercepted would have to act as a guide. The reluctant Portuguese trader had no option but to perform the task that Hawkins demanded of him. As soon as they were reassembled the English fleet followed their pilot cautiously down the coast, and anchored just clear of the shallow water that guarded the mouth of the river. The estuary itself was almost invisible, so low-lying and swampy was the land on either shore.

The channel was difficult to find, for there were no leading marks, and only the leadsman could tell whether the ships were straying from the invisible course. The larger vessels did not attempt to penetrate the river. The Portuguese pilot led the way. After him Hawkins sent only the *Angel*, whose shallow draught could safely ride over most obstacles, and two pinnaces to make a reconnaissance. On board were Robert Barrett and forty men, fully armed, but with only a single piece of artillery—a quick-firing falconet. Next day, if the channel proved navigable, it was proposed to send a stronger party to reinforce them.

Gradually, as they pressed forward, the banks of the river drew together and the four ships were forced into a narrower channel. The mangroves formed an unbroken wall on either hand, rising out of the mud on a network of brine-bleached, stilt-like roots. There were no landing-places or signs of life. Swarms of tiny swamp flies plagued the rowers, but nothing else stirred or broke the heavy silence that surrounded them. For hours they struggled upstream, trying vainly to memorize their featureless course, and sounding as they went.

When they came up to the clearing and wharf that served the trading station of Cacheo, their slow progress had long been observed and there was no question of achieving a surprise. Indeed, before they were within hailing distance of the Portuguese ships that were moored there, the English party were met by a brisk burst of gunfire. The aim was wild, but it was obvious that the Portuguese caravels were heavily armed and eager to defend themselves. Barrett realized that he was hopelessly out-gunned, and chose a moment when there was a lull in firing to attempt a parley. Speaking in Portuguese he shouted across the water that his errand was peaceful. He came, he declared, on behalf of John Hawkins, whose main fleet lay at the river's mouth and his only intention was to trade with them for slaves.

It was a hurried speech, and unfinished, for his words were interrupted by a renewal of firing. Barrett was less patient than his captain. He saw from the splashes, that churned up the still water around the *Angel*, how the sakers and minions were getting his range. To remain where he was would have been suicidal. A prudent man, who had borne in mind his captain's parting instructions, might honourably have withdrawn to await reinforcements; but Barrett chose to attack.

As an act of reckless courage it was unparalleled on the voyage. For forty men in three small boats to attack and overpower seven caravels of more than common aggressive strength was little short of a miracle. As they rowed forward the *Angel* and the two pinnaces were raked with dice-shot from the close range bases— brass guns that in good hands should have wiped out the attackers. But they suffered no casualties, and Barrett urged them forward before the guns had time to reload. At first—as Job Hortop, a pressed man aboard the *Angel*, reported—the Portuguese 'made great fight with us', but as they drew close to their adversaries, and steeled themselves to receive their shot at point-blank range, they became aware that, far from defending themselves further, the Portuguese were deserting their ships and scrambling ashore pell-mell.

Barrett and his men entered into possession of the caravels with their numbers unimpaired. Not a soul was left on board. The guns were still hot and reeking. Provisions, stores, and personal plunder were to be had in plenty, but their greatest hope was unfulfilled: the slave-decks were empty. In themselves seven more ships were no great asset to the English fleet, but obviously they were valuable to their owners and might have bargaining power. Barrett knew very well that the Portuguese factors were forbidden to sell slaves to foreign interlopers, but he felt confident that to save their vessels from destruction they could be persuaded to ignore the prohibition. He therefore forbade looting and quickly sent messengers ashore to make contact with the Portuguese, whom he suspected had retired to the village of Cacheo a mile inland. If they returned to their ships he promised that none of their property would be pillaged. Negroes were the commodity he sought and he offered fair bartering terms.

By nightfall, having received no reply, he moved his own ships and those that he had captured into the middle of the river, set a sharp watch and awaited developments. Next morning at first light a deputation from the shore waited on him and declared their willingness to negotiate. Discussions continued for some hours. At first the Portuguese seemed anxious to come to terms, but gradually, as the talks became more and more protracted and several intervals had elapsed when the negotiators retired to consult with their compatriots ashore, it became evident that their attitude was stiffening and they were talking only to gain time.

Meanwhile Barrett had received reinforcements. Hawkins, true to his word, had sent the *Judith*, the *Swallow* and Drake's caravel, the *Grace of God*, upriver with 200 men between them. With these additions to his numbers Barrett felt confident enough, after his bloodless victory the day before, to impose his will by force. Hawkins had expressly forbidden him to conduct a full scale attack ashore, and had told him not only to exploit the ships near Cacheo, but to go further upstream where the Portuguese factors were actually collecting slaves from the more co-operative of the native petty-chieftains. So far upstream a raid would be un-expected and scarcely defended. But Barrett was angry with the Portuguese he had already encountered at Cacheo, and determined to settle his account with them before embarking on an explor-ation of the upper reaches of the river. He organized a strong landing-party, which he led himself, and left a small rear-guard under Dudley to defend the ships and the landing-stage.

The track between the river and the town was clear enough, but heavily overgrown on either side. A wall of foliage wreathed with creeper almost cut out the sunlight, and provided ideal cover for an ambush. Barrett divided his forces into two groups and pressed forward. Their progress was undisturbed except by the chatter of monkeys, groups of which could occasionally be seen like shipboys high in the shrouds of the trees. Within a mile they came upon the village and the leading party, finding no opposition, started systematically ransacking and burning the deserted huts.

Before the second group could join them the storm broke. During the day the Portuguese had been busy recruiting negroes from the tribes that they could trust and who acted as inter-mediaries in trade. Six or seven thousand fighting men, led by a bare hundred Portuguese, were lying in wait for the English party at the point where they were farthest from their ships. They were armed with their own weapons, spears and arrows for the most part, and only the Portuguese had firearms; but their very inexperience in the face of arquebus fire, and their instinctive bravery in numbers, made them formidable opponents.

No sooner had the ambush been sprung than the sailors who had been busily destroying all that they found in Cacheo retreated to join the main party. Even though they were heavily outnumbered the united English contingent defended their position without great difficulty. As soon as the arquebuses could be reloaded they were discharged, for there was no lack of targets. At times it was impossible to keep the attackers back by small-arms fire alone. Swords and pikes were wielded in desperate efforts to keep the English line unbroken. Often it was hand-to-hand work, and the seamen were glad of their helmets and jerkins to repel the blows of club or axe. Wave after wave of negroes rushed in disordered bravery against the English position and were flung back, leaving their dead behind.

Barrett must have been gratified to watch the steadiness of his men against each onslaught. They had learned much already from their experience on the coast, and fought together as a team. But he had cause for anxiety too. They were beleaguered a mile from their ships; powder and shot would not last long; and, although his serious casualties had been light, there were few men in his ranks who could not show some marks of combat.

A fighting retreat along the path he had come was a dangerous prospect. Nevertheless it seemed inevitable, and Barrett edged his men back towards the river. There was fighting and skirmishing all the way. Most sinister of all was the disappearance of the Portuguese soldiers immediately the Englishmen started to retire. It seemed probable that they had taken some secret track and would cut off the English retreat and hem them in from both sides.

Fortunately, before such a trap could be sprung, the ambushers were themselves surprised. Captain Dudley, hearing the tumult of fighting, realized that Barrett's men might be dangerously placed. With his small rearguard he pushed forward to their aid, stumbled upon the Portuguese ambush, and put it to flight. The fighting that followed was confused and disorderly. Barrett's retreat became speedy, and the negro levies paused before pressing home their advantage. They reached the landing-place in a body, jumped into their boats and pushed off as soon as they were full. Their attackers were hard at their heels. Some of the negroes, not content with the success they had achieved, leaped into the water and swam after the retreating boats, grappling with the oars and striving to delay them.

One such incident, the last in the battle, impressed itself upon the English sailors' minds as typical of the strength and fanaticism of their opponents. A negro, who had jumped into the river to pursue the last of the boats, grasped an oar and wrenched it from the rower's grasp. As he did so a crossbowman fired at him at such short range that the shaft went right through his unprotected body. Despite his wound the negro swam ashore and ran some forty paces along the bank, carrying the oar, before collapsing dead.

The fighting was over, and because their casualties were light the men were inclined to look upon it as a victory. To Barrett, and, later, to Hawkins, to whom a report on the day's proceedings was quickly dispatched down-river, it was an unqualified failure. Hawkins, indeed, according to the men who rowed back with his fresh instructions, was enraged by the whole affair. He blamed Barrett for neglecting to follow out the orders he had been given, and gave notice of his intention to take the *William and John* upstream next morning. He would himself take command of the operations he had originally intended against the slave-collectors higher up the River Cacheo.

He set out as planned, but before he had gone far it was evident that the *William and John* was of too great a draught to cross the bar in safety. Already he was impatient, as the season was advancing and his slave-decks were still almost empty. He had no desire to be delayed still further by going aground. Besides, his temper had cooled and he realized that it would be well-nigh impossible to conduct any orderly or profitable trade after the disturbances of the previous day. He instructed Barrett to bring his ships out of the river, taking with them two or three of the caravels that had been captured at the first encounter.

Hawkins was not hopeful that the Portuguese, who had refused to negotiate for their return when they were in mid-river, would feel differently about their valuable ships if they were towed out beyond the river's mouth; but he waited for a short time after Barrett had rejoined the main fleet in case they changed their minds. No overtures came from the shore, and Hawkins was in no mood to be patient. Once again he set sail, leaving the unlucky River Cacheo behind, and headed cautiously towards the tortuous channels that cut off the Bijouga Islands from the mainland shore. With him went the captured caravels, but only one of them became a permanent addition to his fleet. How he disposed of the others remains a mystery that none of the accounts of the voyage touches upon.

CHAPTER 5

The Walls of Conga

THE details of these slave-seeking forays that Hawkins was driven to undertake amongst the fever-ridden, featureless estuaries of West Africa are necessarily vague and capricious. He himself can often have had only the broadest impression of where he was, and his chroniclers, writing for the most part many years after the event occurred, may be forgiven for remembering most vividly moments when their emotions were stirred by strange incidents rather than considerations of time and place. We can learn, therefore, of the innocent surprise of the Lincolnshire powder-maker, Job Hortop, when he first tasted bananas and discovered that 'sugar is not more delicate in taste than they be'. But he could recollect little of the plan of action that drew him to the river-banks where they grew. Wonder and natural curiosity lasted longer in the mind than the intricacies of navigation.

Memory played strange freaks with each of the men who set down the history of the voyage. At times fitful, at times vague, they relied for their impressions of West Africa not so much on the sequence of events or the wider motives that impelled them, as on a few, lovingly-remembered peculiarities that overshadowed all else in recollection. A trap for hippopotami, the techniques of cannibalism or the method of extracting musk from caged civet-cats with a spoon are vividly remembered, and with emotive guides such as these rather than the aid of map or chart we must follow Hawkins' fleet into the obscure sailings and dealings that henceforward almost conceal his movements and his plans until, after many days, he re-formed his squadron off Sierra Leone.

We hear next of Hawkins receiving on board a petty-chieftain who voluntarily surrendered himself into captivity. His story, as it was translated, was strange but credible. The negro claimed to have secretly committed adultery with one of the numerous wives of the King Zambulo, whose autocratic rule extended over the islands and the shore between which they were passing. Although he believed his actions to have been unobserved, he had just learnt through friends that the offence had come to the King's notice. He knew the punishment he could expect and had consequently fled to Hawkins in order to preserve his life, even at the expense of liberty. Hawkins was naturally interested in the possibility of using his voluntary captive to lead an attack on King Zambulo's township. The negro declared himself willing to guide a raiding party, and from the deck of the *Jesus* was able to point to a place on the mainland where there was a sizeable cluster of huts.

For some reason the raid was deferred for three days, and in the meantime Hawkins dispatched his smaller ships, the *Angel* and *Judith* together with two or three pinnaces, to take an inshore course—probably through the Orango Channel—exploring various creeks and inlets as they went, and meeting the main fleet, after it had dealt with King Zambulo, at Sierra Leone. Only vessels of very shallow draught could hope to do any good amongst the Bijougas. Prudently, Hawkins took no risks with the larger vessels, and was prepared to give the archipelago a wide berth to seaward when the time came for him to go south.

The *Angel* and the *Judith*, accompanied by the small craft that often went ahead to sound a passage, steered a mazy course between the islands. They nosed their way up the River Calousa, the River Casteos and (if it was not in fact the same stream as the latter under a different name), the River Casserroes. They were native names, imperfectly transcribed, and it is now impossible to do more than speculate on what rivers the little ships did in fact penetrate. On two occasions they surprised small groups of Portuguese caravels engaged in trading with the negro tribes ashore, but although they captured several of these craft they gained little treasure and few slaves.

One night, up the River Calousa, they encountered an enemy more dreaded and terrifying to the men than all the Portuguese on the Guinea Coast. One of the pinnaces, with twenty-eight men on board, was shaken by a violent blow from beneath that splintered the planks and threw some of the crew off-balance into the water. A moment later the boat was completely flooded and every man on board jumped into the river. As they did so they saw dimly through the darkness the enormous bulk of a hippopotamus, that had upset the pinnace and now swam ponderously through the wreckage. A second pinnace was standing by, and quickly twenty-six of the swimmers were hauled on board, almost incapacitated by the terror of this nocturnal visitation. Two men, however, were never found. Both were strong swimmers and had last been seen clutching to each other as the boat sank. It was darkly suspected that they had fallen victims to the monster's jaws.

The staved-in pinnace, though waterlogged, was still afloat, and as the distance back to the *Angel* was not great they decided to take her in tow. But before they had gone far the sailors became aware that not only one but many of the monsters were still around them, and seemed to be following their slow progress with malevolent interest. It would have been useless to reassure the frightened seamen, telling them that the hippo was a browsing, harmless creature. They had already seen the strength that it could wield, and caught a glimpse, perhaps, of fanged and open jaws. There were stories to be heard up and down the coast of caravels sunk, and huts demolished, by the blundering power of these river giants. Small wonder that the English sailors, finding themselves amongst them at night when fears and shadows loom large, were on the brink of panic.

There was another lurch, this time from the stern of the surviving pinnace. A sword flashed in the darkness and there was a swirl and confusion of water. A man in the stern-sheets cried out that one of the monsters had put its foot over the gunwale, and that he had cut if off. Through the crowded boat swept a surge of terror. Without a moment's hesitation they cut adrift the waterlogged boat they were towing, and bent furiously at their oars. In a few minutes they seemed to have rowed beyond pursuit, and thankfully regained their ship.

The rest of their explorations met with neither incidents nor success. Gloomily the two small ships, each with its pinnace in tow, made for the meeting-place at Sierra Leone with two casualties to report and a very few slaves.

Hawkins, who had remained with the larger ships to carry out a raid upon King Zambulo's tribe, seems to have had no better fortune. What should have been a climax to the slave-hunting operations along the coast collapsed so completely that the chronicles of the voyage do not even mention it again. We only know that Hawkins took a hundred and twenty of his men ashore and met, instead of the opposition he expected, relics of cannibalism and human sacrifice. Acts of such fearful and unnatural barbarity were discovered that it is possible he and his men fled from them, and left unexplored that evil and deserted shore, impelled by a superstitious dread of the unhallowed things they found there.

Not long after he had dispatched the *Angel* and *Judith* Hawkins led the remainder of his squadron out to sea, rounded the Bijouga Islands, and sailed directly for Sierra Leone. Hereabouts, he knew, lay the last chance of filling his ships with the slaves he needed to justify an expedition to the Indies. So far he had collected a bare hundred and fifty—not enough when sold even to cover his expenses. Further down the coast the rivers became fewer and less navigable, even to small craft. Past Cape Palmas, the farthest point along the coast that his father had reached and farther than he had ever gone, Hawkins knew that he would be swept inexorably round the Bight of Benin, past the strongholds of Portugal in Africa, Axim and Elmina, Shama and Accra. Apart from the danger of such a course it would add many weeks to his sailing time, and the season was already well advanced. He did indeed contemplate a frontal attack on Elmina, but only at the expense of the West Indian venture, and if all else failed.

Meanwhile Hawkins was not entirely discouraged. He had taken a bold step down the coast as he realized the presence of so many Portuguese caravels in the area he had left was a hindrance to good hunting. Around Sierra Leone he hoped to be able to work without disturbance. He knew the coast—a less treacherous one, with distinct landmarks—from his previous voyage, and the negroes he had collected on that occasion fetched a good price in the Indies.

They were a strange, uncouth people these Sapies, for it was from that tribe that slaves were most commonly gathered. Like most of the natives on the coast they wore no clothes except a girdle about their loins. Their ebony-coloured bodies were marbled with tattooing, and even the hair upon their heads was cropped and fretted in strange designs. Noses and ears were commonly pierced and plugged with ornaments of bone or wood. To add to the terror of their appearance the Sapies filed their teeth to make them sharp, and often wore about their necks, like beads, the teeth of enemies they had overcome in battle. The women of the tribe were decorated as grotesquely as the men, with smooth, hairless heads and a nakedness that seemed shameful to European eyes.

Sailing down the coast, well clear of the shore, Hawkins sighted the Los islands shaking themselves free of the lingering fogs that collected amongst the damp, tree-carpeted hills. It was the first landmark that he could enter in the ship's log since he left the Cacheo River a fortnight before. But he paused only long enough to top up his water-barrels. Far off, on the port hand, lay the mainland coast—seeming from a distance more like groups of islands, for the mangrove barrier that connected them together crouched low upon the sea. As the ships neared Sierra Leone the hills behind could be seen in dim outline through the haze.

In the evening they became clearer, and out at sea sunsets of incredible flamboyance lit up the sky. The men called them the smokes, but the word did little justice to the extravagant clash of colour that bathed the ships and even the sea in which they sailed in a reflected glow of crimson, orange and flamingo-tinted light. After the sun had set, and the sky was sombre with the approach of night, a cold wind blew and the sailors hurriedly unpacked from their sea-chests clothes and blankets that they had not expected to use for many months to come. The same pattern repeated itself each day. The wind blew constantly from the north-east, speeding them on their course. By day it was a hot, thirsty breeze, bringing with it a film of red dust that percolated into the furthest recesses of the ship. By night the same wind sent men shivering below.

To Hawkins it was familiar enough. The Harmattan had started to blow, bringing with it the dust and dryness of the great deserts of Africa. In itself it was a helpful wind, but in its wake came tornados and increasingly oppressive heat. It was a warning against lingering long.

The squadron came inshore to anchor off Sierra Leone, or Tagarrin as it was often called. It was two days before Christmas. On the first favourable tide Hawkins sent two or three pinnaces up the river to find out whether any Portuguese ships were trading there; but they returned before long to report that the river was deserted. In some ways this was regrettable for Hawkins lacked the contacts that the Portuguese had established with certain local chiefs who, in return for spirits and coloured cloth, would fill their caravels with pepper and ivory and barter even their own tribesmen into slavery. Hawkins always believed in using the Portuguese traders to good advantage, especially now that time was running short and the task of collecting his own slaves might prove arduous.

Meanwhile, under the cooper's direction, parties were sent ashore to refill the water-barrels; a vital task that was interrupted only on Christmas Day itself. Soon afterwards the *Judith* and *Angel* rejoined the fleet, almost empty-handed, but full of stories of the perils of the River Calousa. Hawkins was impatient of such tales. Before they had settled down amongst the rest of his squadron he dispatched them once again to explore the now unidentifiable River Magrabomba, to the south of Sierra Leone. Here also they drew a blank, and Hawkins began to despair for the success of his venture.

Then their luck turned. A fortnight after they arrived, perhaps longer—for the various accounts differ in their dates—two emissaries came to Hawkins from the Kings of Castros and Sierra Leone. The canoe in which they travelled was scooped out from a single tree-trunk and held a score of men standing upright to paddle. Chanting rhythmically they guided their craft through the ground-swell and alongside the *Jesus*. With a few words of Portuguese and many gestures the ambassadors made their business known. The Kings they represented were allied in war against two neighbouring chieftains, Sacina and Setecama, who had established themselves in the town of Conga on the bank of the River Sierra Leone. It was a more than usually strong position, stockaded with ramparts of timber and heavily garrisoned. The two Kings who besieged it were unable to capture the town by assault. They came, therefore, to ask Hawkins for help. If his ships could bombard Conga from the river side they would surely, between them, quickly overcome its resistance, and would obtain as well as the victory they themselves desired innumerable captives who would be at Hawkins' disposal.

It was a tempting offer, though it sounded more like a full-scale war than Hawkins relished. Nevertheless he could not afford to hesitate. With only a hundred and fifty negroes so far secured, and time running short, here was an opportunity to complete his slaving operations in a single venture. He was fairly certain that there were no Portuguese up the river, and their absence removed his greatest fears of treachery. As far as his interrogations would permit he saw no reason to doubt the story or the promises he had heard. He fixed a time with the ambassadors for his ships to enter the river, and arranged that certain tokens should be displayed on both sides to avoid misunderstandings before his contingent reached its objective.

A few of the smaller ships and pinnaces were considered sufficient for the enterprise, for Hawkins was always loath to take his great ships into confined and uncharted waterways, where they would be defenceless against the perils of surprise or of going aground. A force of ninety men under Robert Barrett were issued with small arms and detailed for the task. At first all went well. Aided by the incoming tide they entered the broad estuary of the river, sounding carefully as they went. Before they had gone far the course of the river turned sharply to the north-east and they lost sight of the main fleet at its anchorage out to sea. Sails were of little help, and after a while they were furled and the crew took to their oars. For some miles the channel was so wide that they could see very little of the banks on either hand. They passed several islands, thickly-wooded, with cliffs of reddish sand, but showing no signs of life. It was a pattern painfully familiar to them after their innumerable abortive excursions up the creeks and rivers along the coast. At first they had laboured at their oars full of expectancy, thinking to find booty and captives round every bend. Now they rowed listlessly, disillusioned by previous failures and enervated by the hot, stagnant air.

As they drew near to the township of Conga a group of natives on the bank exchanged signals of recognition with them and motioned them ashore. Before many minutes Barrett and a party of his men who acted as bodyguard were being led to the presence of the Kings of Castros and Sierra Leone with whom they were allied.

The encampment where the two potentates were holding court was far from splendid. A few mud huts with thickly-thatched roofs of palm and reed stood in a clearing amongst a group of silk-cotton trees. They seemed more like giant skeps than human habitations, and round them swarmed innumerable black warriors armed with clubs and throwing-spears with fire-hardened tips. It was a novel experience to the Englishmen to pass through their ranks without suffering molestation. Both sides stared curiously at each other, gauging their strengths, but offering no sign of welcome or hostility.

Silently a way was cleared to the innermost hut of the group and Barrett was motioned to enter. Stooping, he crossed the mat at the threshold and came into the Kings' presence. It was almost dark inside, but, apart from a few woven palm mats and several earthenware jars, the hut was devoid of furniture. Despite the gloom Barrett was aware that he was being observed by half a hundred eyes, for the old men and dignitaries of the tribe were squatting silently behind the two royal stools on which the Kings sat to receive their visitors. Barrett advanced to touch the out-stretched hands of the two potentates, and broke the silence with a short speech of greeting. They listened attentively, turning to an interpreter to enquire the meaning and to frame a suitable reply. A gourd, filled with palm wine, was first tasted by the Kings, then handed to the Englishmen. When it had circulated they broached the business that had drawn them together.

The discussion was long and laborious, complicated by lack of language and the difficulty of assessing the real strength of their opponents. It was clear to Barrett that his assistance was expected in the land assault as well as bombardment from the river-side. From the advance camp where he was in conference the Kings of Castros and Sierra Leone had already launched a number of fruitless attacks against Conga, but had never breached the stockade that surrounded it. When he asked the number of the defenders Barrett was informed that there were at least six thousand fighting-men within the town, as well as women and children. Obviously it was likely to be a serious undertaking.

Long odds did not usually daunt him. He knew that superiority of fire-power and organization amply offset a lack of men. But the weight of opposition in the proposed encounter made him wish that he had been given a larger contingent from the ships. He never doubted that the battle would be won, but the problem of escorting the prisoners, that he had been promised as the reward of his services, back to the fleet in safety worried him. He proposed that the combined forces should set out immediately for the enemies' fortress to test its strength. With some first-hand knowledge he would be able to send news down-stream to his captain.

For two days Barrett with his small contingent, aided by the forces of the two Kings, skirmished in vain before the wooden walls of Conga. It was a far more difficult task than any they had previously encountered on the African coast. The defence works were sturdily built. Whole tree-trunks had been lashed together with liana to form a wall ten feet high, from the cover of which the defenders could pour forth a hail of arrows without exposing themselves to arquebus fire. Under the walls they had dug many concealed pits into which the unwary might fall, and planted lines of sharpened stakes to break up a determined charge.

From vantage points in the trees outside the stockade it was possible for the attackers to glimpse the closely-set thatched roofs of the huts within the walls, but the inhabitants were well shielded from view. Only their voices could be heard, chanting encouragement to each other as they defended their positions, mingled with the urgent rhythm of drums. By water the town seemed equally impregnable. There was no easy landing-place, and the shot from the few falcons and bases that the small ships carried produced no visible terror or damage.

The defenders were not content to repel the various assaults from the cover of their stockade. Time and again they issued forth and attacked the attackers, driving them back into the cover of the surrounding forest. For the English party it was discouraging work. They had been closely engaged, and twenty of them had been wounded. In themselves the wounds were not very serious; most of them had been caused by arrows which, being small and unbarbed, were easily plucked out. But there was always the fear that they had been poisoned, and the memory of the agonizing death of their companions earlier in the voyage made Barrett's men cautious in exposing themselves. Also they found it difficult to co-ordinate their actions with those of their allies, whose haphazard bravery could not be exploited to full advantage. After two days, with mounting casualties and no progress made, Barrett decided to call on Hawkins for further help.

The appeal did not find Hawkins in the best of tempers. Every time Barrett was sent up-river, it seemed, he asked for reinforcements and let slip the prize. Reluctant though he was to leave his fleet exposed to any chance encounter at the mouth of the estuary, Hawkins determined to lead a relief party himself and, by taking vigorous action, decide the issue one way or the other. A hundred men was all that could be spared, and even this number left the larger ships with only half their complement. Hawkins ordered them into the remaining small craft and headed upstream.

Towards evening he joined Barrett's contingent outside the walls of Conga and sent a message to the encampment where King Sheri and King Yhoma, with whom they were allied, had withdrawn for the night. He announced that he had come in person in order to put a quick end to the fighting. Assuming complete authority for the military operations that would be necessary, he informed the negro Kings that during the afternoon of the following day, at the sound of a trumpet, he would attack from the river, and exhorted them to do likewise from the landward side. To stiffen their morale, and make some liaison possible, he seconded forty of his men to assist his allies. He did not make his plans a matter for discussion. He gave orders and expected them to be obeyed.

The Kings of Castros and Sierra Leone made no objection. They replied to Hawkins welcoming his personal intervention and promising compliance with his scheme. In token of their gratitude they sent with their message a present of gold and some slaves, by both of which they knew Hawkins set great store.

At dusk the English returned to their boats in midstream and passed an uncomfortable, watchful night, trusting neither their allies nor their foes. Next morning forty of them were detached to join the forces of King Yhoma and King Sheri. They arrived in time to witness the dismissal of ambassadors, whom the rival Kings Sacina and Setecama had sent from the beleaguered fortress to negotiate a settlement. Doubtless the arrival of Hawkins' reinforcements had not passed unnoticed. The eve of the attack was no time for negotiations however, and so confident of success was the allied force, and so inflamed for captives and revenge, that the ambassadors were scarcely given a hearing. They were lucky to escape with their lives for the besieging forces were working themselves up into a frenzy of excitement. The warriors were stripped and oiled for battle; some danced passionately to the music of drums and gourd-shaped viols, others chanted and chattered in their strange tongue, drowning even the raucous disputations of the parrots that fluttered like coloured rags in the upper branches of the silk-cotton and baobab trees under which they had set up camp. In the midst of the frantic and disorganized activity of their subjects the two Kings sat in leisurely contemplation. Autocratic and self-assured, they alone amongst their people were clothed: a voluminous shirt and crumpled trousers were their badges of office and, greatly prized, a heavy iron sword—the only metal weapon in the tribe.

If the Englishmen felt like despising them for the rudeness and poverty of their Court, they could not but admire the absolute discipline and obedience that the two Kings commanded. Those who approached the royal presence fell prostrate and spoke their business from the ground: the replies they received were haughty but unquestionable. The territories of these native kingdoms might be limited and ringed with war, their wealth negligible, but the chieftains ruled as despots, and wielded a casual power of life or death over their unprotesting subjects.

When the sun had reached its zenith the land forces moved forward to within a bowshot of the stockade around Conga. Here they halted until a trumpet-note was heard and, a few minutes later, the sonorous sound of gunfire from the ships in the river. The attack had begun.

On the landward side little progress was made. The noise was deafening as wave after wave of negroes rushed towards the defences, shouting battle cries and brandishing their weapons. Some groups attempted to scale the pallisades, others to tear them down, but to make a breach in the defences proved impossible. The defenders threw back each attack with a volley of spears, and the air danced with the shafts of small featherless arrows fired by both sides. It seemed in the pandemonium of the assault that casualties would be catastrophic. Yet when the ground cleared and the two armies paused for a moment's breath there were surprisingly few bodies left on the ground between them. The English party which had been in the thick of the fighting was still almost intact. Five men had arrow-wounds, but they had plucked out the shafts and were still able to use their weapons. Steel helmets and leather jerkins had saved them from more serious harm. Some of their negro allies they could see had suffered fearsome wounds, and Sheri Bangi, the son of the King of Sierra Leone, lay dead at the foot of the stockade. What casualties they had been able to inflict upon the enemy it was difficult to say, but the number of the defenders seemed no less. Undeterred they resumed the attack.

Hawkins with his hundred and fifty men were few in number but better armed than their opponents. They had a stern fight to establish themselves on land, and the narrow bridgehead they won for themselves was entirely within range of the bowmen in the town. Luckily the Englishmen alone possessed firearms, for their position was so exposed that even a single piece of ordnance in the hands of the defenders might have turned the tide of battle. As it was the arrows flew so thickly that there was no hope of avoiding the shafts. Most of the assault party received wounds, but the arrows had little power of penetration and one man in the forefront of the assault received seven or eight shafts in his exposed limbs. Even so, encouraged by Hawkins' leadership, he paused only to pluck out the arrows that encumbered him, and rejoined the battle.

Hawkins led his men forward with unbounded energy. He had been among the first to leap ashore from the landing craft, and now that his men were ashore was actively employed in marshalling his force. His hoarse, peremptory commands rang out as clearly through the hubbub of battle as they did in the teeth of a high wind at sea. Never for a moment did he pause; his stocky figure, moving in a swaggering half-trot, dominated the beach-head. We can envisage him, dressed resplendently in light armour, his cabasset and corselet richly engraved with repoussé work and gleaming in the sunlight, his sword unsheathed in his hand. Under the eye of their admiral the Englishmen were tireless in their attack. Time and again they reached the stockade, learning to avoid the pitfalls and beating down the entanglements of dried thorn that delayed their progress.

They concentrated on what seemed to be the weakest section of the wall, where the earlier bombardment from the boats had shattered the timbers, and after several repulses succeeded in making a breach. At the time they could do no more, but they gained a glimpse of the town within, its huts huddled close together and linked by a labyrinth of alleys. Hawkins did not relish the prospect of a hand-to-hand encounter in such confined spaces. His men would be separated, lost and ambushed long before they could subdue the town. Instead of a renewed assault now that the way had been opened, he called a halt. Gathering his pikemen together he had them issued with flares—bell-mouthed containers stuffed with pitch—which they strapped to the heads of their weapons and lit. The crossbowmen, too, were issued with fire-arrows that could be lit before they were loosed and, like fireworks, burst into flames when the charge ignited. It was with the weapon of fire that Hawkins proposed to overcome the township of Conga. What wind there was blew from behind the attackers, and the palm-thatch roofs were as dry as tinder. If one or two fires could be established they would quickly spread and, Hawkins argued, drive the negroes out of the town and into the hands of their allies on the landward side.

His plan succeeded better than he could have hoped. The advance of the pikemen with their burning staves, and the rain of explosive arrows, threw the defenders into confusion. Against weapons to which they were accustomed they had been resolute, but the tactics Hawkins was adopting brought an enemy into their midst which they were powerless to subdue. The huts nearest to the breach in the stockade were soon ablaze, sending a column of dense smoke into the cloudless sky. The flames seemed pale with the sun on them, but the heat of the con-flagration made the still air shimmer and beat upon the faces of the advancing troops. For a short while, even with their houses burning around them, the negroes within the town resisted Hawkins' assault. But gradually as the English soldiers established their foothold, and the pikemen thrust their burning cressets into more of the dun-coloured, beehive huts, the defending troops slipped away. Some hid themselves and were smoked out or burnt to death, but the majority retreated towards the centre of the town where Hawkins, without further support, was un-willing to follow them.

As soon as they were established within the walls Hawkins was careful to see that his small group did not get separated, either in quest of plunder or through an over-enthusiastic pursuit. He preferred to let the forces of his negro allies round up the defeated foe.

Not until Hawkins had breached the walls, and thick columns

of smoke from the burning town were rising heavily and spreading their shadow over the battlefield, did the forces of King Yhoma and King Sheri make any progress from the landward side. Each time they attacked they had been driven back. But when it became apparent to the defenders that the enemy was already within the town behind them, they silently abandoned the stockade and took refuge in flight. At the next assault, therefore, the storming parties encountered no resistance and were able in a few minutes to tear down the obstructions that lay between themselves and the town. Once the way was clear they rushed forward in an uncontrollable wave. They seemed demented with success and killed blindly any stragglers they overtook. There was no question of surrender. The victors had smelt blood and sought only to increase the slaughter. Those who had taken shelter within their huts were ferretted out and killed, and their womenfolk with them. The air was alive with a confusion of scuffling and screams, the crackle of flames and breathless, ecstatic battle-cries. Over the whole scene hung a pall of smoke, shutting out the sun, and through which, like grimy snowflakes, the ashes thrown up by the holocaust floated down.

The two groups of Englishmen within the stricken town found themselves forgotten and ignored. Sometimes, in their efforts to secure prisoners rather than add to the indiscriminate slaughter, they found themselves skirmishing with their own frenzied allies. Hawkins became increasingly alarmed at the course that victory was taking. He could see hundreds of the slaves he coveted being butchered around him, and gathered from the direction of the loudest tumult that a great proportion of the defeated negroes were being pursued beyond the walls, and herded in a panic-driven flight towards the swamp that adjoined the river and hemmed in the town on the far side. In order to see what was happening and save what he could from the massacre he advanced cautiously in the same direction, combing the ground as he went for stragglers to add to the band of captives that he had already secured. Amongst those that surrendered to him were five Portuguese factors, who had been trapped in the beleaguered fortress and counted themselves fortunate to escape from the turmoil with their lives.

When Hawkins' party reached the outer walls overlooking the swamp they heard, and in part could see, the fearful ending of the pursuit. Floundering in the muddy wilderness of half-sunk land that merged into the river were the poor remnants of their foes. Men, women and children, half-sunk, half-swimming through the ooze and struggling through the silted channels. Some sank helplessly into the black slime. Others clung exhausted to the roots of mangrove bushes. A few of the stronger ones had reached the river and were endeavouring, despite the strong currents, to swim across. They had thrown away their weapons and did not attempt to fight back any more. Their only object was survival, and many hundreds lost that last battle against the swamp itself.

Gradually the sounds of cries and blows isolated themselves and became less frequent. The victorious troops paused in their blood-letting and ceased to pursue the fugitives that remained alive further into the depths of the marsh. Their rage had calmed and they returned to the town, collecting up prisoners and looting the dead. The fires were still burning, but the wind had not been great enough to spread them over the whole area of habitation. Many huts were still standing and the prisoners taken by the negro allies were assembled in increasing quantities. The presence of some, who were persons of note, caused evident satisfaction to the victors, and one tributary King was identified amongst the slain. But of the two Kings, Sacina and Setecama, who were their principal foes, no trace was to be found and it was presumed that they had escaped.

Evening was upon them and the battle was over. The English party, aching and exhausted after a day of hard fighting, gathered together and made a camp for themselves just outside the town. For the first time there was an opportunity to call the muster-roll and find out the number of casualties they had suffered. Four English seamen had been killed at the breach, and as many again, though alive, were thought to be past help. In addition forty men had superficial wounds. Considering the scale of the battle Hawkins felt satisfied that his casualties were as light as could be expected. As for slaves he was entirely happy. He had in his own charge some two hundred and fifty negroes, men, women and children, and he guessed that his allies had six hundred more, of which he was entitled to a share. Together with those that he had already collected he would have the richest lading that he had ever taken to the Indies.

Before darkness fell they lit fires and set about preparing an evening meal. They were all hungry for they had eaten nothing since morning. But for many of the Englishmen all appetite vanished when they heard from members of the contingent attached to the negro forces of the celebrations that were taking place within the looted town. Like the others they were hungry and had gone to their allies to draw the rations of boiled rice and palm-oil which they had been accustomed to receive. Instead they found a banquet of a very different order being actively prepared. Many of the prisoners had been slain and dismembered, and the smell of roasting flesh pervaded the encampment. It was no ordinary feast, but a ritual thanksgiving by which the enemy was humiliated and his strength transferred to the victor through the eating of his flesh. So numerous were the sacrifices, and so barbarous was the orgy that was in progress, that the English party fled from the town and joined their companions on the outskirts. They kept a sharp watch after dark, and for many hours they could see the glow of fires within the captured fortress, and hear the insistent rhythm of drums and the stamping of feet as the gorged and exultant conquerors danced tirelessly through the night. At midnight silence descended, and the watchmen concluded that their allies, drunk with palm-wine and exhausted by their celebrations, had collapsed into sleep.

Then suddenly the fires that had appeared to be dying out sprang up again all over the camping site, seeming to engulf the whole place in flames. But for the lack of noise Hawkins would have concluded that a counter-attack had been launched. He roused all his men and they stood by with their weapons at the ready. There was no need. Before long an emissary came from the two Kings to inform him of their departure back to their own lands. With them went their troops and the captives under their charge. Behind them they left a camping-site in flames, as was their custom.

Hawkins was dumbfounded. He enquired why they were making so sudden a departure, and was told that after the death of Sheri Bangi it would have been unlucky for his father, the King of Sierra Leone, to spend a night in that place. Suppressing his frustrated anger Hawkins then asked the one question that really troubled him—where were the prisoners that were his due? He was told that they would be sorted out at Castros and was advised to call there on his way downstream, whereupon he would receive his share. With such an answer Hawkins had to be content. He suspected evasion and trickery, but it was hopeless with barely two hundred men, in the middle of the night and surrounded by armed men, to attempt to argue. As graciously as he could he returned the compliments and thanks of the departing Kings and resumed his interrupted rest.

Next morning at first light he sent out a scouting party who reported that the town of Conga was deserted and not a living negro was to be seen.

The return journey down-river and out to the ships, swinging at anchor beyond the estuary, was triumphant. The pinnaces were deeply laden, and the sailors tired but cheerful. No one regretted that, now the slave-decks were filled, they would be leaving Africa and heading towards the empty western ocean. The sicknesses of the Guinea Coast were already spreading amongst them. There was hardly a man without sores or ulcers or wounds that would not heal; and many were stricken with sudden, uncontrollable fevers that left them weak and listless. They all longed for the open sea, away from the land breezes that brought pestilence and disease.

Before they finally departed, however, Hawkins determined to call on the King of Castros and hold him to his word regarding his share of the prisoners from Conga. He hated to be tricked, and if the King kept faith he could expect almost to double the number of his slaves. On the subject of this mission all the accounts are reticent. It seems certain that the King of Castros delivered up a number of slaves (probably sixty or seventy in all), but by no means as many as Hawkins felt was his due. He took what he could get and did not worry unduly about the rest.

There was no time to linger, and nothing to be gained by attempting to use force to extract more.

Hawkins did not even spare the time to careen his ships, though during the last few weeks, while they had been anchored close inshore, he could see how quickly barnacles and pulpy weed-like growths had begun to cling to the unsheathed wooden hulls. It was more important to reach the Indies before the tornado season commenced; once among the islands there were various harbours where the laborious task of scraping first one side, then the other, of the beached ships could be undertaken.

Only three things delayed departure: wood, water and an off-shore wind. After a few days' work the first two needs were satisfied, and on February 7, 1568, the wind being fair, Hawkins weighed anchor and led his fleet of ten sail out to sea, steering for the first of many days a westerly course.

CHAPTER 6

The Middle Passage

Two months in time separated the continents of Africa and America. Two months in which the *Jesus* led her convoy of small ships over oily seas whose delicate surface was ruffled only by fitful winds. Neither land nor sail was sighted. The look-outs in the fighting-tops passed their watches in silence. From their high, gently-rolling vantages they peered through the cordage, and round the loosely-hanging sails, scanning the horizon day after day, but found no blemish upon the distant rim of the encircling sea.

They became familiar with loneliness on their slow, western course. At first the tranquility that engulfed their days and nights came as a balm. The tension and discomfort of marauding on a hostile coast was over; the living cargo that they sought was secure below decks. But although they gladly exchanged the flat, fever-ridden coast for the open water, an uneasiness grew within them as they loitered through the huge vacancy of the ocean.

They found no comfort in the sea. It could be challenged and fought, exploited and explored, but it was not companionable. There was no humanity in it. They and their forefathers had used the great waters of the world for centuries, but never tamed them nor lived in harmony with them. All their efforts were defensive: their terms of reference those of a land creature. To be alone at sea was an isolation far harder to bear than to be alone on shore.

The look-outs, exiled for hours on end from all human contact, were first to experience the ache of loneliness on the ocean passage. Their thoughts turned inward, refusing to contemplate the mysteries of sea and sky, and the eye readily followed the mind. The sight of the fleet keeping station around them was comforting; and a surge of fellow-feeling—almost of love—assailed them as they watched the strangely foreshortened figures of their messmates at work on the deck below. Only when the spur of duty prompted did they raise their eyes to the oppressively empty horizon.

There was a pattern to these long days, repetitive and re-assuring; for Hawkins believed, like most sea-captains of his time, that idleness bred many of the diseases that so often scourged ship's companies on tropical voyages. But the tasks were not arduous, and never spiced with danger or urgency. The duties of helmsman or look-out could be dreamily performed as the ships sauntered for mile after mile through open seas. The sails were trimmed to catch whatever wind might blow, and in their shade the seamen of the watch drowsed and meditated, awaiting the next command.

At daybreak the ships that had kept station behind the *Jesus*' stern lantern during the night pressed forward and, as they came abreast the flagship, hailed her three times. The trumpeter on the *Jesus* returned the salute, and the course to steer was shouted across the water. The skirmishers took station ahead, or dropped astern, surrounding the *Jesus* and *Minion* in a protective screen. At six o'clock the sun rose, gilding the cageworks and casting long shadows down the decks. The working day followed the sun, and as the first glimmerings of light crept through the hatches and gunports the quartermasters strode through the dim caverns of the ship rousing the sleepers and hurrying the laggards up on deck. Before work started, or they broke their fast, the crew assembled, and a rush basket filled with books was placed on deck. Those who could read took copies, and together they sang psalms and listened devoutly while an officer recited a prayer in the English tongue. The sailors called it a dry Mass, and twice a week, before they dispersed, the Articles governing the voyage were read to them as well.

As soon as the decks were cleared the swabbers began their work, scrubbing the oak planks and sluicing them down with buckets of sea-water. Some of the duty watch were deputed to work the pumps, for not a day passed without water gathering in the bilges. Others carried trays of burning pitch through the messdecks in an attempt to fumigate and cleanse the fetid atmosphere. Very little daylight or draught penetrated between decks. The accumulated filth of the ship lay rotting on the gravel ballast, and in the larger ships, where the four hundred slaves lay manacled for days on end without freedom of movement, the stench was almost unendurable. In such conditions vermin multiplied, and the stewards fought an unending battle to preserve the victuals against their depredations. On so long a voyage there was small margin for the men themselves, yet rats, mice and cockroaches devoured their tithe, and spoiled as much as they consumed.

The cleansing of the ship was a daily task on which Hawkins insisted, and not until it was completed were other jobs undertaken. The gunner's party was then freed to overhaul the armament, polishing the brass pieces and oiling the trunnions and truck carriages on which they were mounted. The small arms too—crossbows, pikes and arquebuses for the most part—needed constant cleaning against the corrosion of salt air, and there was always work to be done sifting and drying gunpowder, and preparing the cartridge-papers to receive it. Occasionally firing practice would be ordered, and the great guns would send their shot harmlessly out to sea, wreathing the ships in smoke, and causing the Africans in the hold to chatter fearfully amongst themselves in their strange, barbarian speech.

Meanwhile the galley stove that, owing to the danger of fire, had been extinguished overnight was relighted, and the smoke from faggots of green wood that had been cut during the last days ashore rose thickly from the chimney on the forecastle. The cooks were busy preparing the first meal of the day; boiling great cauldrons of beans for the slaves, broaching the steep-tubs of pickled meat, and baking bread in the brick ovens that had been constructed low down in the bows, directly upon the ballast. Sometimes a sailor who had successfully trailed a line astern would beg a little space at the range to cook the fish that he had caught for his mess.

Deep down in the ship, but farther aft than the galley, the stewards weighed out the day's issue of provisions in the storerooms. A pound of bread and a gallon of beer were the rations for each man. But the movement of the ship made the beer acid, and water had taken its place before the middle passage was completed. Even that was flat and evil-tasting, but the tropical sun made men thirsty and none too particular about what they drank. As for the biscuit it was best eaten below decks where the light was dim, for the weevils had claimed it long before it was issued.

Four days a week they ate meat, and, as each cask was opened and the contents put in soak, the sailors grumbled at the dishonesty of the English victuallers who, they claimed, filled every other barrel with bones and fat or rank meat imperfectly preserved. Sailors will always complain about their food, but eat it with gusto just the same. Certainly the flesh days were more popular than the two days when salt cod and hard, sour cheese took their place; or, worst of all, Fridays, when the allowance was halved. It was dull food, but familiar to ocean-going men, and, thanks to Hawkins' vigilance in dealing with contractors and his insistence on keeping his crews small, reasonable both in quantity and quality.

Fresh food could not be stored for more than a day or two under tropical conditions, and Hawkins, who perhaps realized that some virtues connected with good health resided in victuals that had not been steeped in brine or stored in sacks, encouraged the men to fish. The quartermaster issued hooks, and during their off-duty hours the sailors would gather in a patch of shade, watching their trailing lines, and telling tales of the strange lands they had visited and unaccountable things they had seen. Scarcely a day passed without a catch of Spanish mackerel or one of the sleek dolphins that kept company with the ships, and rubbed their smooth sides against the barnacle-encrusted hulls.

Sometimes, in sport, the seamen would bait strong hooks with lumps of meat and troll for sharks. They did not hunt them for meat, indeed they were considered unwholesome as food. But they feared and hated the malevolent great fish, whose presence around the ship was an omen of ill-luck. They found diversion in baiting the thrashing, helpless creatures if they succeeded in hauling them aboard, or else in maiming them and throwing them back overboard where they could watch them being cannibalistically devoured. A less energetic occupation for an idle hour was to play the game called 'Reverent Friars'. A dozen or more men, as one sailor later recalled it, 'would sit round a wheel and each one would be given a name, such as Shaven Friar and Friar such-an-one, ugly names and dirty, such as Lust, Pride, Avarice and other designations . . . and at this game they would play taking such names so that if one made a mistake the others would spank his buttocks'.

Hawkins and his officers, who took their exercise upon the steeply-tilted poop-deck under awnings that had been erected as protection from the sun, would often lean over the rails and watch these sports. Any distraction was welcome; any incident that was worthy of comment was seized upon, as much by the gentlemen as by the crew. Boredom was very frequent, and the constriction of space and company bred petty spites and jealousies. The merchants and soldiers in particular found the time irksome, for their duties at sea were few. Hawkins watched them closely. He could not afford to let another quarrel develop like Dudley's mutiny. Often he must have wished that he had only sailors on board, as on his previous voyages: there were enough routine tasks to keep them busy, however long the middle passage might last. But landsmen were different. He could find little with which to occupy them, and they were unaccustomed to the hard living and tolerant comradeship of a ship at sea.

Hawkins himself was at ease in all quarters of the ship. He talked unaffectedly with his men, calling them by name and using a seaman's jargon in his speech. Some of his gentlemen-companions, he knew, despised him for his familiarity with men of low birth. They themselves preferred to keep to the seclusion of their quarters and exercise their authority at a distance. Such was never Hawkins' way. He gained trust through intimacy and scarcely a man aboard the *Jesus* had not talked with his captain and held him in more respect than was common amongst lower-deck men. In particular he was not ashamed to visit the sick and the dying, praying with them, enquiring about their families, and recording their last messages in his own neat hand-writing. Wherever he went he was conspicuous in his severe, black garments with rich trimmings that contrasted strangely with the ragged and sunburnt half-nakedness of the deck-hands. Hawkins, though no dandy, was scrupulous in his appearance, and set an example that his officers were bound to follow.

In contrast to his informal visits to the lower deck he never overlooked the ceremony which was his due as Admiral of the Queen's fleet. He ate off silver plate, and even if the victuals were not of the best they were served with a flourish, and music was played as he drank his wine. Familiarity, even from friends or kinsmen, he would never tolerate, and to no one did he show favour. His was a lonely eminence, but he did not wish it otherwise. His discipline was sharp and his punishments severe, though seldom crippling. For minor offences a day in irons or a whipping were normal and accepted penalties which he did not hesitate to see administered; but he would not have scrupled to inflict the more barbarous penalties, from which seamen in his day so frequently suffered, if there had been cause. Much of the day he spent in his cabin pondering upon the charts and books of the sea that he had brought with him, until he knew almost by heart the accumulated lore that he and his father and a generation of Plymouth seamen had gleaned from the Spanish main. Hitherto he had sailed with a Spanish pilot on board on whom he could rely for guidance, but this time he depended only on his memory and his native wit.

Each day at noon he took his astrolabe on deck and calculated the latitude in which they sailed; but the longitude, by which he could have determined how far across the wide ocean the fleet had edged its way, he had no means of measuring. From the strength of the wind and current and the sailing qualities of his ships he would hazard a guess, and place a mark each day a little further westward on the chart.

Progress was slow. Often they seemed to drift forward rather than sail, and patches of orange weed closed in around them, clogging the rudder and masking the surface of the sea. Some days the carpet of weed was so thick that it seemed almost possible to walk on it, and as it rotted in the sunlight the rank, briny smell hung heavily in the air around the becalmed ships. But after a time the wind would freshen and the matted fields of kelp split up and drifted apart. Through the channels of clear water the helmsmen guided the ships forward. The bow-waves would froth and splash cheerfully against the strakes, and tiny shoals of silver, skimming fish scattered to left and right of the advancing prows.

The sea, the ships and the men responded equally to the stirring of the heavy, heat-laden air. The water deepened in colour and ruffled as the breeze touched it; the sails bellied out, the yards creaked stiffly as they caught the strain, and the sailors on deck or below roused themselves from the lethargy of waiting and joined cheerfully in the bustle of movement that the wind had created. Canvas wind-scoops were quickly rigged round the ports and hatches to catch the breeze and lead it through the rank, twilight spaces between decks. Even the slaves in their stifling quarters, where day and night were almost indistinguishable, felt the freshness in the air. Up aloft sailors from the duty watch manned the yards, unfurling the last stitch of canvas. Below them strode the boatswain, his silver whistle clenched between his teeth, sending the hands on deck about their tasks with a sudden awakening of energy.

The winds that blow over the equatorial seas are fitful and unsure. They sink to a whisper and die as suddenly as they arrive. By evening the sea would resume its calm transparency, and the coarse canvas sails would hang lazily from the yards, heavy with their own weight. As the sun sank towards the sea, gilding the waters to the west like a highroad before them, the sailors on each ship assembled once again for evening prayers. They had eaten their last meal of the day, and the cook had doused the galley fire for the night. As the last grains ran out the quartermaster turned the hour-glass and handed over the watch. From the waist came the murmur of many voices reciting together the familiar psalms and prayers.

Before the light failed the squadron closed in around the *Jesus*, hailing her and receiving the password for the night. Then they took station astern, and the lantern on the flagship's poop was lit. Candles were issued to the watch on deck, for the sun, once it had plunged into the sea, sucked down the daylight with it. There was a moment of flamboyance as the upper air was coloured with the last rays; then, with scarcely a pause for twilight, a velvet darkness descended upon the world. Against the blindness of the night a few soft, flickering lights from candles burning within lanterns of horn cast a glow upon the compass-card, or followed the duty officer on his rounds.

Below decks only the officers were allowed a naked flame in their cabins. For the crew the darkness on the mess-decks was complete. Hawkins knew only too well that fire was a greater peril at sea even than the enemy. He remembered how, a few years before, the *Primrose* had been burnt out at Tilbury through the neglect of a single candle; and on his previous voyage in the *Jesus* he had all but suffered the same fate, when the gunroom was set alight through carelessness. On that occasion he had ordered all the scuppers to be closed and had had water pumped on to the deck so that it lay ankle-deep; his crew, using every utensil they could lay hands on, had scooped up the water and, at length, extinguished the flames. So strict now were Hawkins' precautions against fire that he forbade pitch to be heated, wood to be chopped or casks to be hooped below decks, and would not allow spirits to be drawn from the barrels by candle-light. There was another dangerous habit that some of his men had picked up in the Indies on his previous voyage, of smoking tobacco leaf; and he feared that if it should be reintroduced the fire risk might be substantially increased.

Very soon after darkness had fallen the last man to be relieved of his watch stumbled past his companions to the sleeping space that was still empty, and threw himself down, fully dressed, on a crumpled palliasse. Further aft the gentlemen, who had long exhausted any desire to converse together far into the night, retired to their cabins early. They lay and sweated upon their bunks or in the new-fangled hammocks ('Brazil beds' they called them), waiting for sleep to intervene. In their boredom they watched the flame of their candle creep closer to the water that surrounded and would soon extinguish it. Over their heads they could hear the passing and repassing of feet; for a ship at sea never wholly sleeps, and under the canopy of stars many watchful eyes guided the fleet forward. In the wake of the ten ships a sluggish, phosphorescent glow was stirred up out of the dark sea, and faded behind them to the east. However frail the airs that drove them forward their aim was constant.

Fifty-two days and nights had to pass after leaving Africa before the look-out on the foretop could cry out that land lay ahead, and scramble exultantly down the ratlins to claim the gold coin that was his promised reward. They had been bland but wearing days, trying both to temper and health. A few men had died, amongst them the unfortunate soldier Edward Dudley, and scurvies and fluxes were beginning to spread. Not a man on board would have wished the middle passage longer. Sailors on ocean voyages were accustomed to the face of death, and none would have accounted a few negroes and one or two of their companions whom they had left behind, shrouded and ballasted after a sea-borne funeral, as an excessive toll to pay. Not until the passage was achieved did they fully realize how strained and weak they had become.

But a landfall was medicine to the sickest man. As the ships drew close to the wild green island that had risen out of the sea before them, no one who could walk remained below decks. The anchor party stood by on the forecastle, the leadsmen in the chains sang out the soundings, and willing hands helped to free the ship's boats from their chocks and clear them for lowering outboard. The island thay had chanced on offered no prospect of treasure or trade. At most they could fill their empty water-barrels and depart. Yet in the air were seabirds and the warm smells of vegetation, and the English seamen greeted Dominica like the promised land.

CHAPTER 7

The Islands and the Main

To a sailing vessel leaving the Guinea coast with the wind blowing from the starboard quarter and steering a west-north-westerly course it was almost inevitable that sooner or later one of the Windward Islands would provide a landfall. This arc of islands, flung like a net to guard the approaches to the Caribbean, was in itself considered of little importance compared to what lay beyond. They were landmarks and watering-places that were welcomed by the voyager but seldom revisited. It was difficult for one thing to beat back against the prevailing winds once one had sailed past them, and no one would cross the Atlantic for their sakes alone.

They were wild and beautiful islands. Columbus, who had sighted Dominica on his second voyage, when asked by the Spanish Queen to describe the appearance of the newly-discovered land had shown her its likeness by crumpling a sheet of parchment in his hand. What he could not show in his impulsive gesture was the verdure that cloaked every spur and valley of the island in a green web. Nor could he show how the rain-clouds shrouded the wooded peaks, breeding under their shadow a choking, exuberant growth of orchids and flowering vines; fields of bamboo that continually rustled and swayed in the breeze and palms in infinite variety that hemmed in the scalloped beaches, each with its thin rim of sand.

There was no gold dust in the beds of the mountain streams that cascaded down from the steamy highlands, and there were no oyster-beds that could be dredged for pearls. Nothing in short that would encourage a treasure-seeker to linger. Indeed there was

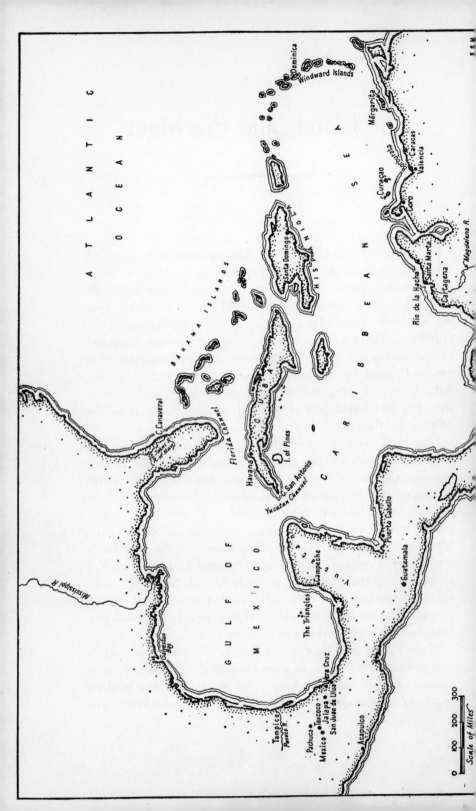

one distinct deterrent. Dominica was one of the last redoubts of the fierce and intractable Caribs, who fought bitterly to retain their ancient freedom.

Before the coming of the Spaniards two main races inhabited the Caribbean islands and the Main, the Caribs and the Arawaks. The latter were a peaceful, docile people, an easy prey for a forceful conqueror. Even before the white man enslaved and exterminated them, their neighbours—the Caribs—were pressing them ever further north, crossing from island to island in their long war-canoes, killing and capturing as they went. When the Spaniards arrived the Arawaks came to meet them with gifts and friendship; but the Caribs greeted the invaders with a shower of arrows poisoned with the juice of the manchineel tree. Many a Spaniard had fallen a victim to their ambushes and raids, and before long they avoided as best they could any unnecessary contact with their war-like neighbours. There were more important and more lucrative tasks to undertake in Mexico and Peru, and troops were too precious to spare for hunting down Caribs on unprofitable islands.

So Dominica, where Columbus had been repelled three-quarters of a century before, was resisting still; and Hawkins would not be likely to forget that just before his last visit in 1565 the crew of a Spanish vessel that was wrecked upon its shores were killed outright, and later eaten, for such was the custom of the Caribs. Stories such as this were rife in the Indies, and so great had Hawkins' caution been on landing that he scarcely penetrated far enough to find water on an island that boasts a stream for every day of the year.

On that occasion he had escaped without attracting notice, but he had stumbled upon a cluster of their huts—high, roomy penthouses of woven rush with eaves that almost touched the ground—but there had not been a soul in sight. He knew none-theless, from the tales he had heard, of the terrifying aspect of the Carib warriors when they broke from cover to launch their surprise attacks. Their olive-coloured, naked bodies were striped with black and white dyes, and circles of crimson outlined their eyes. Lips and noses were pierced and plugged with bone and coral ornaments, and they garlanded themselves with necklaces of human bones and brightly-coloured feathers: a terrifying visitation that he was glad to have avoided.

Now, at the end of March 1568, having been at sea for almost half a year, the English sailors looked on Dominica as a natural halting place. Hawkins, however, knowing the evil reputation of the land, was quick to disillusion them. No sooner had they anchored off shore than he set an armed watch on deck, and told his men that they would stop only long enough to take on water. Even this dangerous operation he would have avoided if he could, but the long middle passage had nearly exhausted their supplies. Many of the remaining casks were foul or brackish, and no one could quench his thirst as he wished. On the slave decks the condition of many of the negroes was pitiable, for, as their sparse rations of food and drink deteriorated, most of the prisoners, already worn down by their long confinement, became racked with dysentery, and, of late, a number of the children and old people had succumbed. Fresh water had, therefore, become an urgent necessity. The boats were slung outboard and the cooper's watering party was rowed ashore, escorted by a company of well-armed soldiers.

Once again they escaped without molestation. Near the beach, under the shadow of a wall of creeper, they found a stream that had carved a bed for itself through the red clay. Ringed around by their escort the seamen carried the empty casks up the beach and rolled them back to the boats when they were filled. It was hot work, but popular with the men for the chance it gave to walk upon the warm sand and see about them the fresh fecundity of growing things. All the boats returned to the fleet well before sunset, for darkness fell suddenly in these latitudes and they had no desire to be benighted ashore.

Next morning the work continued without interruption, and within the day enough water had been brought on board for Hawkins to turn his thoughts towards the real objective of his voyage, the slave-hungry Spanish settlements along the Main. He set a southerly course for his fleet, keeping to leeward of the island-chain, and did not pause until, two days later, the line of hills backing the Venezuelan coastal plain was sighted in the distance, and, nearer at hand, the three rocky little islands of Margarita, Coche and Cubagua.

They were unprepossessing to look upon, for their wealth lay concealed in the waters around them. The oyster beds of Nueva Esparta were famous for their pearls; but already the yield was diminishing. Partly because of the devastation caused by recurrent earthquakes and hurricanes, and partly because the oysters had been torn too greedily from the most accessible places, two of the islands—Coche and Cubagua—had been abandoned for habitation, and only a handful of Spaniards still dwelt at the port of La Asuncion on the eastern coast of Margarita. There was indeed a fort above the town, and a small garrison, but the need for slave labour was greater than the size of the place seemed to warrant. The reason was a grim one: the mortality was so high.

At first pearl-divers had been recruited from the Caribs and Chayma Indians on the mainland, and some of these, branded with the letter C were still to be seen in La Asuncion as a memorial of the great slave market for which Cubagua had been notorious. As the oyster beds grew more difficult to work the divers, huddled naked in their moored canoes, were made to dive deeper in order to find them. Six or even ten fathoms beneath the surface they collected their catch, holding their breath for ever increasing periods. Those in charge of the divers thought to encourage their powers of endurance by allowing them only a little of the driest food, for liquids they considered caused shortness of breath. Day after day of such exertions soon thinned their numbers, and the hazards lurking in the sea itself accounted for as many deaths again.

Before long the mainland colonies could spare no more labour for the islands, and the Guaiquerias who lived in the desolate western half of Margarita, like the Caribs of Dominica, proved too intractable to catch or use. The African negro was the perfect answer, and the Spaniards who worked the pearl-fisheries on the island were always ready to buy more than the official *asiento* would allow them.

Three years before, Hawkins had been able to conduct a profitable trade at Margarita thanks to the co-operation of the mayor. But the Governor of the island had been obstructive and had done as much as he dared to frustrate Hawkins' plans. It was, therefore, uncertain what sort of reception he could expect when he sailed into the rocky bay that sheltered the port of La Asuncion.

Like most of the settlements along the Spanish Main the impermanence of the buildings and the primitive conditions under which the inhabitants lived seemed in strange contrast to the wealth that passed through the town. Margarita was an undistinguished group of huts, all recently built, and only the church and the fort were made of solid materials. All too often the town had been sacked by French corsairs or shaken by hurricanes. Once, too, a renegade Spaniard had pillaged his own fellow-countrymen here and sent them hurrying to the interior with all the wealth they could carry, leaving the town open to his spite. The depredations of nature and of man were of such common occurrence that scarcely a year went by without a material disaster leaving the little settlement in ruins. It was small wonder, therefore, that their buildings were not grand and their treasure deviously concealed.

Dusk was falling when Hawkins' fleet sailed into the sheltered water of the harbour. It was at once evident that their arrival had alarmed the settlement. In the fading light they watched and waited for some indication of the reception they might expect, but none came. Their salute was unanswered, and not a soul was to be seen either at the fort or on the waterfront. Hawkins realized that his ensign might have been indistinguishable from a distance, and he knew too that the fifty Spaniards who lived on Margarita could not have attempted to resist the onslaught of a fleet as powerful as his. He concluded that they had fled inland from a fear that he did not want to exploit. Immediately he could spare himself from the deck he went to his cabin to write a reassuring letter to the Governor of the island, and ordered one of his pinnaces to stand by to deliver it ashore.

'Worshipfull', he commenced, 'I have towched in your ilond only to thentente to refresh my menne with fresh victualles, which for my mony or wares you shall sell me, meanyng to staye only but 5 or 6 dayes here at the furthest. In the which tyme you maye assure youre selfe and so all others that by me or any of myne there shall no domadge be done to any manne, the which alsoe the Quenes Majestie of Inglond, my mystres, at my departure owt of Inglond comaunded me to have great care of.' Thus far he was polite, but firm. Before adding his signature and seal, however, he thought to add the phrase, 'and to serve with my navye the Kinges Majestie of Spaine my olde master, if in places where I came any of his stoode in neade'. What better argument in favour of protective trade, Hawkins must have thought, than the undeniable fact that, only ten years before, his own country had been linked to Spain by a royal marriage?

The boat's crew that took Hawkins' message ashore had scarcely landed at the wharf when they became aware that a small cluster of men on horseback was watching their movements, but keeping well out of bow-shot. The two groups hailed each other and the English party disclosed who they were. On hearing that they brought a message to the Governor one of the Spaniards came forward to receive it, and the whole party rode off into the darkness after promising to bring an answer at first light.

True to their word the Spaniards delivered their Governor's reply next morning. It was a civil, indeed courteous, response; far more accommodating in tone than Hawkins had dared hope. Not only did the Governor propose welcoming the English admiral personally to the town at nine o'clock that morning (although, he claimed, he was so ill that he ought not to stir from his bed), but he freely offered all the facilities that the island could provide and urged Hawkins not to cut short his sojourn. The fleet had already moved as far as was practicable into the shelter of the harbour, and before long Hawkins, meticulously dressed and accompanied by a guard strong enough to deal with any intended treachery, was rowed ashore.

The Governor and almost all the Spanish residents were assembled in the central plaza to greet them. The two leaders embraced each other, and with the aid of Barrett as interpreter they exchanged courtesies. The Governor was, as he had indicated, sick with one of the recurrent fevers that few residents in the Indies escaped, but nevertheless he insisted on accompanying Hawkins on a tour of the little town. There was little enough to see except the ruins of several houses that had been burnt six months before by a raiding party of French corsairs. Hawkins expressed his indignation and reiterated his own peaceful intentions. Before returning to their ships the English party were entertained to a meal that had been hastily improvized. The Spaniards had few delicacies to offer, but the taste of fresh meat was luxury enough, and as his first request Hawkins asked that a quantity of beef and mutton be brought out to his ships for the use of his men. The Governor was eager to oblige, for meat was plentiful in the Indies where the cattle ran wild and bred prodigiously. No one on board the English ships complained when it was served daily—even on fast-days.

Eight busy and profitable days of trading ensued. From out of the holds of the English ships came bales of cloth and linen. These, together with hardware of all sorts, were in great demand amongst the Spaniards and a market was set up in the plaza to display and sell them. Hawkins and the merchants who had been appointed to sail with the expedition superintended the transactions. At first they bartered for meat and maize-flour and water to re-equip their depleted provision-lockers. But when these first necessities had been attended to it is unlikely that the Englishmen would have neglected to traffic for the pearls that made the island famous—Ave Marias and Pater Nosters: the small and the large—heavy and translucent and glowing with white fire. Neither would the Spaniards have been kept in ignorance of the presence of negroes in the English ships. Officially of course all trading was forbidden, and slaves in particular were liable to confiscation; so there is no mention by either side of their being sold at Margarita. It would be surprising nonetheless if a number had not changed hands.

Not many of the four hundred English seamen were allowed ashore. Most of the time when they were not on duty they lounged under the shade of canvas awnings, watching the pearl-diving boats anchored over the oyster-grounds in motionless clusters, while above them innumerable sea-birds glided on narrow wings, plunging from time to time into the still water like falling stones. Sometimes the hunters would themselves be hunted by frigate birds—black acrobats with forked tails and cruel beaks—that flew among them, attacking furiously until a fish was disgorged, only to be snatched up as it fell by the aggressor. Through watching these aerial combats the sailors observed that the victims of the frigate birds' assaults seemed to live in a gregarious colony on a bare rock that stood a mile out to sea. One night several boats' crews rowed out by moonlight to the rock, hoping to surprise them and kill some for food. They landed cautiously, but there was no need, for the birds amply deserved the name 'boobies' that the sailors gave them. They scarcely seemed aware of their danger and allowed the men to walk among them, striking them down with cudgels and loading the boats to the gunwales with their carcasses. They waddled aimlessly, as tame as farmyard geese, around their nesting hollows, where pairs of chalky eggs, blotched with ordure, lay so thickly upon the ground that the sailors trod them carelessly underfoot as they beat down the unprotesting parent-birds. When the lust for killing had died they thought to collect some of the eggs too, and returned with a welcome cargo of fresh food to the ships. Both boobies and their eggs, they declared after they had tasted them next day, were delicious.

Banqueting on a grander, more ceremonious, scale was also indulged in by the officers and gentlemen. Throughout their sojourn Hawkins and the Spanish Governor had been profuse in their courtesies. All the dignitaries of the island came on board the *Jesus* to dine, and Hawkins in his turn was several times entertained ashore. The official proscription against which Hawkins conducted his trade seemed very academic and unreal compared with the cordiality that he encountered at Margarita. There was never any doubt that the ordinary settlers throughout the Indies welcomed him because of the goods that he brought with him; but those who exercised authority could seldom afford to be so self-interested. As representatives of the King of Spain, however humble their post might be, the local governors and mayors could not fail to be aware that Hawkins was a threefold breaker of the law. In the first place without permission from the King he had no right to be in the Indies at all; in the second place he was selling merchandise (at cut rates) that had not been manifested at Seville; and thirdly he was doing business without an official trading licence. For each of these offences against the laws of Spain Hawkins was liable to arrest and his goods to be impounded. Even if such a course happened to be impracticable there was no excuse, it was argued, for conniving with him or aiding his offence.

There was also the problem of religion, a consideration that weighed heavily against Hawkins, as, in Spanish eyes, he was an undoubted heretic. However sincerely he might advance his old allegiance to the Catholic King of Spain it was evident that his present loyalty was to the Protestant Queen of England. To Hawkins, who was no theologian, and regarded a change in dogma as a shifting of the political wind, it did not seem a serious or insuperable matter. Indeed, the farther away from the central authority of Spain that he travelled the more accommodating and tolerant he found the local inhabitants. When his peaceful overtures were rejected and trade was refused, it was fear rather than personal antipathy that obstructed him—fear of the strict, paternal solicitude that Spain extended to her distant colonists, a slow, cumbersome control that sought to guide the detailed policies and moral health of her adventurous sons. The word of the King still commanded absolute loyalty in the Indies. One fifth of the treasure that the country yielded was scrupulously put aside as the royal share, and men who were notorious for their reckless pride, bravery and greed, never thought to question the belated and often inappropriate orders that they received from their far-away homeland in the King's name.

Hawkins was well aware of the official impediments that might hinder his trade. He would certainly have learned from Captain Lovell, who had sailed these same coasts the previous season, that retribution had already struck many of the officials who had shown too friendly a welcome, or been too eager to trade, at the time of his own second slaving voyage. At Borburata, the next port at which he purposed to call, Hawkins knew that he would no longer be welcomed by Alonzo Bernaldez, the Governor who had proved helpful in the past. Bernaldez had been sent back to Spain to answer for his conduct. At Rio de la Hacha the treasurer,

Miguel de Castellanos, had been soured by a fine and an official reprimand. In the light of such treatment there would be few provincial officials who could be expected to welcome Hawkins openly. It was all the more gratifying, therefore, to find at Margarita so little concern about the morrow. Hawkins took good advantage of his opportunity.

On the ninth day after his arrival the fleet weighed anchor and set an easterly course parallel to the mainland shore. Wind and current aided them, and Hawkins had little difficulty in picking out the landmarks that he had laboriously established on his previous voyage when no local pilot had been allowed to guide him. Once having plotted a course Hawkins had no desire to alter it. His cargo was too precious to risk unnecessarily, and Borburata was not only the nearest inhabited place on the coast where he could hope to sell slaves, but also possessed a secluded and sheltered harbour of sufficient depth inshore to allow even the largest of his ships to be beached for careening.

After six months of sailing, mostly in tropical waters, the growth of barnacle and weed that clung to the hulls of the ships could be seen through the clear water as they lay at anchor off La Asuncion. In order to sail swiftly such obstruction needed to be scraped away. But more perilous, though invisible until careening exposed the timbers beneath the waterline, were the ravages of teredo worms—pale, pulpy creatures that tunnelled their way into the strongest planks, weakening the fabric and leaving a network of holes through which the sea could enter. Many an unsheathed ship had foundered from no other cause, and few captains would risk leaving their vessels uninspected for more than a month or two if they were sailing in tropical seas. Careening beaches for a vessel as large as the *Jesus* were few and far between in the Indies, especially if, like Hawkins, one preferred to keep one's distance from the main centres of Spanish provincial government. Borburata was, therefore, an important stopping place for Hawkins. He hoped to stay by invitation, but if necessary he was determined to stay by force.

Burborough Water, as the English sailors called it, was a prosperous little colony of twenty years standing, lying a few miles to the east of the modern harbour of Puerto Cabello. Both the old town and the new served the same purpose: to provide an outlet to the sea for the products of the mines and upland pastures that centred round Valencia, on the far side of the coastal range of hills. A winding track, nearly fifty miles long, linked the two settlements together. During the rainy season it became a morass of red mud, and even when the soil was dry it was a rough and difficult road to travel over. It was dangerous too if one was not well escorted, for the Indian tribes were still unsubdued and sometimes launched surprise attacks against the colonists.

The Governor of Nueva Andalucia, as that portion of the Venezuelan mainland was then called, was Don Diego Ponce de Leon, a native of Estremadura (like so many of his fellow Conquistadors), now in his fiftieth year, the majority of which time he had spent in uninterrupted service in the Indies. His residence was in Coro, a coastal town considerably to the west of Borburata, and in view of his reputation for strict observance of the embargo on unlicensed trade, Hawkins would not have wished to advertise his presence in the province prematurely. His fleet slipped unobtrusively into the snug little inlet between the reefs and sandy cays, and almost before the township was aware that an intrusion had been made upon its privacy, a boat, that had gone ahead to sound out the narrow channel of deep water, had left the main fleet to anchor and rowed ashore to deliver another of Hawkins' persuasive messages.

Hawkins' letter to Don Diego was an ingenious exercise in diplomacy. He admitted quite frankly that he knew the Governor was forbidden by his royal master ('unto whome alsoe I have bene a servaunt') to license the trade that he desired. In the first place the voyage upon which he had embarked had had a quite different objective. But things had gone awry, and rather than lose the considerable costs that had gone into equipping the expedition, Queen Elizabeth had redirected it. It was, Hawkins claimed, far from his purpose to persuade the Governor to break his country's laws; all he required was permission to sell a small fraction of his wares and some sixty negroes—just sufficient to pay the wages of his crew. 'In this you shall not break the comaundement of your prince, but doe him good servyce and advoyd divers inconveniences which happen often tymes thorowghe beyng to precise in observing precepts withowt consideracion. If you may, I most instantly desire you that you will take the paynes to come hether, that I might conferre with you my selfe. Trewly it wolde be lever to me then 10,000 doccatts. If you come you showlde not fynde me ingratefull nor cownte youre travayle lost.'

The hint of bribery in Hawkins' letter could hardly be over-looked. At all events it was courteously done, and the only hope in the circumstances. But the messenger that was to carry the appeal was directed not to Coro, but inland and to the east where the Governor was on tour, inspecting the new lands that Diego de Losada had opened up that same year by founding the city of Santiago de Leon de Caracas. A long journey lay between them, and for the time being at least Hawkins felt secure from molest-ation.

While awaiting the Governor's reply the Englishmen were not idle. Having assured themselves that their presence was not un-welcome to the Borburatans, Hawkins had his ships brought alongside and was able, under strict guard to prevent escape, to exercise his negroes ashore, and ostentatiously to rearrange and display his coveted cargoes. At first after nightfall, and later more openly, the Spanish settlers began to visit his ships and secretly conduct barter deals. As their confidence increased, and the authorities ashore registered no protest, Hawkins began to set up booths and stalls along the quayside and brisk business ensued. Meanwhile those sailors who had not turned merchants were amply employed shipping supplies of fresh water, furnishing armed patrols both by day and by night on the dockside, and re-conditioning the ships for sea.

The supply of fresh meat in the town was not as plentiful as Hawkins could have wished. There was little stock-rearing under-taken on the coastal plains, and for the requirements of the port it was customary to send cattle down from the countryside around Valencia on the hoof. Shortly after the Easter celebrations had been completed (he had arrived on the eve of that festival), Hawkins determined to send for a hundred oxen to serve the needs of his fleet. He also learned of the presence in Valencia of the bishop in whose diocese he had landed. A Catholic bishop might seem the last person who would accede to the importunities of a heretic; but Hawkins, partly from his ingenuous doctrinal views and partly in his cynical belief that most men had their price, was by no means deterred from an attempt to recruit the bishop to his cause. The Cross and the sword wielded independent, and at times conflicting, powers in the Indies; it was possible that one might condone, even if the other condemned, his actions. Hawkins had often found that those who held the highest offices were inclined to be tolerant if approached directly, whereas petty officials were more likely at first to be obstructive. At all events a letter to the 'Right reverend father in God' (for such was the conciliatory manner in which he addressed the bishop) could do no harm. He asked for the hundred oxen to be sent down to him against payment, he requested his correspondent to intercede on his behalf with the Governor, and finally, with another thinly concealed offer of material benefits, he invited the bishop to visit him at Borburata.

The exchange of correspondence was a leisurely business in a country where land communications, even in the dry season, were tenuous. While awaiting replies to his letters Hawkins risked beaching those of his ships that were most fouled by marine growth and, by shifting the ballast and hauling in on ropes from the shore, exposed first one side, then the other, to the careeners. It was a lengthy process as he could only hazard one or two ships at a time in this defenceless position. While he was engaged in these operations messengers returned from the bishop at Valencia bearing his reply.

The bishop was evidently unconcerned with the possible contamination of his flock by heretics. His letter to Hawkins was as cordial as could be wished. Frankly he welcomed the English fleet for the sake of the trading goods and slave-labour that they brought with them. There were few luxuries to be had in the Indies, and supply ships came from Spain so seldom that much of the discontent that sprang up in these small communities arose from feelings of neglect by their own country. Such a lading as

Hawkins brought made everybody happy, and a bishop was not least amongst those who might expect to benefit materially from a peaceful invasion of trade. 'The Cowntrey desire all in generall to trafique', he assured Hawkins, though warning him that it was doubtful if the Governor would echo that desire by granting a licence. Nevertheless the bishop promised to intervene on Hawkins' behalf as best he might. As for visiting the fleet at Borburata, the bishop asked to be excused. Not only age and sickness prevented such a journey; suspicion would inevitably have fallen upon him had he attempted it, and he had no desire to compromise himself.

Hawkins was pleased with the course of his negotiations so far, and saw that the bishop's servants returned to Valencia with a gift for their master of twelve silver spoons and two first quality slaves as an earnest of goodwill. From the Governor, however, no reply was forthcoming. Hawkins thought that his message would have taken no more than four days to reach him, yet it was not until the end of April, a fortnight after they had landed at Borburata, that a reply came through.

The reason for the delay may have been the perplexity and exasperation that the report of his arrival created amongst the administrative officers. Every year and, it seemed, with increasing frequency of late, the harbours and settlements of the province were visited by hostile ships. Some came to trade, others only desired to pillage; some were Huguenots, others were English; but in each case they departed richer than they came and unmolested by the forces of law and order. On each occasion a report was sent to Spain and a reprimand came back. Yet nothing seemed to be done to stop the traffic or to protect the colonists. Unkown to Hawkins the first reaction to his arrival was to cause the royal accountant for the province of Venezuela, Diego Ruiz de Vallejo, doubtless at the prompting of the Governor, to address one more impassioned complaint to his Sovereign. 'These corsairs', he explained, 'come fully supplied with all lines of merchandise, oils and wines and everything else which is lacking in the country. The colonists' needs are great and neither penalties nor punishments suffice to prevent them from buying secretly what they want. As a matter of fact, they make their purchases, but nothing can be learned of them, for they buy at night and cover each other, and no measures suffice to prevent it. Truly, we, your majesty's officials, feel conscientious scruples about putting them on oath, when investigating; all we accomplish, as we think, is to make them perjure themselves.'

The Governor, Ruiz de Vallejo went on to say, had refused Hawkins' request to trade. So he had, but not in the strong terms that the King might have wished. It was, Hawkins decided, a craven, evasive reply; an attempt to keep in favour with both sides. The writer praised Hawkins' merits, but begged to be excused from the smallest gesture of co-operation, quoting proverbs when his own arguments ran dry. From the tenor of the letter there was only one consolation that could be drawn: it was unlikely that any serious resistance would be offered to the continued presence in Borburata of the English fleet, though it seemed likely that an attempt would be made to put an embargo on trade.

Hawkins had met and overcome such tactics before. It so happened that from the gossip he had picked up from those who traded at his booths (and Hawkins was an assiduous listener to such talk), he learned that a party of merchants, well furnished with gold for bartering, had come down from Valencia intending to trade with him, but feared to compromise themselves lest such trafficking was made illegal. They had waited some days and now were reluctantly returning by the way they had come. If trade would not come to him Hawkins was never inclined to sit back and do nothing. A show of force could often persuade even the most timid merchant that he had been made to do business against his will. For his part Hawkins was quite prepared to act the scapegoat if the rewards were big enough.

Without wasting any time a guide who knew the tortuous path to Valencia was hired, and sixty Englishmen were armed and provisioned for the chase. Robert Barrett took charge, and before day broke they had left the town and were making their way in-land towards the hills. Half a day's march took them across the coastal plain and the path began to climb up steep, rocky gorges. From time to time the dense forest that surrounded them on all sides and oppressed them with its humid, windless heat parted sufficiently for the party to be able to look back over the blue Caribbean that stretched out and merged imperceptibly into the equally blue sky. The distant expanse of sea looked cool and desirable to the English soldiers as they glanced back at it and thought of their companions busy careening and bartering at Borburata, now out of sight at the water's edge. A forced march with full equipment was never an agreeable prospect. Not only arms and armour, but provisions for several day's journey needed to be carried, and the way was rough and uphill for the most part. As they progressed farther into the hills the dust which their feet stirred up, and which covered them and their equipment in a red film, gave place to mud. The dry season was coming to an end, and storms in the hills were not uncommon. Soon it became evident that a recent cloud-burst had made the way all but impassable. They trudged on slowly and wearily, conserving their food supplies and sleeping uncomfortably on the wet earth.

Neither Indians nor Spaniards molested them on the road to Valencia. There were however two encounters with wild creatures in the forest that impressed themselves on the men. 'Wee found a monstrous venemous worme with two heads' Job Hortop (who was with the party) reported, and although he undoubtedly exaggerated its size it was not unlikely that an amphisbaena, the two-headed snake of Venezuela, lay across their path—a smooth, pale-bellied, primitive reptile, segmented like an enormous earthworm. Unlike most snakes it could move either forward or backward and had no visible head. Before it could escape Robert Barrett unsheathed his sword and killed it, staining his weapon 'as blacke as if it were coloured with ynke'.

The second encounter was with a jaguar that lay along an overhanging branch in the hope of carrying off a straggler from the main party. Luckily, before it could do damage, it was seen and scared away. Of the other animals and birds that haunted the forest they heard more than they saw. There were flashes of bright colour and shrill warning cries from innumerable small birds, and butterflies of enormous size fluttered past in the patches of sunlight. At night they were bitten by unseen mosquitos and watched the moving pattern of green firefly-lights. The sentries, who kept guard over the sleeping camp, grew accustomed to hearing the challenging cry 'who are you?' from the nightjars, and became less apprehensive of the small animal-movings that accentuated the silence of the uninhabited hills.

Before they reached Valencia, Barrett's party climbed above the forest-level into a more open region of cactus and stony earth. Here they made better progress, but they had been delayed too long to achieve surprise. Somehow their presence had become known along the road, and when at last they reached the town they found, to their chagrin, that it was deserted. Not only the provincial authorities but the merchants, whose treasure they principally sought, had dispersed into the surrounding countryside. Even the bishop, who had been so friendly in his correspondence, had departed. It was to his house that Barrett had gone as soon as he arrived, and found no host but a priest who was too sick to travel. From him the Englishmen learnt that the bishop had been obliged to fly with the rest lest by remaining he should be suspected. Nonetheless he left behind him a well-furnished larder and cellar that he invited Hawkins' representatives to avail themselves of. They were grateful, for they needed refreshments; but even as they partook of the bishop's hospitality they realized that their expedition had been a failure.

A thorough examination of the empty houses convinced them that nothing valuable had been left behind, and as their purpose was not to sack the place it only remained for them to retreat along the path they had so lately trodden. A few days later they reported back to Hawkins at Borburata.

Work on the ships was proceeding well and several of the smaller vessels were once more entirely seaworthy. Rather than have them remain idle while the *Jesus* and *Minion* were beached and repaired, Hawkins sent three of them to the island of Curaçao to buy hides and dried meat, and two others farther down the coast to the little port of Santa Ana de Coro, where, knowing of the Governor's absence, Hawkins considered an exploratory visit was safe. Meanwhile he remained with his great ships at Borburata, still selling his wares covertly, despite the official boycott.

The five small vessels left their moorings in the sheltered waters of Borburata before dawn, taking advantage of the land-breeze that blows only at night in order to gain an offing. Once clear of the coast they steered a north-westerly course, keeping clear of the heavy swell that beat upon the low, sandy verges of the Golfo de Triste. It was an easy passage, though made slow by the northerly wind that blew during daylight hours. Normally Hawkins did not like sailing by night in unknown and dangerous waters, but the advantages of wind and current may have made the risk worth while. Before long two of the ships left the others and turned towards Coro. The remaining three vessels pursued their course until, after two days and nights at sea, they sighted the low-lying and bleak island of Curaçao ahead.

On his previous voyage Hawkins had made the mistake of trying to find a sheltered anchorage for the *Jesus* without the benefit of a local pilot. That there was a harbour for small craft he felt certain, and, once achieved, good trade in hides and boucaned meat. But the inhabitants, whose cattle ran wild over the treeless and gaunt pastures, were not interested in acquiring slaves. The three vessels were stocked with trading-goods and circled the reef-ringed island as closely as they dared in search of sheltered water. At times a stirring of the air would bring a waft of corruption with it from the land, and later the sailors learnt that this was caused by the multitude of rotting carcasses that the Curaçaoans, after stripping the hides from their slaughtered animals, left in discarded heaps, greater than the carrion fowl that flocked there could devour.

The dry, windswept island with its gently-rolling, dun-coloured hills was very different from any other island that they had seen in the Antilles, and when at last the three little ships found a haven, and enquired ashore about trade, they met with a friendly reception and were able to linger profitably for a week or two. The sailors ate prodigiously of the fresh beef and mutton that the islanders almost gave away, and dried more to take with them. Between the decks they packed a fine lading of hides, and having accomplished their task settled down to await the arrival of the main fleet, for they could not easily beat back to Borburata against wind and current.

It was not until the beginning of June that Hawkins was satisfied that he had exhausted the possibilities of Borburata. Before leaving he took the precaution of obtaining letters of recommendation from the bishop at Valencia and certificates of good conduct from the authorities in the port. Such documents might well prove useful later on in persuading other Spaniards of his honest intention, or at least would provide arguments against the recriminations that he fully expected from the Spanish Ambassador when he returned home. Even more valuable than the letters was a pilot, whom Hawkins had been able to persuade to accompany his fleet as far as Rio de la Hacha, his next important call on the mainland coast. This pilot, who had already bought twenty-two slaves from Hawkins, was eager to obtain more and had been promised a reward in kind to repay his services.

All things being ready, the *Jesus* and *Minion*, accompanied by the three ships that remained with them, set out to sea, picking up the two craft that had been detached at Coro and re-uniting as a fleet of ten sail at Curaçao. There was a pause here, during which time Hawkins sent the *Angel* and *Judith*—the latter now under the command of his young kinsman, Francis Drake—forward to Rio de la Hacha in advance of the main party.

His reasons for choosing Drake to make the first approaches to the obstinate and embittered Treasurer and Captain-General of Rio de la Hacha, Miguel de Castellanos, are obscure. Four years before, Hawkins had parted from Castellanos on reasonably amicable terms. Since then the Treasurer had been reproved for his conduct by the Spanish Governor and had succeeded only the year before in frustrating John Lovell's attempt at trade, and caused him to leave ninety negroes behind, for which no payment had been made. Drake had sailed with Lovell that year and would have had no sympathy for Castellanos' perfidious conduct. There was a debt to be paid, and Drake was young and angry enough to be eager to claim it. If Hawkins had intended his ambassador to come in peace he made a most unaccountable choice.

CHAPTER 8

The Treasurer

NUESTRA Señora de los Remedios del Rio de la Hacha was a city of some sixty huts. Like Margarita it was famous beyond its size for the pearls that it annually sent back to enrich the Spanish treasury. For the past fourteen years Miguel de Castellanos had held authority as Treasurer of the town and Commander of the tiny garrison. He lived in the only substantial building, apart from the church, that had been constructed within the palisade that surrounded the settlement. The other houses were straw-thatched and built with a careless fatalism caused by the recurrent devastation of corsairs. The river from which the town took its name flowed into the sea on the eastern side, and it was possible for small craft, using the channel that it cut for itself, to come close inshore; but it was a difficult approach through heavy surf and a bad anchorage, especially early in the year. For many months Rio de la Hacha was almost cut off from the outside world, and during the season when shipping called there more hostile than friendly sails were sighted.

During his years of office Castellanos had continually pleaded to be given the forces and the equipment to defend himself against the annual devastation to which he was subjected. But he had met with little support. He had been able to equip a few horse-men with white leather shields and javelins; these were useful against Indian raids, but ineffectual against corsairs. Since his reproof, and the twenty thousand pesos fine that he had suffered as a result of trading with Hawkins, he had managed to secure a supply of arquebuses; but even so his total force of fighting men amounted to little more than a hundred, together with negro and

Indian slaves to whom he did not dare issue firearms. Nevertheless his success of the year before, when both Lovell and Captain Bontemps had been turned away, made him confident and truculent, and as he no longer dared to negotiate with unlicensed traders he made diligent preparations to repel them as best he could.

The arrival of Drake with two small ships did not deter him in his resolve. The *Judith* and *Angel*, on account of their shallow draught, were able to come to anchor hard by the town, and immediately sent ashore with a request for water. By way of reply Castellanos ordered his three pieces of artillery to be fired at the ships, and attempted to seize the boat's crew that had gone ashore with the message. An arquebus shot wounded one of the Englishmen, and Drake, not without some satisfaction, found ample reason to return the fire. One of the first targets he gave his gunners was the Treasurer's house.

It was a desultory and ineffectual exchange of shot. The *Judith* and *Angel* had only one gun each that could be brought to bear, and although they succeeded in destroying a few of the habitations ashore, they had not the fire power to do any great damage. The Spaniards, likewise, did not possess the heavy cannon that might have sunk the two little boats. As soon as they began to get the range Drake weighed anchor and moved out of gunshot, having wisely decided to wait for reinforcements.

In the outer harbour he kept a five-day vigil, disturbed by only a single incident. A small craft, carrying routine messages and stores from the islands, sailed innocently into the harbour. By the time she realized her danger the *Judith* and *Angel* had weighed anchor and were moving to intercept her. There was a quick attempt to beach her under cover of arquebus fire from the land, but the English ships cut her out before she grounded and ransacked her thoroughly before resuming their blockade.

Meanwhile Hawkins, for lack of wind or other reasons, pursued a leisurely course from Curaçao to Rio de la Hacha. He might not have risked sailing by night, and even in daytime, would often send a pinnace ahead of his great ships to scout out the reefs and shoals. Soon after leaving Curaçao the island of Aruba would have provided a landmark, and then, on the port hand, the long, low-lying and deserted Cape de la Vela with the Sierras rising faintly and distantly behind.

The sea through which the eight ships so quietly passed teemed with life. Sometimes a giant ray would leap from the water like a plate of flexible steel, catching the sun for an instant before plunging into the translucent blue depths. On the surface of the water turtles drowsed, and flying fish rose and scudded away from under the bows like showers of meteors. Those old enemies of sailors, the sharks, still balefully followed the ships, turning their great moon-coloured bellies uppermost to seize the slops that were thrown overboard. But more dangerous than any fish were the patches of disturbed or discoloured water that appeared from time to time, disclosing sandbanks and coral reefs un-recorded except in the memory of those who frequently coasted in these waters. Even with a pilot aboard Hawkins proceeded cautiously.

He arrived at the roadstead of Rio de la Hacha on the evening of June 9th, and was immediately told by Drake of the events that had preceded his coming. Outwardly Hawkins appeared very little moved by the account. He knew the Treasurer of old, he thought, and was confident of how to deal with him. First of all, before nightfall, he had a letter delivered to him ashore. The wording was familiar: a blunt and disarming acknowledg-ment of the main problem, followed by an ingenious, face-saving solution (backed by a threat of force) whereby trade might be initiated. To a Spaniard, accustomed to the discursive courtesies of official communications, Hawkins' letter might have appeared brusque and peremptory, but its meaning was certainly clear. The outstanding matter of payment for the negroes that Captain Lovell had left behind the year before was dismissed as an un-fortunate misunderstanding which Hawkins, for his part, did not intend to pursue. On this occasion all he desired was per-mission to sell sixty negroes to defray his immediate expenses. 'If you se in the morninge armed menne alond,' Hawkins blandly continued, 'lett it nothing trowbell you, for as you shall comaund they shall retorne abourde againe. Shewing me this pleasure, you shall comaunde any thinge I have.'

The Treasurer's reply was far more defiant than Hawkins anticipated. If selling negroes ashore was the only way Hawkins had of providing wages for his crew, Castellanos remarked, he had far better leave them unpaid. If they attempted to land they would be resisted by Spaniards as brave and well equipped as any Englishmen. Hawkins shrugged aside the boasts and bravado of the letter and made his dispositions for a landing next day. At this stage at least it was obviously going to be impossible to trade peacefully.

A frontal attack through the shallows against the palisades that surrounded the town might well have proved costly. Hawkins planned to make a landing with some two hundred men a mile or two down the coast and march, under cover of the guns of the fleet, to take the town from the landward side. At noon on June 10th the pinnaces bearing Hawkins' assault-party made an unopposed landing. The Englishmen, well-armed with arquebuses, pikes, crossbows and halberds, formed up on the beach before starting to march eastward to the town. A group of twenty Spanish horsemen, led by Castellanos himself, shadowed them just out of bowshot, but did not interfere.

Before setting forth Hawkins sent the Spanish pilot, whom he had brought from Borburata, to talk with the Treasurer and try to persuade him that peaceful trading was the more profitable and honourable course for him to adopt. But Castellanos was determined to resist and sent the pilot back to Hawkins, telling him to do what he liked but never to expect a licence to trade from him.

A quarter of a mile along the path to the town the Spaniards had thrown up a roadblock, behind which almost the entire force of arquebusiers that Rio de la Hacha boasted, together with some negro and Indian levies, lay waiting to receive the English assault. Over the breastwork that had hastily been constructed across the line of advance flew the flag of Castile. The struggle promised to be bitter. To save himself casualties, however, Hawkins directed the heavy guns from his fleet to fire against the barricades, and waited until they were partially destroyed before turning to the assault. After a preliminary round of shaft and shot the Englishmen pressed forward with hand weapons and, in a confused and sudden struggle, put the defenders to flight. The Spanish horsemen never pressed home an attack, but contented themselves with skirmishing. When the resistance at the road-block broke they fled, like the foot-soldiers, for the protection of the town. Hawkins, who had won the day more swiftly than he expected, found the path to Rio de la Hacha open before him, and hastened, unopposed, in pursuit of his routed adversaries.

So swiftly did the Englishmen advance that the Spaniards had no time to regroup themselves and defend the palisades. Most of the foot-soldiers were forced to disperse into the open country in order to avoid capture, and the horsemen, unable by themselves to conduct an effectual defence, did likewise. One Spaniard was captured unwounded and entered the abandoned city as Hawkins' prisoner, though later he was released.

No sooner had they established themselves in Rio de la Hacha than a single horseman, with a white flag tied to his lance, rode towards the town. The message that Castellanos sent under the flag of truce was as truculent as ever. It exhorted Hawkins to depart at once, for under no circumstances would Castellanos treat with him. Hawkins was not unduly disturbed by the recalcitrance of the Treasurer. A war of words was a game that he felt himself well equipped to play. He paid more attention to the messenger than the message, and took pains to ingratiate himself with the Spaniard, arguing plausibly about the benefits of trade and emphasizing his reluctance to do damage or cause unnecessary hardship. When the emissary returned to Castellanos, Hawkins was confident that he had sown a seed of discontent amongst the settlers against their Treasurer's unreasonable defiance. The Spanish pilot from Borburata was sent once again to Castellanos with Hawkins' reply—a reiterated demand for permission to trade, backed by a threat of setting the town on fire. That one of their own countrymen should voluntarily carry Hawkins' message could not fail to impress the dispossessed and disconsolate Spaniards, who waited aimlessly outside their captured walls. But the Treasurer did not hesitate long with his answer. If Hawkins set all the Indies on fire, he declared, he would still get no licence to trade.

While Hawkins was busy with these diplomatic exchanges his men were engaged in a thorough investigation of the town. To their regret they discovered no treasure and scarcely anything worth claiming as personal booty. But doubtless a few casks of wine were found and broached, and the exhilaration of the chase had hardly cooled. Possibly they had heard and misunderstood the threat to destroy the town. At all events, before Hawkins was aware of what was happening, a number of the tinder-dry hutments were in flames and the fire began to spread rapidly. Hawkins immediately ordered his men to put out the blaze, but before they could do so one third of the buildings had been consumed, and the thick pillar of smoke that rose from within the palisade told its own story to the Spaniards hiding in the woods outside.

Yet another deputation arrived under the flag of truce with a message from the Treasurer, couched in even more intemperate language. The burning of the town, he told Hawkins, pleased him very well, because even if it was totally destroyed the King of Spain would build it again at his own expense, and better than before. For good measure he added the vague threat that the longer Hawkins stayed the more he would regret it, as plans for his annihilation were afoot.

A number of the most important citizens of Rio de la Hacha carried the message, impelled by a curious dread to discover whether their own houses had been destroyed. None of them, Hawkins could see, was a fanatic like the Treasurer; they all appeared more miserable than hostile. Hawkins received them in the most friendly manner, read Castellanos' message aloud, and discussed it openly with them. It was, he claimed, not only a stubborn but a disloyal letter. To express pleasure at the prospect of destruction could only mean that the Treasurer was already planning to make a profit out of the charges that he expected to put forward to cover the rebuilding of the town. Such conduct, Hawkins emphatically declared, could not be tolerated. The King of Spain was his master too, and he would not see him cheated by a man who had carefully removed his own fortune and possessions to safety and now proposed speculating over property that did not belong to him. He was prepared to answer to the King himself for his conduct—Hawkins spoke with warmth—but never through the Treasurer, whom he proposed to hunt out wherever he might hide and force from him a licence to trade.

It was impossible to doubt the determination of a man so persuasive and forthright as Hawkins, but in case any of his audience still doubted his goodwill he added in a milder manner that he was prepared to recompense any individual whose house might have been damaged or destroyed by the fire. Before they left the town he pressed various small gifts on the Spaniards, and escorted them courteously to the gates of the palisade. Some of them at least seemed sorry to depart.

Next morning, after a watchful night, Hawkins landed two small field-guns together with their carriages, and had them trained to cover the landward approaches to the town. In the afternoon he led a sortie to investigate three outlying houses that lay beyond the palisade. He met no opposition, and discovered nothing except a small, hastily-concealed cache of small arms that the retreating Spaniards had left behind, together with the personal ensign of the Treasurer. He displayed this trophy all the way back to Rio de la Hacha, in the hope that his arch-enemy was watching.

For a few days neither side took positive action. Spanish horsemen began to patrol the ground close under the guns of the town and were warned to keep their distance, but otherwise both parties seemed content to wait. Hawkins sent Barrett back to the ships in case bad weather blew up.

Five days after they landed, a negro slave, the personal property of Castellanos himself, deserted and sought sanctuary within the English lines. The negro was brought before Hawkins and interrogated. From his answers it became apparent that he knew where the Treasurer had secreted the royal fifth—that share of the accumulated treasure reserved for the King—and a quantity of other valuables. As the price of his freedom the runaway promised to lead Hawkins to the spot. At last the chance Hawkins had so patiently waited for seemed to have come.

He assembled a hundred and twenty men, but kept them

within the shelter of the town until night fell. If surprise was to be achieved it was essential that the Spaniards were given no warning of the direction of the raid. The negro led the Englishmen through unfrequented forest paths for six miles. They travelled nervously, with arquebuses primed, for an ambush would have been easy. But their guide, whom they kept under close guard throughout the journey, was true to his word. In a clearing among the trees they discovered two or three tents, and without a shot being fired they surrounded and captured the sleeping inhabitants. For the most part these were women and children, with their personal servants and the few belongings that they had managed to carry with them in their flight. In charge of them were one or two of the elder citizens of Rio de la Hacha, and in a tent by itself was the prize that they especially sought—the iron-bound chests that held the town's wealth.

By lantern-light they broke open the hasps and examined the contents. There were little goatskin bags heavy with graded pearls, boxes of gold-dust, some nuggets and some emeralds; also silver and gold coins, almost without number. The Englishmen let them slide through their fingers, exultant yet awed by their success.

The first thing to do was to send Hawkins the news, and to warn him to bring transport if he came to remove the treasure. Two carts would be needed, they reckoned, to take the chests over the rough track to Rio de la Hacha. Meanwhile, as dawn had not yet broken, the English party placed a guard over the Spaniards they had captured, and posted sentries in case the Treasurer's forces should attempt to regain their lost wealth. It was a necessary precaution to take. The day was not far advanced, and Hawkins not yet arrived at the scene, when Castellanos with a few arquebusiers and some Indian levies made an attempt to recapture the treasure by force—an attempt that, thanks to their vigilance, the Englishmen were easily able to frustrate.

The night had not been uneventful even for Hawkins at Rio de la Hacha. Another deserter, this time a half-caste with a grudge against the Treasurer, had come through the lines, and Hawkins

was busy interrogating him when the news of the successful
seizure of the treasure reached him. He immediately ordered the
mulatto to come with him and set off up country with a suitable
bodyguard, two ox-carts, and his ever-obliging friend and witness
the Spanish pilot from Borburata.

He arrived after Castellanos' counter-stroke had been beaten
back, but the Spaniards were still in the field, though they
kept out of bowshot. While the two carts were being loaded
with the treasure and loot that had been captured, Hawkins sent
the Spanish deserter, together with some of his own men, under a
flag of truce to seek out Castellanos and tell him, in the presence
of as many of his followers as possible, that all the riches the
Englishmen had captured were being conveyed for safe-keeping
to the ships, but that they would be returned to their rightful
owners immediately the Treasurer consented to trade. Until a
free and honourable basis for trade was established, Hawkins
declared, he had no intention of departing; if Castellanos, or
any of the Spanish dignitaries that were with him, doubted his
good faith they had only to enquire of those who had had experience of dealing with him in the past. His prices were fair,
and he was willing to pay without demur the $7\frac{1}{2}$ per cent customs
duty normally imposed on the selling-price of each slave. If he
refused to issue a licence on these terms it was the citizens of
Rio de la Hacha (though not, he was led to believe, the Treasurer
himself) who would be the losers.

When these latest overtures had been heard, and it seemed that
Castellanos was likely to remain obdurate, a murmuring arose
amongst the principal citizens of the town who stood near him.
A week of discomfort, camping on the fringes of the forest
almost within sight of their homes, with little food and daily
rumours reaching them of the losses they were suffering, made
most of the Spaniards very willing to come to terms with an
enemy who was, by all accounts, honourable. Fanatical opposition, such as the Treasurer urged on them, could do no good,
and might bring utter ruin if the reasonableness that the Englishmen had hitherto displayed gave way to reprisals against their
goods or womenfolk, both of which were now at Hawkins' mercy.

Castellanos found himself surrounded by voices telling him to temporize, to meet Hawkins and negotiate with him. They were mutterings of despair that he dreaded hearing, for his own resolve was unshaken. Yet he had felt the stirrings of discontent amongst his followers ever since his emissaries had returned from the English camp, charmed by the persuasiveness of Hawkins' speech. Angry and alone, Castellanos realized that the last battle was being won by Hawkins without a shot being fired. Turning to his counsellors he cried out in hopeless rage, 'None of you knows John Hawkins. He is the sort of man, who, when he talks to you, makes it impossible to deny him what he wants. That is the reason why I have been so careful to keep my distance from him—not because I suspected his motives, but because it would be most dangerous to do what he wanted rather than what the King demands. Do not, I pray you, ask me to go to him now.'

His followers did not heed his advice. 'If Hawkins is as honourable as you make out,' they said, 'and if he promises you safe-conduct, what harm can there be in going to talk with him, now, before our goods are carried away?' With a heavy heart the Treasurer agreed to meet Hawkins in a nearby clearing between the two armies that same afternoon.

The two men conferred together for an hour but kept their counsel about what, if anything, had been agreed between them. Hawkins, however, appeared well satisfied with the result of the meeting, and inferred to his companions-in-arms that they might expect to start trading again before long. He had taken care that the Treasurer was not the only Spaniard who knew the details of his proposals, which included full recompense for the personal damage that his forces might have inflicted on property and the release of the non-combatants whom he had seized. When they took counsel amongst themselves, therefore, and the results of the discussion were disclosed, the Treasurer found himself under irresistible pressure to accept Hawkins' conditions and grant him a licence in return. A message was sent to the English camp to signify the Treasurer's capitulation, and a little later, under renewed pressure, Castellanos himself rode forth to seal the compact by a display of friendship. The two enemies em-

braced each other, and Hawkins set free his captives and returned to their owners all the personal booty that he had appropriated. In particular he instructed his men on pain of death to
return to the Church the furnishings and holy images that, with
the mixed motives of covetousness and Protestant zeal, they had
appropriated.

But the full details of the agreement remained unpublished;
partly because Castellanos did not wish to be publicly associated
with them, and partly, perhaps, because certain clauses to which
Hawkins agreed were not so honourable as he might have wished.

The royal treasure chests returned with Hawkins to Rio
de la Hacha, and Castellanos promised to follow and claim them
the next day. He was true to his word, and in an atmosphere of
strained cordiality received them in the King's name. Hawkins
first removed four thousand gold pesos, in exchange for which he
landed and handed over to the Treasurer sixty negro slaves. It was an
enforced sale, and part of the contract that had been agreed. If
Castellanos was pleased with the bargain he certainly disguised the
fact when, later, he reported to his masters in Spain on the events
that had taken place. The slaves that Hawkins landed, he claimed,
were dying on his hands, and had been given away to save the
trouble of throwing them overboard. 'Old men and infants at
their mothers' breasts, and among them all there was not a slave
worth anything at all.' Naturally enough Castellanos did not
mention that he had, in addition, bought twenty more slaves from
Hawkins for a thousand pesos of his own money, and, as on the
last occasion for which he had been reproved, exchanged presents
with the notorious corsair. Hawkins' gift consisted of a velvet
cloak, embroidered with pearls and with gold buttons, together
with a fur-lined, taffeta gown. In return the Treasurer sent him a
great curiosity, which Hawkins proudly displayed to Barrett and
his other officers as soon as he returned on board the *Jesus*; it was a
woman's girdle entirely faced with pearls of a size and quality
seldom seen outside King Philip's treasury.

With these exchanges trading was officially initiated, and,
although Castellanos himself left Rio de la Hacha next day and
refused to re-enter it until Hawkins departed, the citizens whom

he had hitherto restrained now eagerly crowded the booths and stalls that were hastily improvised in the market place. Boat-loads of negroes were ferried ashore from the *Jesus* and *Minion* and paraded for the inspection of buyers. The daily total of sales, and the good prices that slaves of all sorts fetched, very soon justified Hawkins' stubbornness in insisting on trading at this port. A hundred and fifty negroes changed hands in a few days, and many bales of linen and cloth. In exchange, Hawkins accumulated in the locked chests that he kept in his own cabin on the *Jesus* a solid and rewarding weight of gold coins, with lesser quantities of pearls and silver.

The likelihood of fighting being resumed now seemed slight. Most of the sailors returned to their ships to wait until the trafficking ashore was over and they could again resume their voyage. They employed themselves as best they could with occupations of their own devising. One group, more enterprising than the rest, borrowed a pinnace and rowed a short distance up river in search of alligators. They took one of the small, stray dogs, that lived a scavenging life around the settlement, with them as a bait. When they reached a suitable spot they strapped the unfortunate creature to a butcher's hook, the end of which was secured to a chain and a strong line. The dog was thrown overboard and allowed to swim; the end of the line was secured to the boat. It was not long before the victim was observed. A line of puckered water drove straight at the terrified animal, there was a swirl, the glimpse of a reptilian jaw layered with teeth, then a sudden silence. The dog no longer swam behind the boat. No sooner had the alligator seized its victim than the boat's crew, pulling hard at their oars, drew the line tight and hooked it. Immediately the water broke into life around them. In its struggle to free itself the alligator seemed to dance half in and half out of the river, thrashing and jerking at the line. Then it sounded and drew the boat after it for a space. Alternately hauling in and slackening the line the seven sailors held on to their prey, and before long its struggles ceased. They rowed to the bank and were able to haul the carcass ashore. Never before had they seen an alligator at close quarters. All the men were deeply impressed by the size and ugliness of the animal. It was, they reckoned, twenty-three feet long, and of its strength and ferocity they had ample evidence. They were determined to take the skin back on board and stuff it, in order to show it off when they reached home again. Accordingly they gutted the creature on the spot and as the light of the day was waning rowed back to their ship in no little triumph.

The skin was duly stuffed with straw and stowed away on the ballast; but unhappily, for reasons that no one could then foresee, this proved to be its last resting place.

With such diversions the sailors beguiled the time while Hawkins and the merchants busied themselves ashore. They were not anxious to linger long, but a good price could never be obtained by hurrying a bargain, so it was not until the beginning of July, after nearly two weeks of trading, that Hawkins was satisfied that he had sold all he could. By now two-thirds of his cargo had been disposed of, and already the voyage had well paid for itself. He had good reason to feel content with his progress.

Before he left the port he performed the last, distasteful act of his bargain with the Treasurer. In addition to a number of slaves that he freely gave as recompense to those whose houses had suffered damage at his hands, he handed over the two deserters, the negro and the mulatto, who had betrayed Castellanos for an assurance of safety. Although Hawkins was going back on his word it is doubtful if he would have regarded his deed as reprehensible. An act of treachery by a servant against his master, whether enemy or friend, was not a thing to be encouraged, even though it might on occasion be useful to exploit it. It would have come as no surprise to Hawkins if he had heard of the fate of the two men at the Treasurer's hands after his departure: the negro was quartered and the mulatto hanged.

When Hawkins' ten sail had finally disappeared, and the people of Rio de la Hacha surveyed yet again their half-ruined town, their despondency was not unmixed with a fearful satisfaction. There were few citizens who had not profited by Hawkins' scrupulously fair trading. The only difficulty was how to disguise the fact from the inevitable commission of investigation that would descend on them in due course. Those in authority were especially aware that their trafficking had been illegal, and many features of it awkward to explain. It was not until nearly three months later that they compiled their official report on Hawkins' sojourn—at a time when, had they known it, their enemies' fortunes had taken a singular turn for the worse. They thought it best to interpret the four thousand pesos that had been taken out of the King's share as a ransom for sparing the lives of hostages and of the remaining buildings in the town. Separately they mentioned a number of slaves that Hawkins had landed before he departed—children under six and old women of over a hundred was Castellanos' picturesque description. These they proposed selling by auction for the benefit of His Majesty's treasury. It all sounded plausible, but they must have prayed that the details would not be investigated too minutely.

All the same they hoped for a quieter life in the years to come. Hawkins' visits might be profitable, but they were always dangerous; and Hawkins was not the least welcome of an unscrupulous fraternity of sea-raiders that molested their shores. One can only sympathize with the settlers in their forlorn plea for the protection that their mother-country never seemed able to afford. 'We entreat your majesty to remedy the grievous conditions prevailing today in Indies. For every two ships that come hither from Spain, twenty corsairs appear. For this reason not a town on all this coast is safe, for whenever they please to do so they take and plunder these settlements. They go so far as to boast that they are lords of the sea and of the land.——Unless your majesty deign to favour all this coast by remedying the situation, all these settlements must necessarily be abandoned.'

CHAPTER 9

The Desperate Choice

FURTHER west along the mainland coast Hawkins had never sailed. On his last voyage, after leaving Rio de la Hacha, he had made for the islands of Hispaniola and Cuba, hoping to buy a cargo of hides before returning home. But on this occasion he had a hundred and fifty negroes still on board. Since it was doubtful if he would ever get permission to sell these slaves under the very eyes of the Governor in Santo Domingo, he resolved to continue his course along the coast of Nueva Andalucia, where the need for negro labour was evidently great and the chances of undisturbed negotiation more likely. Hitherto results had been satisfactory, but the delays he had experienced were serious. The hurricane season was almost upon him, and he had no wish to prolong his voyage unnecessarily. Besides, he reckoned that the presence of his fleet in the Indies was by now well known, and he had no wish to fight his way out through the Florida Channel.

His fears as it turned out were not unjustified, though the danger came from no scratch fleet that the Indies could muster to protect themselves against corsairs. Even as his ten ships, using the trade winds to swell their sails, passed between Rio de la Hacha and Santa Marta, the next settlement along the coast, the annual Spanish convoy, that was to bring back the accumulated wealth of the new lands beyond the great ocean, cleared the river Guadalquivir and headed west.

A few days sailing brought Hawkins' ships at dusk on the evening of July 10th to the roadstead of Santa Marta. It was an easy port to find, even for those to whom the coast was strange. Although they were keeping several miles out to sea a great range

of snow-capped mountains, the Sierra Nevadas, was an unmistakable distant landmark, and nearer at hand a line of white
cliffs led them into the sheltered bay that contained the port.

Santa Marta had not grown to the size and importance of its
neighbouring towns on either side. It consisted of some forty-five
buildings, few of which were of solid construction. It was, however, the oldest foundation on the mainland coast, for in 1525
Rodrigo de Bastidas, searching out the creeks and havens along
the shore, chose this natural harbour above all others as a place
for settlement. Although it had not prospered it had survived.
From time to time it was sacked by corsairs, and equally frequently
it was almost overwhelmed by Indian raids. But the harbour, with
its careening beaches, was too precious to abandon. Each time the
buildings were destroyed they were rebuilt, and gradually a
significant quantity of gold and copper from the interior began to
pass through the town.

Some of the nearby Indians established themselves as peaceful
neighbours and reserved their poisoned arrows for hunting the
wild pig and deer that abounded in the undulating, open country
between the town and the high Sierras. They grew crops too,
in particular maize and sweet potatoes, which the Spaniards
bought from them for trifles. The tiny garrison was always
watchful, both to seaward and to landward, but so long as they
remained unmolested the citizens of Santa Marta lived a pleasant
enough life. It is true that malaria was endemic, but there were
few settlements along the coast that could not say the same, and
attacks of fever, like those of Indians, were regarded as one of the
inevitable discomforts associated with living in the Indies.

The pattern of Hawkins' entry into a Spanish port was once
again repeated at Santa Marta. Before darkness fell he sent a
message ashore to the Governor. It was a bland and friendly
letter requesting a licence to dispose of the remnant of his human
cargo and to buy the food and water that he needed to reprovision
his fleet. He had not expected a reply before morning, but an
hour or two later a boat's lantern was seen coming towards the
anchored ships, and the Governor's response was delivered.
Hawkins' arrival was not, it seemed, entirely unexpected; nor was

the Governor ill-disposed towards the proposal of trade. But there were factions within the town that were fearful of the outcome; in order to arrange matters to their satisfaction it was proposed that the two leaders should meet ashore at ten o'clock next morning to discuss procedure. Hawkins was inwardly delighted and sent the boat back with his agreement. In view of the overpowering odds against them he had judged that the Spaniards at Santa Marta would not resist, but he feared they might have taken flight instead. So indeed they might if they had had any security to fly to, but the inhabitants regarded exposing themselves to an Indian attack as a worse peril than trading illegally with the English.

At the appointed hour Hawkins, with a suitable armed escort, went ashore and met the Governor. They greeted each other courteously, exchanged words in private and returned to their respective bases. On reaching the *Jesus* Hawkins summoned his captains and with wry humour outlined the agreed plan of action. Later that day a landing-party of 150 men, armed and equipped for an assault, was to embark in the pinnaces and longboats and make for the sandy beaches that bordered the town. At the same time the ship's guns were to be brought into action and fire a dozen rounds in the general direction of the houses, but taking care to aim high and thus avoid unnecessary damage. One isolated building on the edge of the town was scheduled as a target, in case evidence was needed later of the fury of the attack. Meanwhile the landing-party was to advance to the central square where it would be met by an emissary from the Governor.

The assault went forward as planned. Hawkins, in full armour despite the intense midday heat, led his troops unopposed to the market place, where a Spaniard with a white flag was waiting to receive them. Hawkins summoned him to explain his mission. He replied that the Governor and the chief citizens of Santa Marta were waiting at the far end of the town and wished to discuss terms. Under the flag of truce Hawkins advanced towards them. The Governor thereupon delivered an impassioned plea that the settlement be spared. If their houses should be burnt, he declared, they would be at the mercy of the Indians and forced to seek passage with Hawkins rather than await their inevitable doom. To this Hawkins replied that the destruction of property gave him no pleasure and was far from his thoughts. His only desire was to realize some money by the sale of slaves, in order to be able to pay his seamen's wages.

With this assurance honour was satisfied and the act was over. The Governor granted Hawkins a licence to trade and Hawkins dismissed all but a few of his men back to their ships.

At Santa Marta the Englishmen were received with an unfeigned friendliness and hospitality from all the citizens, such as they had not experienced since leaving Margarita. Each side feasted the other, and trade continued briskly and harmoniously for nearly a fortnight. During that time the English sailors were not stinted of fresh provisions. Beef was plentiful, and there were more unusual foods for those who were adventurous in what they ate: guavas, papaya and pineapples could be purchased from the Indians, and were esteemed as delicacies by some.

Meanwhile the usual watering-parties were assigned the task of filling the casks that were empty or had become foul. On one such expedition to a stream that lay beyond the town Job Hortop, whose wonderment at the wild life he saw around him never decreased, recounts how 'two of our company killed a monstrous adder, going towards his cave with a Conie in his mouth'.

Their sojourn at Santa Marta was a pleasant interlude, but it could not be prolonged. At one time Hawkins hoped he might be able to empty his slave-decks completely; but although he disposed of a hundred and ten negroes, half of them to the Governor himself, there were half a hundred left which it was clearly beyond the means of the little town to buy. Reluctantly he prepared to move on to Cartagena where, if he was admitted to trade, he knew he would have no difficulty in selling them. Before he departed he exchanged gifts, as was customary, with the Governor, and received a certificate of honourable conduct which he hoped might prove useful at his next port of call.

Soon after they had cleared the port of Santa Marta the English fleet, although they sailed well clear of the coast, encountered a belt of disturbed and discoloured water that marked the disemboguing of the River Magdalena. As though it still ran through an invisible channel the green, turbulent river water cut into the blue Gulf and forced aside the Caribbean current, sucking and swirling the calm water into confused races. A concealed reef breaks the surface of the sea in just such a manner, and at first Hawkins may have feared that he had led his fleet amongst uncharted rocks. But his ships did not founder, although the whip-staffs were almost wrenched from the helmsmen's hands as they forged through the patches of broken water. More dangerous than the races was the flotsam that the great river brought with it to the sea. Whole trees, wrenched out by the roots, needed to be carefully avoided, since a blow from such floating rams would have staved in the smaller craft. Here and there were bushes and mats of green reed like small, moving islands, and when the sailors lowered buckets over the side and tasted the water they found no trace of salt.

Nearly a week of daytime sailing brought Hawkins' fleet to Cartagena. Three gashes of rock, that interrupted the smooth coastline a few miles to the east of the port, established their position and they moved closer inshore, following the fringe of mangrove and low cliffs up to the town itself.

Cartagena was a town almost surrounded by water. There was no landing place on the sea front that faced the Caribbean. The houses clustering along the low-lying northern shore kept watch over the open sea, but offered no haven from it. Behind them rose a green hill, and around them the stilt-rooted mangroves marked out the swampy coast. To reach the sanctuary of the harbour—and Cartagena harbour was the safest and most commodious of any along the main—a ship needed to sail on, past the town, and choose one of two channels leading into a sheltered lagoon that lay behind the natural line of the shore and bent back to touch the southern aspect of the town. In this great natural bay there was a protected anchorage for any fleet that called, but to approach Cartagena closely it was necessary to pass through a narrow channel into an inner harbour. This channel was fortified with squat stone towers, each with a battery of guns, that sealed off the town itself from armed incursion.

Hawkins had heard of these well-nigh impregnable defences, but was sufficiently encouraged by the results of his negotiations along the coast to anticipate no need to test them. He realized his visit would be no surprise: he hoped it might be welcome. As his flagship came abreast the seaward aspect of the town he dipped his ensign, struck his topsails, and fired six guns in salute. The town replied with a similar courtesy and Hawkins sailed past to seek out the channels that led to the lagoon. He chose the first and wider entrance, the Boca Grande, for the sand bar and the obstructions with which this channel was later blocked were at the time no hindrance to shipping.

Hawkins did not attempt to take his fleet past the twin forts into the inner harbour. He had no wish to sail into a trap. At first it was enough to anchor in the still, green waters of the main bay, and send a pinnace inshore with the customary message to the Governor. From where his fleet lay he could partly see the town and the batteries that defended it. Without question it was a stronger and richer settlement than any he had yet visited. He made sure that his messengers were well acquainted with the gifts that he proposed giving to the principal inhabitants in exchange for a licence to trade, and instructed them to make no secret of their munificence. In his letter to the Governor Hawkins made no mention of the last remaining negroes that he wished to sell. He contented himself with requesting provisions for his homeward voyage for which he offered straightforward payment. To ask too much from a town that had no cause to fear him was to invite refusal.

The pinnace returned to the flagship sooner than Hawkins expected. The letter it brought back was a hastily-written but categorical refusal either to trade or even to let the English vessels take on water. In view of these prohibitions Hawkins was requested to take his departure forthwith. The messengers who brought back the uncompromising reply added that at first Don Martin de las Alas, the Governor, who seemed a sick and petulant man, had refused so much as to open Hawkins' letter. Only under pressure from the chief citizens of Cartagena who stood near him did he condescend to read it and reply. While he was signing and handing over his rejection of Hawkins' overtures, Don Martin made it plain to the English messenger that he would receive no further communication on the subject which he now considered closed. But he let them discover before they left that the garrison of Cartagena was far from small. As well as a troop of horse he held at his command five hundred well-equipped Spaniards, a like number of reliable negro slaves, and six thousand loyal Indian levies. For the first time Hawkins found his total complement of three hundred and seventy men insufficient even to cause his enemy alarm.

The English fleet was baffled and, for a while, irresolute. Hawkins hated to admit defeat and turned over in his mind one ingenious scheme after another that might break the deadlock. The season was so far advanced that he could not afford the time to cruise much longer from port to port, yet it would be ignominious to return to Plymouth with a tithe of his trading goods, unconverted into profits, still on board. Besides he needed water and some dry provisions for the voyage home. In the end he made a half-hearted attempt to bluff Cartagena into compliance. He moved the smaller ships of his fleet close in under the defence works of the inner harbour and gave the *Minion* the task of using her demi-culverins at extreme range to bombard the town. The Spaniards, he knew, had no guns that could effectively reply.

If he hoped to scare the Spaniards into a negotiated truce his manoeuvre was a failure; but by bringing his ships closer inshore Hawkins was at least able to satisfy himself that a direct assault with his meagre resources was out of the question. As soon as it became apparent that the desultory bombardment from the *Minion* was ineffectual he called his ships off and sent them to all corners of the lagoon in search of anything that might prove useful, either for its own sake, or as a means to exert pressure on the Governor of the town.

While he was waiting for them to come back Hawkins, with the tenacity of a convinced negotiator, wrote once again to Don Martin. It was a forlorn hope, but there was perhaps a chance that a proud Spaniard might be shamed into giving way at least with regard to water. Water could not be denied even to an infidel. Surely, Hawkins rhetorically reasoned, he would not refuse a fellow-Christian.

But Hawkins was himself too proud to write a begging letter: 'Well,' he concluded, 'I will not be beholding vnto you at this tyme.' He was strengthened in this resolve by a report that reached him from one of his scouting party that there were undefended wells of fresh water on the island of Tierra Bomba that divided the two entrance channels into the lagoon. The letter was sent ashore to the Governor and, as Hawkins must have anticipated, received no reply. But he did not wait for one; already he was on his way to the island with all the pinnaces from the *Jesus* piled high with empty water-barrels following after him.

Those of his men who had already landed were delighted with the place. They welcomed their captain ashore, and told him that not only was there abundant water but a series of pleasant orchards and the summer residence of some notable citizen of Cartagena. They had captured the negro caretaker who had revealed to them the only booty that the island possessed—a cool cellar well furnished with crocks and goatskins filled with oil and wine. These at all events were worth removing. Hawkins agreed, and soon the pinnaces were being rowed back to the flagship deeply laden with their unexpected and welcome cargo.

As always Hawkins was scrupulous in paying in kind for the goods he had taken. His anger against the town of Cartagena did not extend to vindictiveness against any individual citizen. The negro servant was taken ashore and sent to his master with a request from Hawkins to know what commodities would be acceptable in return for the stores that he had appropriated. The Spaniard chose sailcloth and linen, and a suitable quantity was deposited on the island.

No further business proved possible at Cartagena, but a contrary wind kept them within the harbour for nearly a week. Even then Hawkins left before the breeze was established, and before it had gone far the fleet was becalmed. Hawkins, who hated idleness, used the two days of inactivity that ensued to good purpose. He considered that the caravel he had taken from the Portuguese fishermen off Cape Blanco had served its useful

purpose. Now that the majority of the slaves had been sold there
was more than enough room in his own ships for the less bulky
cargoes he had received in return. The battering of the sea and the
boring of teredo worm had left this little ship the weakest member
of the fleet. It would be an unnecessary risk to take her back
across the Atlantic. Accordingly Hawkins had her ransacked of
all valuables, the crew were transferred to other vessels, and the
carpenter cut through her wooden planks to let in the sea. She
sank gently, scarcely disturbing the oily swell.

During the calm spell the smaller of the two French vessels
that had hitherto faithfully taken their place in Hawkins' fleet
indicated its wish to stay in the Indies, where it hoped to be able
to indulge in some minor piracy on its own account. Hawkins was
well aware that his policy of peaceful trade was not entirely
pleasing to his French allies. Several times he had had to restrain
their ardour to attack and appropriate, and to remind them that
so long as they sailed under his flag they were bound by considerations of policy to more devious ways towards wealth. Like
the English, the French nation was at peace with Spain. But the
terms of the treaty of Cateau-Cambresis applied only within the
bounds of certain 'lines of amity' that were drawn just west of the
Azores. Beyond these lines there was no treaty and no peace.
Every French sail that found its way to the Indies was an outlaw,
and all things Spanish its prey. When the French caravel decided
to part company Hawkins did not demur. He handed over the
agreed share of the profits from the voyage and wished the
adventurers good luck. But the little ship was dangerously small
and ill-equipped to be a corsair. Captain Bland declined to
accompany his fellow countrymen with the second and larger
vessel, the *Grace of God*. He preferred the security of Hawkins'
fleet for the voyage home. When the wind came and stirred the
limp, extended sails only seven ships followed the *Jesus* on her
northerly course. The ninth and smallest of them all remained
behind. As it turned out her career of piracy was short-lived.
The Spaniards captured her before many weeks had passed.

The winds were not always kind to those who sought, late in
the season, to escape from the Indies. To round the tip of Cuba and

steer eastward against the prevailing trade wind required time, good seamanship and some luck. The Florida channel is not wide, and the coast on either hand is ill-provided with anchorages where a sailing ship could wait for a favourable moment.

From their becalmed anchorage off Cartagena Hawkins set his fleet a northerly course, with a fair and seasonal cross-breeze blowing from the east. For a few days they sailed out of sight of land hoping, if the wind did not freshen, to pass through the Yucatan channel and round Cape San Antonio, the western extremity of Cuba, without pause. After they had doubled the Cape they hoped to claw to windward, aided by the current, and beat a laborious way through the Florida channel into the open sea and the zone of westerly winds.

They reached the Isle of Pines without incident and sighted Cape San Antonio before the weather deteriorated and troubles beset them. The sky, which had been benign and cloudless, became lowering and a series of squalls, each more tempestuous than the last, drove up from the south-east, blotting out the shore-line and enveloping the ships in hard-flung bursts of rain. At the first onset the crews were sent aloft to reef and furl the canvas, but several sails carried away before ever they could be secured, and the flapping remnants were cut from the yards. Unlike most squalls, which pass as suddenly as they arrive, the wind and blinding scud showed no signs of abating. The sea, that had been whipped up into a confused froth of waves, beat against the planks with an increasing rhythm; and, by the time the urgent tasks of taking in sail and battening down had been accomplished, it became apparent that they would have to keep beating against the wind in order to retain their position at the mouth of the Florida channel until, hours or days later, the wind allowed them to pass.

Meanwhile the eight ships kept open station and tried by repeated tacking to keep within the narrow confines of the channel. Visibility was poor, and at times the fume of the sea and the driving rain seemed to encase and isolate each separate vessel—almost to suffocate it with moving water. Two or three men struggled with each whipstaff, endeavouring to hold a course between Florida to the north-west and Cuba to the south. But neither coast was now visible, and as hours dragged into days the various captains grew apprehensive lest they be forced on to a lee shore, and urged their rain-blinded look-outs to increasing vigilance.

The same wild battle with the elements that had so nearly overcome them soon after their voyage began engulfed them again, and as before the *Jesus* proved a perilous ship in a heavy sea. High up in the aftercastle Hawkins and his officers were swung and buffeted like leaves on a tree-top. Each wave jarred the framework of the ship; and the noise of grinding and creaking timbers, the sluicing of water in the bilges and the percussion of the battering sea merged and separated in a demoniac symphony of sound. On the flats and messdecks, where the lurching of the ship was less fearsome, the stench and sliminess of the dark living-quarters proved intolerable. The sea pounded like thunder all around them, and in the blind pandemonium it seemed as though every bale and barrel had broken from its lashings and was sliding and splintering in a self-destructive frenzy.

On deck conditions were no better. The wind shrieked through the shrouds, and tore at the slips of sail that remained set in order to give the ship steerage way. The yards and masts shuddered and bent: it seemed only a matter of time before they snapped like dry twigs. Hawkins ordered men aloft in the teeth of the storm to cut down some of the top hamper to reduce the strain. But the greatest danger to the *Jesus* lay below decks. The timbers that had sprung, and in particular those around the stern post, had been only roughly repaired. The old wounds were quick to open again. Before long the carpenters, who laboured to staunch the flow of water, sent messages to Hawkins that the rifts were so wide that with the streams of seawater living fish had been forced through, and now floundered upon the ballast.

The situation was grave indeed, and Hawkins must often have wished that he had abandoned his crank flagship when her work in the Indies had been done and he lay in calm water off Cartagena. As an ocean-going vessel she was obviously past repair, and once stripped of her cargo and fittings her actual value was small. But she was the Queen's ship, not his, and Hawkins was not willing to abandon her lightly. His resolution in this respect was entirely disinterested, for, according to the usual charter parties under which royal ships were loaned to private syndicates, no restitution was demanded in the case of loss; but if the vessel came safely home it was the responsibility of the syndicate to see that she was fully repaired. As each wave opened up fresh seams in the *Jesus* and wrenched her old planks apart, her captain, who in honour and stubbornness refused to yield her to the sea, must have imagined the profits from his voyage swallowed up in an endless bill for repairs.

So long as the storm lasted there was no question of abandoning the *Jesus*. In her lay the only hope of survival. But fighting against the wind could not be continued in a ship so likely to founder. The station they were attempting to keep at the mouth of the Florida channel was useful only to ships that could exploit a favourable wind and head for the open sea. The *Jesus* obviously was in no state to undertake an ocean passage. She would need to find a harbour first. Although by no means certain of his position, Hawkins at length decided that the only course for the *Jesus* was to run before the wind, and he reckoned that he was still sufficiently far within the Gulf to do so without danger. Accordingly one evening, as the gloom of another storm-wracked night shut down upon the fleet, Hawkins signalled his intention to bear up. Six ships followed him as he abandoned the struggle and let the *Jesus'* head swing to the north. But the *William and John* failed to observe the signal in the gathering dusk and, unawares, was left to battle her way out of the Caribbean alone.

The seven ships fled blindly into the darkness, following as best they could the bucketting stern lantern of their flagship. Neither the stars that night nor the sun next morning revealed themselves to allow Hawkins to estimate his position; the leadsmen in the chains were the first to disclose the proximity of the Florida coast. They cried out that the ships had come within soundings, and soon afterwards the look-outs descried the low line of the shore. A little of the venom had been drawn from the storm, and although the wind still drove the bedraggled convoy decisively forward on its northerly course it was possible to keep the larger ships clear of the treacherous inshore reefs, while risking the smaller craft, sounding as they went, on the urgent task of finding some secure anchorage on this wild and unknown shore.

For two days and nights they ran parallel to the coast, ever watchful and fearful for their lives. The call of the leadsmen in the chains and the rhythmical clatter of the pumps was a constant accompaniment. There were times when the cry 'by the mark, four' was heard, and the ships seemed to be speeding towards certain destruction; but the hidden reefs allowed them to pass over in safety, and the uneasy search for a harbour led them helplessly on.

The wind seemed gradually to blow itself out, but before the stricken fleet could collect itself and seek out some more hospitable shore the weather took another and more sinister turn. The breeze veered swiftly, pressing them for a moment back on to the reefs of Florida which they had struggled so long to avoid. But while they laboured to keep sea-room the wind shifted to the north, and then to the north-east. It blew cold and strong, in strange contrast to the humid warmth of the breezes that preceded it. As its forerunners came flocks of birds flying southward, and gusts of ripples broke out over the swelling water, glistening on the surface with a wan, metallic radiance. In the north the clouds, that had for so many days oppressed them, showed signs of breaking up; but even so hopeful a portent was ominous. To Hawkins, who was well versed in the sailing conditions that prevailed in these waters, it was evident that the first of the endemic winter winds, the northers, was about to blow. There was little he could do but furl the few sails he had set, batten down all hatches and prepare, with God's help, to run free before the tempest as long as his ship would carry him.

The main force of the wind, when it struck the expectant ships, allowed no alternative. Like autumn leaves the seven vessels were thrown out into the open waters of the Gulf and driven at the whim of the elements towards the south-west. Not knowing what might lie in their path they could do nothing to direct their course, but for three days and nights they endured a battering beyond all expectation of endurance. The following seas searched out every weakness, and the carpenters despaired of ever plugging the gashes between the riven planks. The wind that shrieked through the bare poles strained at the towering after-castles of the older ships, wrenching them this way and that, and sending them yawing through the scend of the sea. Many a time they almost broached to, and were only saved by the weary and desperate efforts of the seamen struggling with the whipstaff as it plunged like a dowser's rod in a frenzy beyond human control.

Northers, though they blow fiercely, do not normally last long. On the third day the wind died away, and as the ships gathered together to exchange tidings they found themselves once more in sight of land. This time it was no shore line that they sighted but two long, exposed reefs, not more than a few feet above sea level, against which the waves ceaselessly broke. As they approached these obstacles they observed that a narrow channel of water divided the nearer reef into two parts. None of the sailors had sailed in this part of the Gulf before, and Hawkins himself did not learn till later that they had sighted the Triangles, a cluster of coral reefs fifty miles from the coast of Yucatan and deep in the south-western corner of the Gulf.

It was a desperate situation. Few ships ever sailed these waters, and none that needed succour more urgently than Hawkins' storm-battered fleet. There were no harbours to welcome them, since the unhealthy coastal regions had scarcely been settled by the Spaniards. Water and provisions were running short after three weeks of storm; they did not know which way to turn in the hope of obtaining any. Most menacing of all was the lateness of the season. It was September 11th, and already the northers were upon them. By the time they reached the Atlantic the winter gales could easily complete the destruction they had so narrowly escaped from the Gulf winds. Yet a harbour had to be found first. Doubtless an unfriendly port that would quickly detect their weakness and need; but that danger was less than an immediate attempt to reach the open sea.

The breeze had shifted to a more easterly quarter and Hawkins was loath to run before it to the farthest extremity of the Gulf without knowing whither he was bound. Half-heartedly he edged his ships against it, thinking perhaps to find shelter in the lee of Yucatan. They made little headway that night, but next morning, though still in sight of the Triangles, two small craft were seen sailing down-wind towards them. Immediately Hawkins detached his swiftest pinnaces with orders to intercept, and anxiously watched the ensuing chase. One of the Spaniards (for such their colours proclaimed them to be) drew ahead of her pursuers and escaped; but the second, a more sluggish sailer, hove to as the English vessels began to overhaul her and allowed herself to be boarded. The captain, Francisco Maldonado, a young man from Cadiz of about Hawkins' age, was brought across to the *Jesus* where Hawkins eagerly began to interrogate him.

Maldonado's ship, it transpired, was a trading-craft carrying a cargo of wines from the islands to the port that stood at the gateway to Mexico, San Juan de Ulua. He was off course, because the norther that had driven Hawkins across the Gulf had forced the Spaniard to take shelter at Campeche about a hundred miles astern, whence he was now continuing to his destination.

These preliminary questions soon gave way to those that were more urgent to Hawkins in his present situation. He enquired about the ports up and down the coast—what facilities they had for repairs, and where provisions could be purchased. The answers he received were of little comfort to him. Apart from Campeche, which lay aweather of his present position and could not accommodate his largest ships, only one port—San Juan de Ulua—lay ahead. Here shelter, provisions and repairs could be obtained, and four days' sailing would bring them there.

But San Juan was not only a well-defended port, it was also expecting visitors. Some time during the month the *flota*—the annual convoy of well-armed galleons from Spain—would arrive, bringing stores, equipment and reinforcements for the Mexican garrisons. It was a fleet strong enough on its return voyage to protect the accumulated wealth that each year was sent back to the King's treasuries. Hawkins' ships would be out-numbered and out-gunned, and, should he cross the track of this proud armada, he could not hope for a friendly reception.

The chance of an encounter was so great that Hawkins would normally never have risked entering so perilous a harbour. He faced ignominious destruction; but there was a chance, if he was granted ten or twelve days at San Juan before the arrival of the *flota*, that he might be able to effect the immediate repairs his ships needed, take on provisions and water, and escape in peace. If he did not accept the risk it would be necessary to abandon the *Jesus*, and possibly the *Minion* too, careen and reprovision the small ships at Campeche, return to an irate Queen having failed her trust, and live through a reputation for cowardice and irresolution. The choice was inevitable. He ordered the Spanish wine-ship to sail with him, but brought the Campeche pilot across to join Maldonado on board the *Jesus*. Setting a south-westerly course Hawkins made the best speed possible towards San Juan de Ulua.

As they neared their destination, after some days and nights of tranquil sailing, the English fleet encountered two small boats. In both cases Hawkins intercepted them, took their captains on board his flagship, and made them follow him in company to San Juan. He was determined at least to make an unheralded entry into the port, and hoped that the hundred passengers and crew, that between them they contained, might afford him some bargaining power if he used them as hostages.

On board one of these vessels was a passenger of some consequence. His name was Agustin de Villanueva and he was bound, in company with two friars, for Santo Domingo. The reason for his journey, or as some have it his flight, is obscure. Job Hortop was certainly mistaken in declaring that Villanueva 'was the man that betrayed all the Noble men in the Indies, and caused them to be beheaded'. It is true that Villanueva, not long before, had empeached the tyrant Muñoz and forced him to relinquish his powers. But he had done so legitimately, in the King's name, and it was Muñoz rather than Villanueva who deserved Hortop's reproach. Whatever version of the story Hawkins himself may have heard or believed, he resolved to treat his captive guest with more than usual solicitude, though insisting that he return to San Juan with the English fleet.

On September 15th Hawkins' ships sighted land, and just before nightfall, with the pilot's aid, chose an anchorage within sight of their objective. He did not send his customary message ashore to announce his approach. The time for trading-licences and protracted negotiations was past. Next morning his fleet would enter the harbour, fighting its way in if necessary. So far as he could see, as he strained his eyes against the setting sun, no cluster of masts rose above the low ground that concealed the mooring berths, and when he turned his gaze to seaward the horizons were empty. The Spanish fleet had not yet arrived.

CHAPTER 10

The Second Fleet

SAN JUAN DE ULUA was a desolate but necessary harbour. The road from Mexico City to the sea was the artery through which Spanish power was maintained over the kingdom that had been wrested from Montezuma. By this road the extorted wealth of gold and silver, cochineal and hides that Mexico yielded every year to Spain was laboriously conveyed, to await in the treasure-houses of Vera Cruz the arrival of the annual fleet.

Vera Cruz, an unhealthy town of some three hundred house-holds, commemorated in its name the planting of the true cross on the soil of Mexico. It could boast of few other glories. Lying on an unsheltered coast and surrounded by low sand-dunes and clumps of coarse, colourless grass, it offered no protection from wind or weather. The humid sea-breezes that blew almost every day brought no refreshment with them, but stirred up the sand and flies and the smells of rotting vegetation that rose from the beaches and pervaded the town. During the summer months the intolerable damp heat and the inevitable onslaught of disease combined to force most of the Spaniards to leave town for higher, healthier ground. Only the poor and gentle Totonac Indians who had greeted Cortes on these beaches fifty years before remained behind, fishing lazily from their canoes, unaffected by the agues and fluxes that caused so many Spanish deaths.

The approach of autumn brought better conditions, and with the prospect of the arrival of the *flota* the factors and merchants returned to the coast. As often as not their womenfolk stayed behind, since conditions never wholly ameliorated. No child born to Spanish parents in Vera Cruz had yet survived infancy, and sickness was written on every adult's face. In their ignorance the inhabitants considered that their afflictions arose from the evil vapours of the earth, and strove to eradicate them by driving herds of cattle through the dusty streets each morning. All such precautions were in vain. Once already the site of the town had been adjusted to a supposedly healthier spot. Many years later it was moved yet again and grew up where it now stands, fifteen miles down the coast at San Juan de Ulua.

In 1568 when Hawkins sought refuge at San Juan it was the port for Vera Cruz and nothing else. A garrison of fifty Spaniards and a labour force of a hundred and fifty negro slaves were accommodated in hutments ashore and on the island. There were a few workshops, a chapel, some fortifications, but no permanent settlement. The coastline was as flat and unindented as around Vera Cruz to the north-west, and in itself provided no shelter from the north winds. But a group of reefs, some of which rose a few feet above tide-level, was scattered offshore. One in particular, the Arrecife de la Gallega, lying a quarter of a mile from the coast, provided a low shingle barrier athwart the prevailing wind. The shelter that this reef afforded was only some 250 yards in length, but the water was deep on the lee side and ships could lie close in, moored by headropes to the island itself and secured against swinging by stern anchors.

Such was the port of San Juan de Ulua. It seemed wretchedly insecure, for the ships towered above the protecting reef and their forecastles overhung it. From the wind there was no shelter; but the bank of shingle broke even the wildest sea, and, although the island might seem awash with the waves breaking over it, the deep water in which the ships rode was never disturbed.

Viewed from a mile or two to seaward San Juan de Ulua was scarcely recognizable as a harbour. A few dismasted hulks, too battered and weather-worn to be seaworthy but useful as depot-ships, were to be seen close inshore protected by the almost invisible reef. Approaching nearer, a few buildings became apparent, and the pattern of surf outlined the shoals through which a course needed to be steered. In fine weather it was not a difficult approach, but in the teeth of a norther it was impossible to make the harbour in safety. When it started to blow, a wise captain would not risk his ship so close inshore.

Some warning of the arrival of these dreaded winter winds could be gained from the unnatural clarity of the distant view. Sixty miles inland from San Juan de Ulua, beyond the barren seaboard and the fever-ridden jungle that lay behind, the land reared up to a broad plateau, guarded by volcanic peaks. The greatest of these mountains, Orizaba, a pyramid of dazzling whiteness, was a landmark many miles out to sea. But the cold clarity of its snows never seemed so luminous or sharply-etched as when a norther was about to blow. Then the mountain seemed to march forward and brood over the sultry, flyblown port, and the sky above it was blue and scoured of mist by the oncoming winds.

The arrival of a fleet offshore had not passed unnoticed amongst the watchers on San Juan de Ulua. It was late in the evening of September 15th when it was first sighted, and as the weather was fair it was natural that the ships should delay their entry until morning, when the dangers of the reefs, and of the land-breezes that often sprang up at night, could be avoided.

The fleet was of course expected, and a more than usually cere-monious greeting had been prepared for it. This year it would bring not only the ever-welcome stores and luxuries, new colonists and news from home, but on board the flagship was travelling a most distinguished passenger—Don Martin Enriquez, son of the Marquis of Alcanizes and newly appointed Viceroy of New Spain. It was essential that such a nobleman, the King's legate and over-lord of all their future actions, should be well-pleased by the loyalty of his reception.

In the fading light the negro slaves who were employed to maintain the mooring berths on the island were hustled into last-minute preparations. Captain Delgadillo, the young inspector and military commander of the island, coached his soldiers in the ceremony they were to observe next day when the *flota* entered harbour. It was an occasion of some dignity for him, and he may have hoped, through the scrupulous performance of his duty, to gain some praise and preferment. Meanwhile messengers were dispatched to Vera Cruz with news of the fleet's arrival, the small craft that were sheltering in the harbour were cleared from the main berths and the hulks, including a cumbersome great carrack of some six hundred tons, were prepared as floating storerooms. It seems unlikely that, as some reports have it, they were already laden with gold and silver awaiting transhipment to the *flota*. More probably the treasure was still safely housed in Vera Cruz.

At first light the fleet was seen to weigh anchor and set sail. Only ten vessels, two of which were great ships, had made a landfall together. Others might be expected to straggle in later, because often a storm at sea would separate one group of ships from another. The progress of the ten ships was slow, and was further delayed by the arrival of a small sailing boat that had set out from Vera Cruz to welcome the new Viceroy at sea. On board this craft were two of the principal citizens of the town, Francisco de Bustamante, the treasurer, and Martin de Marçana, the deputy mayor. They intercepted the fleet just before it had reached the outlying reefs, and were seen to go alongside and board the flagship which hove to to receive them.

What the watchers on the island could not see was the astonishment and terror of Bustamante and his companions when, having secured their boat alongside and cast their eyes upwards, they observed too late that the threadbare, weather-stained flag flying at the maintop was the Royal Standard, and the voices that greeted them from the deck spoke, not in Castilian, but in English.

After a while the fleet resumed its slow progress towards the land. The *Capitana*, flying its flag at the mainmast, came first followed at a distance by the *Almirante*—the second in command—carrying its ensign at the foretop. Behind her, in line astern, came the smaller vessels. They took the northern channel between the Galleguila and Blanquilla reefs. The garrison on the island under the command of Delgadillo was so preoccupied priming its guns and standing by to receive mooring lines that no one observed the incongruity of the open gunports and the anonymity of the indecipherable flags borne by the approaching ships.

As the *Jesus* came abreast the battery of five guns mounted at the south-eastern extremity of the island, Hawkins was close enough inshore to see the gunners receive their orders and touch their matches to the powder. It was a crucial moment. If his true identity had been discovered he would receive a point-blank salvo that might fatally cripple his ship. If, on the other hand, he was being greeted with a salute his deception still held good and might enable him to establish himself as master of the port without incident.

Even at first glance as he sailed into this strange anchorage, Hawkins realized that the shingle bank against which the ships moored was the strategic key to the harbour. Whoever commanded the island commanded the gateway to Mexico. Ranged against him was a modest but well-positioned battery. If it resisted his entry he must have considered the possibility of beaching the *Jesus* and storming the emplacements before the guns had time to reload. It might have been possible, but fortunately there was no need. The guns ashore roared, engulfing themselves for an instant in their own smoke. But it was a harmless courtesy. The shot that Hawkins half-expected would tear through the timbers of his ship had been carefully removed. A great weight of apprehension fell from him as he realized that nothing could now stop him from using the haven he so badly needed. He ordered the salute to be returned, luffed, and nosed his way as quickly as possible into an empty mooring-space.

Hard behind the *Jesus* came the *Minion*, and both these great ships were within hailing distance of the island before the Spanish garrison realized its mistake. Who first identified the English fleet no one could remember, but the news spread along the length of the island in an instant, and swept the garrison with panic. 'The Lutherans are upon us', they cried to one another; and indeed the towering forecastles of the Queen's ships loomed ominously above them, with armed landing parties gathered in the bows waiting to leap ashore. Resistance was useless, and almost every man turned and fled to the mainland. Slaves and soldiers piled indiscriminately into rowing-boats and pinnaces and betook themselves ashore as fast as they were able. Many plunged straight into the water and swam the two furlongs that separated them from safety.

Captain Delgadillo and the men who stood by the saluting-guns were as thunderstruck as the rest when an escaping boat-load called out the bad news as it passed. In an instant the guns' crew melted away and joined the flight. Delgadillo himself made a half-hearted attempt to rally his men, but only eight stood by him. With such numbers he could not hope to re-train the guns, load them with shot, and fire even once, before he was over-whelmed. Preserving as much dignity as possible he and his small group remained at their post and watched the English ships lowering their boats, taking lines ashore and laying out kedge anchors astern. Seeing the ease with which they accomplished these feats Delgadillo concluded that the English vessels must have aboard some captive seamen familiar with the intricacies of the port.

As soon as the *Jesus* was secured and the first patrols were seen to issue forth, Delgadillo sent two of his men across to the flag-ship to enquire the purpose of the English fleet's visit and to request that a formal conference might take place between a representative of the English captain and himself. The Spaniards quickly returned bringing Robert Barrett with them who was able to converse with Delgadillo in his own language. Before they met, the two Spanish emissaries whispered that they had been court-eously received, but had seen enough of the war-like preparations on board, and the number of their fellow countrymen held under restraint, to realize that the English ships were not idle visitors and would not be deflected from their unknown purpose by threats or cajolery.

The interview between Delgadillo and Barrett proved less fearsome than the Spaniard had dared hope. After explaining who he was and the nature of his mission Barrett expressed regret that the arrival of Hawkins' fleet should have caused such fear and flight. They themselves had attempted, he said, to halt the exodus from the island by calling out reassurances to the fugitives, but in vain. Even now Hawkins was sending a placatory mission across to the mainland to stress his peaceful intentions and to try to arrange the purchase of provisions of which he stood in immediate need. Barrett asked for Delgadillo's help in this matter, assuring him that everything taken would be paid for.

Furthermore, Delgadillo learnt, Hawkins had, at the suggestion of his distinguished 'guests' from Vera Cruz, freely empowered the deputy mayor to make his way overland to that city, and thence send messages to Mexico explaining the situation that had arisen and passing on Hawkins' request for a licence to conduct the trading necessary for his refit. He asked also for instructions to cover the possible arrival of the Spanish *flota* at San Juan before he was ready to depart. It would be difficult, he foresaw, for two proud navies to ride together in one anchorage without strict political control.

Clearly Hawkins did not intend to wait in idleness for the reply; indeed, secretly, he hoped to be gone by the time it arrived; but as always he liked to respect the forms of courtesy, and on his own account wrote personally to the *Audiencia* in Mexico in a similar vein. This letter he entrusted to Francisco Maldonado, the sea-captain whose boat he had intercepted off Campeche, to be delivered personally. But neither Maldonado nor the letter travelled further than the mainland shore, and Hawkins' account of his circumstances seems quickly to have been suppressed.

Delgadillo had one further enquiry, regarding the disposition of the rival forces on the island. Barrett reassured him by saying that, apart from placing guards on the mooring-ropes, no English soldiers would remain on the strand. Delgadillo was free to call back his men and resume his duties as garrison commander. It would not have escaped his attention, however, that his exposed batteries were well covered by the guns of the *Jesus* and *Minion*.

The day had already passed by the time the last of Hawkins' fleet, and the three Spanish craft that he had forced to follow him, had warped themselves into position facing the sea-wall. Together with the eight Spanish vessels that were already there they comfortably filled the berthing space that was available, with anchors fore and aft and well secured to the fixed chains and ropes ashore. So peaceful was the invasion that many of the Spaniards

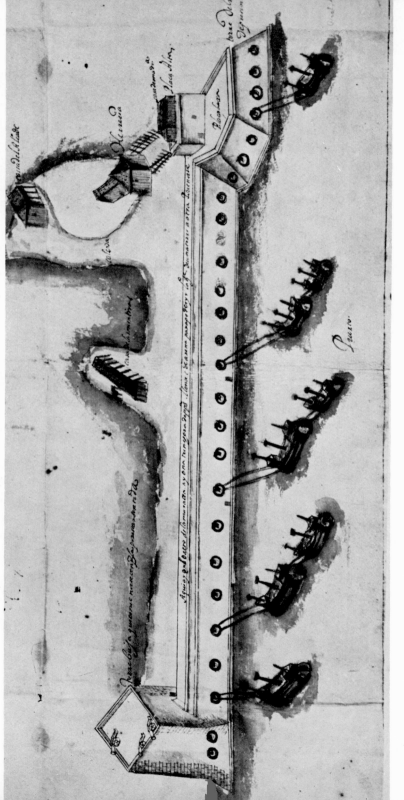

The moorings at San Juan de Ulua in 1590. The sea-wall and fortifications would have been less impressive in 1568

Do Martin, Enrriquez ae Almansa 4. Proire
et Dux genealis Ano 1568

Don Martin Enriquez, Viceroy of Mexico

and negroes who had previously left the island returned and continued their normal tasks. Hawkins' ships obtained enough food and water to satisfy their immediate needs, and apart from keeping a vigilant watch his men worried very little about their equivocal position. By now they were accustomed to find security in dangerous places.

The ease with which he had settled down at San Juan, coupled with the shortage of food that his fleet was experiencing, led Hawkins to release all but the most eminent of the hostages he had brought with him. The three ships he had captured were restored to their masters, and the Spaniards sent ashore. For the time being he kept the treasurer Bustamante, Agustin de Villanueva, and one or two others on board the *Jesus*.

That night Hawkins had good reason to feel pleased at the way Providence had smiled on him. He had only one fear left, and as he listened to the wind singing in the cordage, bringing with it a threat of blustery weather out at sea, even that shadow lifted a little from him. His cabin was hot, with the stagnant heaviness of the day trapped between decks; but Hawkins slept soundly with no trepidation of what the morning might bring.

At daybreak on Friday, September 17th, Francisco de Luxan, admiral in command of the Spanish plate fleet bound for Mexico, was awakened with a report that land had been sighted. The news was expected, but nonetheless welcome. His ships had been more than ten weeks at sea, and he looked forward to a spell in harbour, not only for the benefit of his vessels and their crews, but because he would have discharged a task that at times he had found embarrassing. Under his command, as a passenger, he carried aboard his flagship a man who was his superior both by birth and by appointment—Don Martin Enriquez, the Viceroy-elect of New Spain. From the beginning Luxan had feared lest his authority as admiral of the fleet might be usurped, but hitherto, with the exercise of tact, very little friction had disturbed their relations. Administration would be easier, however, once the Viceroy had taken the road to his capital.

As soon as he was dressed Luxan left his cabin and went on

M

deck. A sharp cross-wind was blowing which made progress slow, as all the ships were deeply laden and sailed sluggishly. Looking about him he observed that nine of his fleet were following fairly closely, but during the night two of the merchantmen had fallen far astern, and could only just be descried upon the horizon. The vice-admiral, Juan de Ubilla, who commanded the second of the escort vessels and sailed in the rear of the convoy, had very properly waited behind to watch over the laggards. Turning his gaze ahead Luxan caught a glimpse through the billowing canvas of the shore line, still many miles ahead. Above it, and gilded by the morning sun, stood the peak of Orizaba, floating, it seemed, over the mists of the earth.

While he was glancing about him the look-outs, invisible in their high, sail-shrouded nests, sang out that a small boat seemed to have left the harbour for which they were bound and was tacking towards them. It was early in the day, Luxan thought, for reception-committees, yet undoubtedly something of that sort was approaching. He had forgotten all about it when, unceremoniously and with a noticeable lack of fine phrases, the crew of the pinnace he had watched approaching at a distance was hustled into his presence. In a few words they repeated their message as Antonio Delgadillo had instructed them. For Delgadillo had been the first to see the sails of the approaching *flota* outlined against the streaks of dawn in the north-eastern sky, and in great secrecy had sent a pinnace out to warn the fleet that the port of San Juan was in the hands of the notorious English corsair 'Juan Aquines'. The matter sounded so serious that Luxan departed at once to inform the Viceroy of the unwelcome news.

Don Martin's first reaction, on being appraised of the situation, was to take command personally. He was able to do so by the use of a *cedula* with which he had carefully provided himself before he left Spain in case such an emergency arose. Although he was no sailor and a naval battle seemed possible, honour demanded that the responsibility and, he hoped, the glory, of any encounter should be his. With the best grace possible Luxan was obliged to bow before the assertion of viceregal power. The fleet was ordered to hove to and all captains were summoned aboard the flagship.

Only Ubilla, the vice-admiral, and the captains of the two merchantmen that he was escorting, were too far behind the main
fleet to comply.

While the conference was being organized a second boat was
seen to be approaching from the shore. On board was Antonio
Delgadillo. No sooner had he arrived than he was taken below to
where the Viceroy, Luxan and the assembled captains were
awaiting him. After having given an account of the circumstances that had led to Hawkins' peaceful entry into San Juan
de Ulua the day before, and excused his apparent dereliction as
best he could, Delgadillo described how he had caused a warning
to be sent to the fleet immediately he sighted it, and how, not
long afterwards, there had been a stir of activity on board the
moored English ships, and four or five men, one of whom was
Bustamante the captive treasurer of Vera Cruz, had rowed ashore
and escorted Delgadillo back to the English flagship.

The war-like activity that he witnessed on board the *Jesus*
astonished and impressed him. Chains of men were bringing
powder and shot up from the magazine in bulge barrels and
stacking the ammunition beside the guns. The armoury had been
opened, and small-arms and equipment laid out along the decks
under cover of wooden blinders, that had been erected to shield
the exposed decks. Some men were busy filling tubs with vinegar
and water, and sprinkling sawdust on the deck around the gun
carriages; others were hauling crossbows and heavy stones up into
the fighting tops. He saw all this, Delgadillo said, only in
passing, for he was taken straight away to Hawkins, a stocky,
incisive young man whom he found, to his surprise, on deck
and mingling with his seamen as he directed their activities.

Hawkins had asked him what ships they were that had appeared
from seaward overnight. He replied that he assumed it was the
flota from Spain. This answer did not outwardly discompose
Hawkins, but he gave Delgadillo notice that he would be obliged
to occupy the island of San Juan with his own men and take over
the batteries. This, he stressed, was merely a precautionary
measure as he had no wish to come into conflict with the forces of
Spain, to whose King he was himself bound by his old allegiance.

He had proposed, therefore, sending Delgadillo as his emissary to work out satisfactory terms whereby the two fleets might, for as long as was necessary, share the same harbour. If these safeguards were not accepted he gave notice that he would deny the Spanish ships entry and defend the port by force. As to the nature of the terms, he had seemed, Delgadillo informed his audience, quite determined; and although he had had little enough time to ponder the problem his attitude was already inflexible. There must be an exchange of twelve hostages, a complete physical segregation of Spanish and English ships at the moorings, and the English would retain the armed possession of the island.

As he put forward each of Hawkins' conditions Delgadillo was aware of the stupefied incredulity of the assembled captains. Even though they had been told of the preparations that the English corsairs were making to resist them, they could scarcely believe that any band of interlopers would dare to offer defiance to the force and majesty of the fleet of the King of Spain—let alone propose humiliating conditions. To accept such terms was unthinkable; even to debate them seemed a loss of dignity.

Don Martin, we may well imagine, spoke first without waiting, as would be customary at such a council, for his captains to express their own opinions in reverse order of seniority. To him the answer was simple. As soon as the vice-admiral had rejoined the fleet they would sail forward and eject the English pirates by force of arms. Had they not been told that the English flagship was unseaworthy, and five of the seven ships of small fighting power? The English captain was attempting a bluff. Call it, and it would quickly be apparent how desperate were his circumstances.

The less-experienced commanders, who were then called upon to appraise the situation, may, understandably, have echoed the Viceroy's truculence. But Luxan and one or two senior captains who had sailed to Mexico before realized how unrealistic such proposals were.

Deferentially the admiral began to acquaint Don Martin with the nature of the port of San Juan. He described the lay-out of the anchorage, and emphasized that whoever held the batteries on the

island could easily repel a fleet, however powerful, that attempted
to force an entry. In view of his impregnable position he marvelled
that the English commander was even interested in a peaceful
settlement, and, with the Viceroy's permission, Luxan questioned
Delgadillo as to the probability of a trap being engineered,
whereby the *flota* might be lured into range of the corsairs' guns.
Certainly this was a possibility, but perhaps an inevitable hazard.
Already, the admiral pointed out, the wind was freshening, and
although not a norther it blew sufficiently athwart their course to
make an unopposed entrance difficult. Soon it might become impossible. A harbour was the first essential and San Juan de Ulua,
alone along the coast, would serve. The exchange of hostages
might at least defer any English act of treachery until the fleet
was safely moored. What action it was expedient to take thereafter he must naturally leave to the judgment of the Viceroy.

Admiral Luxan's advice seemed acceptable even to the impetuous Don Martin, though the blow to his dignity and pride
in being forced to accede to the humiliation of dictated peace
was a wound that admitted only a single remedy. The give and
take of the market place, to which Hawkins might cheerfully
submit, or the expediency that might influence a Spanish provincial governor to comply with terms imposed upon him, were
base considerations to which the character of a high-born
aristocrat of Spain was alien. There was no shrugging away an
insult. There was no tolerance between Lutheran and Catholic.
There was no deceit when honour needed to be avenged. Don
Martin did not scruple, therefore, while accepting Hawkins'
conditions, to lay plans for disregarding them as soon as the
advantage lay with him in doing so.

The conference had turned to the details of the proposed pact
when the arrival of the vice-admiral, Juan de Ubilla, was
announced. His rearguard had at last rejoined the main fleet,
bringing it up to its full strength of thirteen vessels. He was
flustered by the rumours that he had heard and the urgent
summons he had received to come aboard the flagship. As a
professional sailor he found himself very little at ease in the
formal atmosphere of the Viceroy's conference, and the excuses

he made for his late arrival were coldly received. For his benefit the position was once again reviewed and the decisions that had been taken were put to him. He agreed without demur. Delgadillo, who had by now spent the best part of the day on board the flagship, was instructed to return to Hawkins with a message that the Viceroy was prepared in principle to accept the terms proposed and would welcome a deputation from the English fleet to ratify the details.

Meanwhile in the Viceroy's day-cabin the discussion continued, and centred largely upon the nature and quality of the hostages that should be exchanged. Don Martin, who made no secret of his intention of breaking the pact as soon as was convenient, had suggested that as the hostages would be liable to instant reprisal it would be advisable to dress up a number of seamen in gentlemen's attire and thereby minimize the loss. Lots were drawn amongst a selected group of personable hands, and the chosen men were summoned to the conference to learn their fate. It was quite obvious that the proposed hostages regarded it as no honour to be picked. So loath were they to go that Ubilla realized that they might easily disclose their insignificance in order to safeguard their lives. To the Viceroy he proposed that, whereas it was obviously politic to send men of secondary importance, the hostages should at least be gentlemen. He himself would volunteer to go, but as that might be impractical he offered to send his own nephew who was serving under him and three other gentlemen-retainers from his own entourage. Don Martin thanked him and accepted the four men. The remainder were quickly chosen, and the conference adjourned until Delgadillo came back.

It was a long and strenuous haul through choppy seas to regain the sheltered water in the harbour of San Juan. As he came to the approaches of the port Delgadillo could see what a transformation had been effected in his absence. The island was alive with men, and all of them were English. The five guns he had commanded were now supplemented by six brass pieces commandeered from the dismasted carrack that lay alongside. These eleven guns were disposed in three batteries, one at the smithy, another near the most substantial building on the island known as the House of Lies, and at the far end of the strand a third battery was based on the blockhouse, La Ventanilla. Around each group of guns a protective bank of shingle had been dug up, and a palisade gave cover for small-arms fire from within the House of Lies. Delgadillo estimated that there must be about fifty Englishmen manning the fortifications on the island.

The ships themselves, especially the two fighting vessels, were equally ready for action. The *Jesus'* battery of twenty-two guns seemed to have been reinforced on the port side, but it was difficult to see what other warlike preparations had been undertaken as the blinders hid from view all upper-deck activities. There were sounds of forging and hammering, however, the purpose of which it was not difficult to guess. Some of the small ships seemed curiously empty, and Delgadillo concluded that Hawkins was concentrating his fighting power.

Most of Friday evening he spent in conference on board the *Jesus*. Following his instructions he protested against the proposals to forbid the Spaniards to land on the island once they had moored. But Hawkins was adamant and the only concession that he would make was to allow access to any who were totally unarmed. On the question of hostages Delgadillo persuaded Hawkins to reduce the number to be exchanged to ten on each side.

Next morning Delgadillo, together with two English gentlemen empowered by Hawkins to conclude the pact, departed once again for the Spanish fleet that lay waiting nine miles to the north of the port. Ten more Englishmen, nominated at their own request from among the officers, merchants and gentlemen who had undertaken to share the hazards of the voyage with Hawkins, accompanied the delegation to act as hostages should the agreement be signed. One of these volunteers was George Fitzwilliam.

The Viceroy meanwhile had not been idle. In anticipation of the coming battle he had sent a pinnace ashore to Vera Cruz, carrying much personal treasure and equipment that he had no wish to hazard under fire, and also a number of non-combatants, including his own son—a lad of ten or twelve years and not yet fledged in arms.

This boat-load was received ashore by Don Luis Zegri, the mayor of the city, who had been absent inland at Jalapa when Hawkins had first appeared at San Juan, but who had hurried back to Vera Cruz as soon as the news reached him. He had found his city in a state of disorganization and panic. The capture of San Juan de Ulua had caused the burghers of Vera Cruz to fly to the interior to hide their treasure and preserve their lives. Those who had no riches to conceal grew fat on the carelessness of the more prosperous. Meanwhile no food supplies reached the city, and business was at a standstill. The arrival of the *flota* and the return of the mayor helped to restore confidence, and in a second wave the citizens departed to retrieve the wealth they had secreted so diligently the day before.

The Viceroy had sent a personal message with the boat, instructing the mayor to recruit every man in the town capable of bearing arms. Some of these soldiers were to be ferried out to join the fleet at sea; the remainder were to be marched down the coast road to San Juan de Ulua, but to be kept out of sight of the harbour for the time being. Don Luis Zegri hastened to obey his orders. As fast as they could be assembled and equipped the young men of Vera Cruz led by Captain Pedro de Yebra were dispatched, a few at a time in small boats, to reinforce the *flota*. Nearly two hundred were taken on board before the weather became so bad that no further contingents dared embark.

With these reinforcements Don Martin, whose training was that of a soldier, became confident that he had sufficient superiority in numbers to overcome the English intruders. Weight of manpower, he considered, was the key to any engagement whether by land or sea. After the first grappling the technique in naval battles was very much the same as when two armies met. The sailors in the Spanish fleet were mere auxiliaries who, having brought their ship alongside the enemy, were not of sufficient importance even to merit protective armour. The actual fighting was a soldier's job.

It might have surprised Don Martin to know how differently his opponents regarded an engagement between fighting vessels. He would have been shocked, professionally, to learn that Hawkins held the close-range slings, bases and fowlers, with

which his flagship was plentifully equipped, in so little favour
that he had not even troubled to lift them from the ballast where
they lay. The great proportion of the armament with which the
Jesus and *Minion* made ready to defend themselves were long-
range culverins and sakers, guns designed to sink ships rather than
disperse men clustered together before boarding. And the men
who fired these weapons—and made the accuracy of English
gunnery famous and feared—were common seamen.

The second conference on board the *capitana*, under the direction
of Don Martin Enriquez and in the presence of the twelve
Englishmen, was both formal and brief. The basis of agreement
had been thrashed out by Delgadillo, and it only remained to
ratify the undertakings on both sides. The Viceroy received
assurances that as soon as Hawkins had effected the repairs that
were necessary to his fleet, and had purchased provisions, he would
depart in peace. All this he had put in writing, and in return the
English delegates were handed a letter, addressed to their
captain, couched in the florid and courteous language proper to
such official documents. In view of subsequent events it is interesting, though not edifying, to read this communication in its
entirety.

'I well believe that your honour's arrival in that port was
forced by the great need your honour had of subsistence and other
things, as your honour writes me. So also I am certain that, as your
honour says, your honour has not mistreated any vassal of his
majesty's, nor done any damage with your fleet in those ports and
parts where it has called, but that your honour has engaged solely
in bartering slaves and other merchandise carried, paying in same
for the subsistence taken, at its just value; and further that your
honour had paid the dues payable to his majesty's royal revenues.

'Wherefore I am content to accept the proposal which your
honour makes in your letter, asking me to deliver hostages and
to enter the port in peace, although I was determined to the
contrary. Therefore I send ten principal persons and rely upon
what your honour states, that those your honour sends me are
similar persons. I well believe that although the people of this
fleet enter without arms into the island, they will not be pre-

vented from going about their affairs, nor harassed in any fashion. And I am very confident that when we meet, friendship will augment between these fleets, since both are so well disciplined.'

Ten well-attired Spanish hostages were brought forward, and, after the two English delegates had bidden their own compatriots farewell, they returned in their pinnace to San Juan, bearing with them the tokens of amity. As soon as was convenient after they had arrived, the Viceroy told them, he would direct his fleet to sail for the shelter of the harbour.

But the negotiations had been too protracted; or perhaps in his greed for reinforcements from Vera Cruz the Viceroy lingered longer than was wise in his exposed anchorage. Whatever the cause of delay the cross-wind, against which the lightly-laden pinnace had battled on its errands between San Juan and the *flota* offshore, freshened sufficiently to make it impossible for the unmanoeuvreable, heavily-charged galleons and carracks to attempt to enter the port that night. Some, who had experience of sailing in the Gulf, declared that a norther was likely to blow, in which case it would be wise for the fleet to keep well clear of the shore.

For three days the wind prevented the Spanish ships from gaining the shelter of San Juan de Ulua. Hawkins, who watched them hourly from within the protective shelter of his moorings, must often have wished that a tempest such as he had lately experienced would rise up and scour the seas, driving the *flota* into the far recesses of the Gulf and taking with it the burden of the uneasy truce that his conscience had forced upon him. How simple it would have been to have denied the port utterly to the helpless fleet. If they had chosen to fight he could have defended it with ease, and humiliated Spain at the very gateway of her empire. But if they had turned away he knew from his own experience how far they would have to search to find a haven. For him such a triumph would have been baneful and short-lived. It was the expediency of a pirate, which he personally deplored, and from the political repercussions of which he would suffer irremediably after his return.

Now, with the Viceroy's pact secure in his possession, he could afford to pray for a north wind. But after three indecisive days his prayers were rejected. The wind dropped, and on Tuesday September 21st, with the morning tide, the fleet of Spain entered San Juan de Ulua.

The courtesies of the sea were scrupulously observed. Salutes were exchanged, and when the preliminary mooring had taken place trumpets were sounded and the text of the agreement was read aloud to the men of both nations. Visits were exchanged, and despite the barriers of language and religion both sides were at pains to show their friendliness and their determination to give no reason for offence.

The task of mooring was not easily accomplished in a manner that safeguarded the ships and satisfied the wariness of the out-numbered English contingent. The harbour was by now considerably overcrowded. There had been eight ships, including one large carrack, already berthed before Hawkins arrived with seven of his own vessels and the three small craft that he had intercepted. Now thirteen ships from the *flota* brought the total to more than thirty sail. The length of the island was a little more than a quarter of a mile, thus making it impossible for every one of the vessels to lie with her head-ropes secured ashore. Hawkins insisted that his own fleet was moored together, and chose to occupy the berths at the south-eastern extremity of the island where he was least hemmed in. At the seaward end he placed his virtually defenceless small craft, and screened them from the Spanish ships with the towering wooden flanks of the *Jesus* and *Minion*.

It was the *Minion* that marked the division of the two fleets, and here, though at no other point, there was a space between two of the moored ships. Parallel with the *Minion* across these few yards of open water, lay the hulk that seemed to have become an inert part of the furniture of the port. Beyond her were ranged the ships of the *flota*, so close together that, except for the one gap it would have been possible to pass from deck to deck down the entire line. The smallest Spanish vessels, for whom there were no mooring berths, anchored as best they could within the harbour or against the mainland shore.

Warping and kedging the ships into their agreed positions was a slow and laborious task. While these activities were in progress there was little chance of buying stores or undertaking repairs. But at last, after working all day Tuesday and much of Wednesday, the arrangement was completed. The last of the network of hawsers that led from ship to shore was secured, and each vessel had placed a sheet anchor astern on a short stay. The Spanish berthing parties, whose activities were closely watched by the English garrison on the island, returned to their ships, and a gradual calm spread over the two fleets.

A casual observer might never have guessed the tension and hostility that divided them had he not realized the significance of the axe that lay beside the head warps in the bows of each English ship, or the capstan securing the inboard end of the stern anchor whose spoke-like wooden bars were left unshipped.

CHAPTER 11

The Fight at San Juan

THE day before the two fleets came together Hawkins released Bustamante and allowed him to join his compatriots. As soon as the Spanish ships entered the harbour he hastened to pay his respects to the Viceroy, and shortly afterwards, when the fleet was finally moored, he was summoned back to the flagship for an urgent conference.

Walking across the shingle by the quayside the treasurer would have seen that the seamen of both nations were fraternizing and mingling together with every show of cordiality. The Englishmen wore side-arms and the Spaniards had no weapons, but in all other respects the coarsely-dressed, weatherbeaten and bearded men were indistinguishable.

The first ship on the Spanish side of the gap that separated the two fleets, Bustamante observed, was Diego Felipe's hulk, the dismasted, all but deserted, ruin of a noble ship. Next to her came the *Almirante* and then the *Capitana*—the only two fighting-ships in the Spanish fleet. Both were powerful vessels, not unlike the *Minion* in fire-power and size. It was to the *Capitana* that Bustamante directed his steps.

At the conference table he recognized Don Luis Zegri the mayor, and several other notables of his city. To those he did not know, the captains of the newly-arrived ships, the Viceroy, who presided over the deliberations, introduced him. The meeting was, he soon discovered, a council of war. Everyone present assumed that no alternative to the destruction of the English corsairs would be creditable either to themselves or to Spain; all that was necessary was to plan the nature and timing of the assault.

189

Thursday September 23rd, two days later, had been deemed the appropriate day, and Don Martin was already determined on his method of attack. It was to be a soldiers' battle; and by using the advantage of surprise he did not anticipate that a single vessel would stir from her moorings before the issue was decided. In choosing to fight on land the Viceroy was confident of himself and of his numbers. Afloat he was inexperienced, and not uninfluenced by the stories he had heard of Hawkins' fabulous skill with ships. Don Martin required the glory of the battle for himself. He would not risk its outcome at the hands of sailors in whom, as a landsman, he had little faith.

On Wednesday night in great secrecy, the Viceroy declared, some two hundred men were to be transferred into the hulk and kept under cover until eleven the next morning. Luxan and Ubilla would be in charge. There was some murmuring at this proposal, and Ubilla was bold enough to question whether the unusual course of appointing both the admiral and the vice-admiral to a command away from their own ships was wise. But the Viceroy would have no truck with such objections, and gave a short reply. Realizing that criticism of a plan already perfected in Don Martin's mind was unacceptable, the assembled company heard the remaining details of the proposed assault, but made no further comments on them. Each officer was given his task and the conference was on the point of disbanding when the Viceroy called them back for a final word. The English he reminded them, were not fools and kept a strict watch. It was imperative that they should have no inkling of the project either through careless speech or action before the moment of the assault. At eleven o'clock, he reiterated, turning to where Luxan, with Ubilla next to him, sat at the table, you will signal from the hulk with a white napkin that your men are ready to attack. On seeing the token I shall sound a trumpet and the battle will commence.

Wednesday, the first full day that the two fleets had lain together, passed watchfully but without incident. On the English side every man went about armed, and every gun remained loaded before its open port-hole. The guards and duty-men were reinforced, and Hawkins himself was almost always to be found on deck scrutinizing every movement on board the Spanish ships and searching for some sign whereby he could anticipate the sudden attack that he hourly expected.

All that day he heard and saw nothing positively hostile. An unnatural calm had descended upon the Spaniards. He had experienced treachery before and recognized the atmosphere in which it germinated. The over-hearty greeting shouted across the water, the busy secretiveness of officers passing from ship to ship, the concealed smiles and glances over the shoulder among whispering groups of men; all these Hawkins read as tokens of a plot destined to engulf him. Yet he had no cause for complaint: the conditions of his agreement were being scrupulously observed.

He slept little and uneasily that night. Several times he was called, and stood amongst the group of silent watchers on deck listening to slight, persistent noises that came from across the narrow strip of water that separated the *Minion* from the hulk. Undoubtedly there was movement aboard the Spanish vessel. Occasionally he saw the flashes of a dark lantern and heard the scraping of metal on metal or the creaking of wood. He guessed that armed men were being moved into the hulk, and as the noises persisted over a long period he estimated their numbers to be considerable. The Spaniards, he reckoned, would be unlikely to launch a night attack, and until day dawned there was little that he could do. By then his own men would be up and about.

Daylight disclosed no obvious changes on board the Spanish ships, but by several small tokens Hawkins became convinced that Diego Felipe's hulk did indeed conceal an armed host. As soon as the sun had risen, and the early attack he had half-expected showed no signs of materializing, Hawkins dispatched Barrett to the Spanish flagship to deliver a verbal protest against the various suspicious acts that he had observed, hoping by demonstrating his awareness of the Spaniards' designs to discourage them from proceeding. Before he left, Barrett received from the garrison ashore even more positive evidence of the Viceroy's hostile intent. Overnight new embrasures had been cut in the bows of certain ships, through which guns were seen to be trained against the island emplacements.

All these threats to the peace Barrett related to Don Martin as he delivered Hawkins' complaint. The Viceroy, Barrett said afterwards, had seemed genuinely concerned to learn of them and immediately ordered all such menacing deeds to be countermanded. To Barrett personally he had been courteous and conciliatory, and told him to assure his captain that by his faith as a Viceroy he would protect him against any treachery.

With such promises Barrett had to be content, and indeed, for the next hour or two, there was noticeably less coming and going of men and equipment between the Spanish ships; but whether this marked a change of heart or an increase of caution it was difficult to say. So close together did the Spanish vessels lie that they largely screened each other from inquisitive eyes.

Hawkins himself was far from reassured by the Viceroy's bland words. He waited a little longer, but, as the Spaniards made no attempt to remove whatever threat they had concealed overnight in the hulk, he instructed Barrett to call once more on Don Martin with a demand to know whether or not there were troops on board.

It was then half past nine, and, after waiting a while for the Master of the *Jesus* to return, Hawkins retired to his cabin where an early dinner awaited him. He assumed that Barrett had been invited to dine aboard the Spanish flagship. Hawkins was joined, as was his custom, by his officers and gentlemen—fewer than usual, for some were on duty and others had gone as hostages to the Spanish ships. Their places were taken by the Spanish sureties and by Agustin de Villanueva, who had evinced no desire to leave the *Jesus* and was treated as an honoured guest. He sat near to Hawkins at table, and it was thought that the two men in their secret conversations were each seeking to discover how best he could use the other to advance his own schemes.

The meal had scarcely begun, and the stewards were passing behind the diners with piles of dishes, when a struggle flared up between two men at Hawkins' side. All conversation stopped instantly and in the silence that ensued a dagger was seen to fall to the deck. In a moment every man was on his feet and swords were drawn, but before they could do more than exclaim at the outrage Hawkins called them to silence. Beside him Agustin de Villanueva was held pinioned by John Chamberlain, one of the cabin stewards. As he passed behind him, Chamberlain declared, he had seen the dagger concealed in Villanueva's sleeve. There was no doubt for whom it was intended.✝

Hawkins did not wait to hear Villanueva's excuses. He shouted to two stewards to bind the traitor and keep him prisoner. Without a moment's hesitation he strode over the upturned chairs, seized a crossbow from the arms-rack at the door and before his dining companions could recover from their astonishment had scrambled up the companionway on to the open deck.

The same ominous quiet embraced the two fleets. But now Hawkins' last doubts were removed. He knew there was treachery afoot and he had no intention of being surprised by it. Passing from the *Jesus* over on to the *Minion* he summoned some of the men on watch and led the way to the forecastle where the best view could be obtained. He was immediately aware that the crew of the hulk were engaged in singling up their head-ropes and preparing, with as much concealment as possible, to warp their vessel alongside the *Minion*. By a lucky chance Hawkins caught a glimpse in the bows of the hulk of a figure whom he recognized. Sternly he hailed him across the water. Vice-Admiral Ubilla, not a little flustered at having been detected, stood up and acknowledged himself. He was fully armed.

Without Barrett at his side Hawkins could only speak in a rough and ready Spanish. He was sufficiently fluent in that tongue, however, to inform Ubilla that he was not conducting himself like a gentleman and to accuse him of trickery. Ubilla, touched on a point of pride, replied that he was following his calling like a captain and a fighter. This retort was partly lost on Hawkins, but he caught the last word and his long pent-up emotions were released. 'You are quite right', he shouted back, and levelling his crossbow discharged a bolt at the vice-admiral. A moment later an arquebusier standing near Hawkins fired in support, and a man at Ubilla's side fell to the deck.

* acc. to Corbett the Spaniards had been plying the English with w[...]

THE DEFEAT OF JOHN HAWKINS

There was no time to reload. The Spaniards took cover, and the last Hawkins saw of the vice-admiral was his arm waving a white cloth in the direction of the *Capitana*. On the steeply-tilted deck of the Spanish flagship a small figure seemed to acknowledge the signal, and a moment later a trumpet call rang out clearly and decisively. The truce was over.

The events of the next few minutes were confused, yet they determined the eventual outcome of the battle. The single shot and the trumpet call released a spring of expectancy that had inwardly constrained every man and boy aboard the English ships for the past two days. Without waiting for orders they ran headlong to their action stations—an exercise so often rehearsed that it required no thought. There was a drumming of many feet, the clash of arms, urgent words of command and the creaking of heavy gear being shifted. Then came gunfire, and the clamour of battle drowned the small noises of preparation.

The first clash was on land. Hawkins saw at a glance that the shore batteries were hard pressed. There was hand to hand skirmishing all over the island, even in the emplacements themselves. A few of the guns were discharged, but whether against the moored ships, or whether they chose as targets the groups of Spaniards hurrying from the main fleet to reinforce their companions ashore, he could not tell. The smoke from the guns soon made it difficult to distinguish friend from foe. His own garrison, Hawkins knew, numbered no more than fifty men and the Spaniards were coming ashore in hundreds, some from small boats, some swimming, others leaping from the overhanging bowsprits. Unless he could reinforce them or cause a diversion he feared that his men would be overwhelmed, since artillery was useless at very close range. Inwardly he raged at his lack of foresight in allowing such treacherous neighbours even conditional use of the island. ✗

There was no hope of aiding the island garrison now. The ships themselves were in deadly peril. Hawkins had not regained his flagship before, looking back, he saw the hulk swinging slowly across the narrow strip of water that separated her from the *Minton*, her upper deck thronged with armed men. There was a lurch as the bows of the two ships touched and with exultant cries of 'Santiago' a throng of Spanish soldiers leapt across on to the English deck. There seemed painfully few sailors available to repel the boarders. Drawing his sword, Hawkins called out in a loud and confident voice to his own men on the *Jesus*—'God and Saint George, upon those traitorous villains and rescue the *Minion*. I trust in God the day shall be ours.' His words carried above the noise of battle, and in an instant sailors from the high-decked flagship were leaping down to the support of their captain and the embattled crew of the *Minion*. Fortunately, before the full weight of the Spanish assault could be brought to bear, the two vessels started to drift apart. The invaders from the hulk jumped for safety, though a few were killed in the fierce sword-play, and for the time being the English ships remained unscathed.

Immediately the action began the *Jesus* and the *Minion* had cut their headropes, and below decks the crew at the after capstans were straining at the bars in a slow effort to haul the vessels away from the mooring quay into the open waters of the harbour, where they could set their sails and gain a little manoeuvring space. As they inched their way backward the unwieldly hulk swung clear of the *Minion* and drifted against the *Jesus*. Another scuffle ensued, with the Spaniards attempting to grapple and board Hawkins' flagship, aided in their attack by two pinnaces that fastened like terriers against the *Jesus'* sides. But Hawkins had way on and was able to disengage his ship without great difficulty.

Meanwhile the Spanish *Almirante* had been exposed, broadside on, and was evidently unprepared for a close-range duel. The gunners on the *Minion* had had no chance as yet to prove their worth. Their pieces were primed and ready, but they were too hemmed in to bring them to bear. The sudden appearance of a target was the signal for slow matches to be plunged in every touch-hole on the port side and from both decks a ragged burst of fire shook the ship.

Before the acrid fume had drifted away and the guns' crews reloaded, the *Jesus* joined in the bombardment. Almost immediately she achieved an impressive success. A cannister of grape-shot fired from one of the two great cannon-periers on the lower deck ignited a barrel of powder on board the *Almirante*. There was an immediate explosion and a flash of fire before a column of black smoke engulfed the ship. A lucky chance, but it cheered the Englishmen in their desperate plight to see one of their adversaries' greatest ships shattered, burning, and incapable of doing them harm.

Within five minutes the guns were reloaded and one by one, as they were ready, they continued their cannonade, this time choosing the next vessel down the line, the *Capitana*, as their target. The range was close, the English ships were moving slowly away from their berths, but the Spanish vessel never stirred nor did her big guns reply. Shot after shot from the culverins of the two English ships pierced the wooden sides of Don Martin's flagship, breaking through the timbers at the water-line and splintering the carved and gilded upper works. Concentrating their fire upon the one target they set about a methodical task of destruction.

Only to the guns' crews, stripped to the waist, blackened by smoke and powder and streaked with sweat, did the pace of the action seem hectic. To those ordering the battle from the after-castle there were minutes at a time when no gun fired and it was possible to take in the larger picture of the struggle that was developing on the island and in the ships. Afloat, at least, the English fleet seemed to have out-manoeuvred the Spaniards. All Hawkins' ships except the *Swallow* had successfully cut loose from their moorings and were in process of hauling themselves clear of the land. Indeed, thanks to the onslaught that the *Jesus* and *Minion* had directed against the two principal Spanish warships, the English vessels were encountering singularly little return fire. There was some light artillery and small-shot directed against them, as was to be expected; but although this caused casualties among the exposed members of the crew on deck it was not sufficient to jeopardize the ships themselves. To many of the sailors the fact that the Spaniards had all but deserted their ships seemed a cheering indication that the tide of battle was swinging in their favour. Not so Hawkins. His eyes were ever on the island, straining to read through the eddying smoke the result of the struggle ashore. He realized that the first victory lay not with him, but with the Spaniards who had forced him to abandon his out-numbered garrison on the shingle bank of San Juan. And whoever commanded the island held the key to final victory.

Again and again the guns of the *Jesus* and *Minion* were loaded, trained and fired. The *Capitana*, passively defiant, sank lower in the water. The *Almirante* was afire from stem to stern and had been abandoned by her crew. On the island all noise of battle seemed to have ceased, but the outcome remained obscure.

The first news came to Hawkins from three of his men who swam out to the *Jesus* and were picked up, exhausted, from the sea. The island, they said, was overrun and the batteries captured intact. They alone had escaped. A few minutes later the guns that Hawkins had so carefully positioned for his defence were turned against him, and the English fleet came under heavy and accurate fire.

Not a little agitated by his narrow escape Vice-Admiral Ubilla ducked under cover and glanced around for his superior officer, General Luxan among the press of soldiers on the lower deck of the hulk. Failing to find him, and realizing that the Englishmen could no longer be caught by surprise, he had no alternative but to give the signal for the assault. It was inconvenient, as many of his men were not yet armed, believing that they had an hour's wait still before them; but battles, he may have reflected, however meticulously devised, seldom follow a premeditated course. He had, perhaps, been rash to linger on the upper deck in full armour once he had arrived on board, but soldiers were notoriously careless in singling up ropes, and it needed skill such as only a sailor could provide to warp the hulk securely alongside the English ships. Seizing a white napkin, and taking pains to keep his body under cover, Ubilla waved it towards the flagship.

Don Luis Zegri and certain other gentlemen were gathered on the poop when the vice-admiral gave the signal to attack. As it was still an hour before the prearranged time Don Martin was in his cabin, but hearing an arquebus shot he hurried on deck and realized at once that there was no hope of concealing his purpose any longer. He ordered the trumpet to be sounded and waited anxiously to see how the assault parties would react to the sudden and premature signal.

To one man on the *Capitana* the trumpet-call came as no surprise. No sooner had Robert Barrett come aboard the Spanish flagship to deliver Hawkins' second protest than he was arrested, bound hand and foot, and chained to the deck in the dark, airless caverns of the hull. He had lain there, unable to warn his captain, for many long and anxious minutes before he heard the first sounds of battle; and throughout the action he, like the English hostages who later joined him in his confinement, was able to judge the slow progress of the fight only by the intermittent noise of gunfire, and the urgent, half-muffled voices that from time to time he overheard on the decks above. There were moments when the guns of their own ships came near to destroying them; yet as the day drew on and such perils became fewer, their fears and despondency increased.

Luckily for Don Martin most of his men were positioned in good time. Bustamante, who had been given no specific assignment, joined his friend from Vera Cruz, Captain Pedro de Yebra, whose men lay concealed in a cluster of small boats between two of the merchant craft. Further down the line Captain Delgadillo commanded a similar assault group. The trumpet call took them unawares; there was some hasty buckling on of swords and armour, but within a few seconds the boats had cast off, and a few strokes brought them to the island. It was not an orderly landing; the leaders scrambled ashore, followed by their men, and ran as fast as their equipment and the loose pebbles would allow towards the gun emplacements that they had been given as their objective. At some points their task had been accomplished before they arrived. It had been arranged that those Spaniards who innocently went ashore that morning to exercise and converse with the English garrison should carry concealed weapons. When the trumpet sounded swords and pistols were drawn and the Englishmen were fiercely assailed where they stood. Even the guns' crews were so busy defending themselves that many of the pieces were never fired, and before long, with the help of reinforcements from the ships, each battery was overwhelmed by vigorous Spanish assaults. Only a few isolated bands of Englishmen managed to hold out, killing a number of the attackers before they could be eliminated or persuaded to surrender.

As soon as the batteries were in Spanish hands, several groups of soldiers made their way to the seaward end of the island where the smaller, less defensible English ships were moored. As they ran they noticed that the hulk had failed to grapple with either of the great ships and, being without motive force of her own, was swinging broadside on against the sea wall under the bows of the retreating enemy. Although the English ships had cut their headfasts and were hauling themselves clear, only a few yards separated them from the land, and their guns commanded the foreshore. In the fighting-tops the English marksmen forced the soldiers on board the hulk to keep below decks, and a murderous fire of dice-shot greeted any attempt by the Spaniards to rush down the line of mooring berths and overrun the small craft. The check was temporary, and before long the two English ships had withdrawn to less effective range for their light armament; but it was sufficient time for most of the remaining ships to cast off and evade capture. They prevented one vessel from escaping and took her intact, but it was galling to watch six others hauling themselves away, hoisting their yards preparatory to setting sail, and firing defiantly with all the guns they could bring to bear.

Cooped impatiently between decks on Diego Felipe's hulk the two admirals of Spain, who had so notably failed to perform the task demanded of them, fretted impatiently. They had been instructed to grapple and overwhelm first the *Minion* and from her the *Jesus*. Instead they were swinging slowly and helplessly at the mercy of their enemies' guns. Their situation was uncomfortable and not without its dangers. Although the hulk was massive and well able to withstand the desultory bombardment that she attracted, she was not the most urgent target for the English gunners. Before long it became possible to secure her alongside once again, and both Luxan and Ubilla, feeling an urgent need to redeem themselves in the eyes of the Viceroy, cast about to find means whereby they might influence the course of battle. The two hundred men who had manned the hulk had no such qualms. Without waiting to receive instructions they streamed ashore, swelling the ranks of the assault parties who swirled aimlessly over the already subdued island.

Before he had a chance to regain his own ship Ubilla saw her blown up and the wreckage of her upper works swept with fire. Those on board who had survived the explosion jumped ashore and she was abandoned at her moorings. From one of his crew Ubilla learnt that more than thirty men were unaccounted for and were presumed to have been killed. To Ubilla the hazards of war were nothing new, and while the fight was on he allowed himself no pause for repining. Later there would be time to assess his losses, and he foresaw that they would be grievous. The destruction of friends and possessions made him all the more anxious to save his honour. With desperate energy he turned his attentions to the business of making war.

The sight of smoke billowing down-wind from his burning ship brought to mind an old stratagem, often used to dislodge a well-placed enemy, that might prove effective in the confined waters of San Juan, and for which, if it should be successful, he could claim a full measure of glory. Summoning a mulatto who stood nearby, he led the way down the line of merchantmen until he found a small craft directly upwind of the English ships. At his direction the mulatto procured two barrels of powder, and between them they heaped up inflammable materials and laid a train. It was all done in haste and they loosed the boat from its moorings before the fire on board was properly established. As she drifted into the harbour they saw the flames smoulder and die.

Before he had time to organize a second fireship Ubilla was hailed by name from the forecastle of the *Capitana*. Turning towards the flagship he saw the navigating officer crouching behind cover, for the upper decks were raked with fire from the English fighting-tops. He implored the vice-admiral to come to the succour of Don Martin, who had been abandoned by his men yet resolutely remained on board despite the danger. Obedient to his sense of duty Ubilla abandoned his activities and hastily set about the task of recruiting some of the many hundreds of men who, leaderless, had sought safety on land. They were reluctant to return to the flagship, which was so evidently the main target of the English guns, and invented a score of imperative reasons for avoiding Ubilla's conscription. At length, with many threats, a band of reinforcements was assembled, and before they could melt away Ubilla drove them unwillingly aboard the *Capitana*.

The ship was almost deserted and in places the wreckage was catastrophic. Between decks the daylight filtered through ragged holes in the timbers and lit up the destructive havoc that the sakers and culverins had caused. Stores, guns and personal goods lay in forlorn abandon, and the bitter smell of saltpetre and charred wood permeated the air.

Scrambling as quickly as he could through the gloomy labyrinth, Ubilla made his way aft to the Viceroy's cabin. It was as deserted as the rest of the ship, and being at the nearest point to the English guns was jarred and shaken by the impact of every salvo that was fired. Still searching for Don Martin, Ubilla retreated to the *plaza de armas*, the lowest part of the upper deck between the towering bastions of forecastle and poop. Here, where the soldiers would assemble before a boarding operation at sea, Ubilla discovered the Viceroy, in full armour and outwardly composed, with a few members of his staff around him. He was relatively protected where he stood with his back to the mainmast, but his view of the battle was restricted. From time to time he ordered a man to step to a higher vantage place where he could report the progress of the battle. An observer thus exposed always drew the fire of enemy marksmen, and while Ubilla was talking to the Viceroy one such man came tumbling down to cover after the pike he was carrying had been shot from his hand.

At the Viceroy's request Ubilla described the course of the battle. The failure of his own manoeuvres he sketched over lightly, but dwelt at length on the success that had attended the operations ashore. Undoubtedly, he claimed, it was a victory, and in a short while it would be complete. Although he heard him out Don Martin was far from satisfied with this optimistic account. Since the start of the action he had been harassed by his enemies' guns and his fighting ships irreparably damaged. It was intolerable that a Lutheran pirate should humiliate him, and through him the Kingdom of Spain and the true Faith. Where, he demanded, was General Luxan, and why had the batteries on the island not been brought to bear on the enemy? Vice-Admiral Ubilla was dispatched ashore to investigate.

General Luxan had not been idle since escaping from Diego Felipe's hulk. He made his way across the shingle to inspect the newly-captured gun positions, passing as he went small groups of English prisoners under guard, and an ever increasing number of his own men, unofficered and purposeless, who had drifted ashore and added to the prevalent air of confusion on the small island. A number he ordered back to their ships, but as many again took their place. Cursing their ill-discipline Luxan came to the House of Lies where the last resistance had just been overcome. He was gratified to find that in the suddenness of the attack the Englishmen had neglected to spike the guns. The batteries were intact, and as some of the pieces had never been fired there was ample powder and shot besides. All that was needed was to find experienced gunners, retrain the weapons against the English ships, and throw up earthworks in this new direction to protect them from return fire. There were plenty of soldiers who could be organized for this work, and having put it in hand Luxan sought out Delgadillo, instructing him to do likewise at one of the other batteries.

Progress was swift, and before Ubilla found him to deliver the Viceroy's message Luxan had opened fire against the enemy. A few minutes later Delgadillo's battery joined in the bombardment. From that moment the island was never silent long. One gun thundered after another, leaping backwards in its shallow pit. Through the drifting smoke the crew closed in with sponge and rammer, thrust a new charge down the muzzle, hauled the carriage forward, and trained it afresh. Again and again the slow rhythm was repeated. There was no dearth of targets. The English ships had not hauled themselves far, and the range was short enough to bring every shot home.

But a duel by gunfire between pertinacious adversaries was

seldom determined quickly. Only the smallest pieces of ordnance were speedy to reload. The weightier guns spoke infrequently, despite the untiring attention of their crews. Unless dismasted by some freak of chance or, as in the case of the *Almirante*, blown up, a great ship was expected to withstand as well as to give punishment, and could endure over a period of hours the laboured ravages of firepower equal to her own. The damage and the casualties would accumulate, but slowly, and, as long as she retained her mobility, in God's good time. Similarly ashore; a well-entrenched battery might expect to survive a direct bombardment. The earthworks would absorb the iron round-shot that alone could destroy a gun unless, by a hazard beyond the skill of any gunlayer, a direct hit was obtained.

Thus between ship and shore a long, intermittent, but nonetheless implacable, duel developed which continued long after the sun had passed its zenith and, in a daze of heat, dipped westward towards Orizaba, whose snow-cone, unnaturally bright, stood out against the lucid sky.

The *Jesus* was lying about two lengths away from the Spanish ships when the first shots from the island hit her. She was an easy target, and Hawkins was disturbed to see that the gunners were firing chain-shot for the most part, in an attempt to dismast the English vessel before she could make good her escape. As he watched each shot strike home, and felt the wooden bulwarks around him wrench and shudder at the impact, Hawkins realized that he was far too exposed and lacking in mobility to stand and fight. He ordered his guns to engage the land batteries and ignore the huddle of half-wrecked shipping into which they had been hurling their shot. And he exhorted the men at the capstan to still greater efforts. The alum-drenched fighting sails were bent ready for hoisting, but the wind was blowing up from the north and the *Jesus* was not yet sufficiently clear of obstruction to cut her cable and rely on her sails for safety.

The other ships of the English fleet that had succeeded in casting off from the island were in the same condition of perilous suspense. Drake's little vessel, the *Judith*, was the first to get clear. Being at the end of the mooring line she had attracted little attention from the Spanish guns, and as she was virtually un-armed could concentrate her efforts on saving herself. Under sail she made her way out of range and anchored in a sheltered position until the outcome of the battle was decided.

The two smallest ships had been less fortunate. The caravel captured from the Portuguese in the River Cacheo was damaged and hastily abandoned by her prize crew. The *Angel*, just as she was preparing to cast loose, was holed at the water-line by a round-shot and sank speedily in deep water. A few of the men were able to save themselves by swimming to the larger ships.

The *Grace of God* and the *Minion*, exchanging shot for shot with the Spanish batteries, seemed, despite some damage, to be hauling themselves away to safety. The towering upper-works of the *Jesus* gave them protection from certain quarters, which they gratefully took. Although Hawkins willingly offered his flagship as a shield his own retreat was slowed down by the unwieldy nature of his ship. The *Jesus* was not agile in close manoeuvring, and this weakness, together with the flag she flew, made her the chief target for the island guns. Her own response was limited partly by a choppy sea that made accurate gunlaying difficult, and partly by an inability, that she would not have suffered under sail, to bring both broadsides to bear. *This is nonsense!*

Standing in the waist near the foremast, Hawkins began to be alarmed by the reports he received of the havoc that was being caused on board. He was careful to conceal his feelings from the crew. To those who saw him, or heard his voice bellowing orders and encouragement above the hubbub, he seemed buoyant and confident. The close-counselled, shrewd negotiator was trans-formed magically into a man of war. His armour had been brought to him on deck when the action commenced, and he was now easy to identify as he strode from one vantage point to another. Wherever he went his bearing coloured the action of his followers and bred an enthusiasm that even the round-shot of the enemy could not quench.

The shipwrights reported that the mainmast had been struck in several places and was dangerously weak. Hawkins hastened to

× Hortop puts it much more vigorously; "He...... willed the Gunners to stand by their Ordinance lustily like men."

THE FIGHT AT SAN JUAN

inspect the damage. As he went he called Samuel, his negro page, demanding a tankard of beer, for the weight of his armour and the oppressiveness of the day had made him thirsty. The drink was brought in a silver cup, and Hawkins, lifting it in the sight of those around him, toasted the gunners and urged them to re-double their efforts. He set down the empty cup and a second later a cannon-ball struck it away, along with a carpenter's plane that stood beside it. Only a couple of feet had stood between Hawkins and destruction. The men who had paused a moment to watch him drinking were aghast, but they found their captain as calm as ever. 'Have no fear,' he enjoined them in a voice that never wavered, 'for God, who has preserved me from this shot, will also deliver us from these traitors and villains.'

A message was whispered in his ear and Hawkins hurried off. A chain-shot, aimed high against the rigging, had severed the foremast just below the hounds.

The length of the upper deck was scarred and splintered by shot. The blinders had been half shot away. Several stays had been cut through and lay with ravelled ends where they had fallen. Under foot the water, slopped from the tubs beside each gun, mingling with spilt gunpowder gave off a bitter smell. Discarded weapons, clothes and occasional streaks of blood, told their own story of death and of those who lay wounded in the cockpit low down in the bows, awaiting the surgeon's ministrations.

As he made his way forward to inspect the damage, Hawkins shouted encouragements to the guns' crews. These groups of four (more surely) weary and unrecognizably-grimed men had been living ever since the fight started in isolated, hectic worlds of their own. They scarcely knew how the battle progressed. Briefly, as the gunport was opened they glimpsed their target, the piece was trained and fired, they leapt back to avoid the recoil and were engulfed in choking smoke. Then the ports were closed again to protect them, and in the half-dark, with ears singing from the explosion, they sponged down, reloaded and hauled their gun back into position. So intent were they upon their work that they hardly noticed the return fire. Occasionally they broke off to smother a smouldering timber set alight by incendiary shot. Or a grenade

+ This is all wrong. The Spaniards had neither the facilities or the time to heat shot, and and shells were not in common use.

THE DEFEAT OF JOHN HAWKINS

would burst nearby sending its deadly splinters into the barricade of mattresses and bales of cloth that they had piled around them.⨯ Now and then an unlucky shot burst in the midst of them; but before the dead and dying could be hauled away a fresh crew was ready to recharge the gun.

There was not a man idle. Even the cooks and stewards were employed carrying loads of powder and shot from the magazines to replenish the lockers beside each gun, and sprinkling sand on the slippery deck. The shipwrights' parties were scattered throughout the ship patching the most dangerous shot-holes, particularly those near the water-line, with lead sheeting and plugs of oakum. From the exposed upper deck, under the boatswain's directions, seamen were going aloft to reeve fresh stays and shrouds.

Twelve men had died when the foremast fell, and the ruin of wood and cordage had not been cut clear when Hawkins reached the scene. He realized at once that with the foremast down, and the mainmast so weakened by shot that it would not stand the strain of canvas, the *Jesus* was incapable of escaping. She had hauled herself as far out from the island as her cable permitted, but she was still well within range of the shore batteries. For a time she could continue to resist, but not for long.

There was nothing he could do on the forecastle. He ordered that the flag of St. George, which had fallen with the mast, should be hoisted again on the stump. Then he looked outboard to see how the remnant of his fleet was faring. The *Minion* and the *Judith* were clear of immediate danger. The French ship was also clear and had hoisted sail, but was performing a strange, un-accountable manoeuvre. Instead of anchoring out of range like the others, the *Grace of God* was beating up wind in an attempt, Hawkins could only conclude, to escape by the northern channel. It was an almost impossible feat in view of the strengthening wind, and she was running the gauntlet of a good deal of shot. Even as he watched, Hawkins saw her sails shiver and fold and the whole mainmast, struck off at deck level, crash overboard. Before she could drift far an anchor was dropped, and from the smoke that billowed out in several places it seemed that she was being set on fire to prevent her falling into enemy hands. After a while her pinnace was launched and the entire crew rowed over to the *Jesus* and boarded her on the lee side.

Hawkins, furious at the Frenchman's conduct, summoned Captain Bland and rated him for running away. But Bland defended himself vigorously. His intention, he said, was not to escape, but to claw his way up-wind of the Spanish ships at anchor, grapple with the weathermost, and at the same time set fire to the *Grace of God*. By this means, if he had succeeded, the fortune of battle might have been reversed and all the Spanish fleet destroyed by fire. He did not deserve rebuke for the ill-chance of having failed.

Hawkins did not pursue the argument; there were many more urgent matters to attend to. The afternoon was by now well advanced, and the position of the three remaining vessels was becoming untenable. How long the *Jesus* could continue to defend herself was uncertain, but he knew that she would never be able to leave the harbour again. His only hope of escape lay in the *Minion*, and he saw with anxiety that she was still the object of long-range bombardment from the island. It was essential that until nightfall she should be protected from any further damage. The only available screen was the *Jesus* herself.

At Hawkins' command John Hampton weighed anchor and brought the *Minion* alongside the *Jesus*. No sooner was she in position than Drake followed suit and secured the *Judith* under the lee of the *Minion*. The towering flank of the crippled flagship concealed and protected them from every hostile gun. Acknowledging defeat, the Englishmen used the respite they had achieved to salvage what they could from the *Jesus* and prepare for an orderly retreat by night. Food and water were the first essentials. The provision rooms were thrown open and working parties carried the remnants of their store over into the *Judith*. Tools and equipment followed after, and some of the bulkier purchases and trading goods that lay in the holds. In their urgency some men snatched what was most essential, others what was nearest to hand. There was no hope of transferring everything of value. Before very long the little *Judith* was laden as deeply as was considered safe. Hawkins told Drake to cast off and anchor at

John Hawkins and Francis Drake

the harbour mouth, where he would join him as soon as the *Minion* was ready. The *Judith* set sail, and the evacuation of goods and possessions into the *Minion* continued apace. It seems unlikely that he neglected to transfer from his cabin most of the small chests and bags that contained the wealth of gold and silver coin accumulated in trade, nor would Hawkins have forgotten his books and instruments of the sea. But a great trunk full of silver plate proved too heavy to move, and many of his belongings and the luxurious fitments that he provided at his own expense were left behind.

To shift all articles of value from one ship to another inevitably took time. A start had been made; the crew swarmed through the dark labyrinths below, ransacking and passing up on deck bundles of personal gear and every scrap of food; but much had to be abandoned. The last forty-five negro slaves were not trans-shipped, neither were the Spanish hostages. Provisions were too short to share with them, and there was no good use to which they could now be put. It was intended to transfer the wounded last of all. All those who could not walk lay close together on strips of sailcloth, enduring their private agonies in the hot, evil-smelling gloom of the cockpit. But before their companions were ready to lift them into the *Minion* the last act in the battle cut short their preparations, and in a surge of panic they were all abandoned to the enemy.

Twice already during the fight a fireship had been devised. In neither case had it been a success. Now the Spaniards at last succeeded in igniting a fair-sized ship and set her adrift upwind of the two English ships. She was ablaze from stem to stern and the freshening wind drove her like a floating holocaust directly at the *Minion*. Smoke and showers of sparks preceded her, and when, from time to time, a powder-barrel exploded, a sheet of flame flared up. To the tired and dispirited English sailors she seemed like an inexorable symbol of doom. In the gathering dusk the flames that obscured her outline blazed with unnatural brilliance, and gusts of hot air fanned the panic-stricken faces of the watchers on the English decks.

Hawkins and his most experienced fellow officers were least

disturbed by this development. They knew that despite the terror of its appearance a fireship seldom caused actual damage. But it required strong nerves to wait, half-blinded by choking smoke and scorched by fire, until the floating torch had blundered its way past, or to fend it off with long poles if it threatened to lodge alongside. The English seamen were too demoralized by defeat and a day of unremitting combat to endure such a trial. Spontaneously, without awaiting orders, the crew of the *Minion* slipped the ropes that secured her to the *Jesus*, and with desperate energy scrambled aloft to cut the lashings that held the heavy sails furled at the yards.

Seeing the *Minion* about to cast off, a number of men from the *Jesus* threw down their loads and leapt over the rails in order not to be left behind. Panic began to spread. Confused by the shouting and the smoke each man, determined to save himself, jostled for a place to jump on to the *Minion's* deck. At first Hawkins attempted to stem the tide. He ordered the *Minion* not to move, and tried to stop his terrified crew from boarding her. But his voice went unheard, and it was soon apparent that he no longer had authority over his men. The rumour of sudden flight had swept over the *Jesus*. The gunners abandoned their weapons intact; there was no shipwright left to scuttle her. Only in the *Minion* lay a hope of safety, and already she was edging her way clear of the flagship without waiting for late-comers.

Bewildered and ignored, Hawkins' eleven year old nephew Paul, who had sailed as his uncle's page, stood on the deck of the *Jesus* clutching a rich goblet and a plate of fine crystal studded with precious stones and pearls that he had been instructed to carry across to the *Minion*. But 'while holding them in his hands ready to jump he saw an Englishman killed and being afraid that he might be killed . . . he threw the plate and goblet into the sea and stayed on board'.

Unaware that his nephew had not preceded him, and seeing there was no alternative, John Hawkins stumbled through the enveloping smoke and leapt across the narrow gap that now separated the two ships.

With the wind filling her shot-torn sails the *Minion* quickly steered clear of the fireship's path. She paused long enough to pick up a last boatload of men, who rowed out to join her from the *Jesus*, then fled to the extremity of the harbour where the *Judith* already lay at anchor. The fireship, they observed, drifted harmlessly past the *Jesus*. But there was no question of going back. It remained to be seen how far forward their luck would carry them, against a rising north wind and a perilous sea.

CHAPTER 12

The Homecoming of the *Minion*

THE gathering darkness silenced all guns. Although the two surviving English ships were known to have anchored within range of the heavier pieces ashore, their outline could not be discerned and they showed no lights. Exhilarated by their success in clearing the corsairs from San Juan the Spaniards would have liked to follow up the retreating enemy. But their best fighting vessels were burnt out or sunk, and the armed merchantmen that had survived were too deeply-laden and slow to be employed. As the night wore on an added peril confirmed their resolve to be content with what had already been achieved. The norther that had been threatening all day began to blow in earnest at midnight. If they did not drag their anchors the English vessels had some protection where they lay, but by daylight they would again become easy targets. If they attempted to escape from the harbour they would almost certainly be blown ashore on the coastal reefs of La Caxa. The Viceroy organized a troop of horsemen to ride down the coast from San Juan to round up any shipwrecked survivors, and waited confidently for daybreak to complete his victory.

The dawn of Friday September 24th disclosed one unexpected development during the night. The smaller of the two English ships, Francis Drake's *Judith*, had disappeared. At first it was assumed that she had been driven ashore, but no wreckage was sighted and gradually the explanation that she had escaped from the harbour before the full fury of the wind set in gained credence. Her flight was of little consequence to the Spaniards, who did not attach to the name of her young captain the dread that in later years it grew to deserve. The shallop that had escaped was of little more than 50 tons burthen; the ship that remained was the more worthy prize.

But as the batteries on the island prepared to reopen the bombardment the Englishman was seen to be on the move. To escape from her anchorage into the open sea was deemed to be a desperate act. With storm-sails set she sped over the confused waters, her deck canted and awash as she struggled to keep her head away from the reefs on to which she was driven by the howling wind. It was a grim, tense battle for survival and for many minutes the issue was in doubt. To the watchers on the island it seemed that the ship was running along the very line of surf that marked the rocks. But her shallow draught, the press of sail that she had risked setting and a measure of good luck preserved her. Gradually she gained ground and was seen to have come under the lee of an offshore island where she anchored, and, for the remainder of the day, rode out the storm from that uneasy shelter.

In the harbour of San Juan, undisturbed by the tempest that was raging around them, the Spaniards were tasting the fruits of victory. A boarding party headed by the two admirals had rowed across to the English flagship as soon as she ceased to defend herself and, against expectation, found their hostages alive and unmolested. They took possession of the ruined *Jesus* in the name of the King. Luxan left Ubilla in charge, and the ransacking of all valuables that Hawkins had commenced continued under the encouragement of the vice-admiral of Spain.

Ubilla regarded the personal effects on board the *Jesus* as his for disposal, since by his action he had been instrumental in capturing her intact. When the battle was at its height he had sought out the owner of one of the less seaworthy ships at the moorings, negotiated a purchase price, and caused her to be cut adrift. This time success had rewarded him; his fireship had broken up the English fleet's last stand. But although the looting of clothes and trinkets was a matter for indulgence, Ubilla's conscience was troubled by the wholesale appropriation that Agustin de Villanueva began to conduct immediately he was released from his confinement. Before the vice-admiral was aware of what was happening Villanueva had ferried seventeen of the best remaining slaves ashore, as well as a chest—suspected of containing treasure—that was smuggled out of the *Jesus* covered over by an embroidered cloth. Ubilla had him arrested, but to his disgust the Viceroy, whom he darkly suspected of complicity, ordered his release. Soon afterwards Ubilla was relieved of his duties on board the *Jesus*, but not before he had seen the rest of the slaves and many bales of trading goods quietly conveyed ashore.

His expostulations were ill-timed, and even his friends considered them untactful. By choosing to fall out with the man who wielded the King's power Ubilla lost the support of all his fellow officers. When he returned to the fleet and found his own ship gutted by fire he sought in vain a suitable alternative vessel from which to fly his flag. At length he appropriated the *Swallow*, an unpretentious command for a vice-admiral, but one of the few ships that had sustained no damage during the engagement. Not long afterwards he learnt from the gossip that went round how, far from being praised for his part in the battle, he was being publicly condemned for having given the signal to engage the enemy too soon and without authority.

General Luxan, who had returned to the *Jesus* the day after the battle in company with the Public Scrivener for the purpose of making an inventory, was also instructed by the Viceroy to return to his own flagship. Unlike Ubilla he was careful to obey with good grace, and the Scrivener went with him though his task had not been completed.

Don Martin very evidently regarded the prizes as his particular charge and would not tolerate the slightest interference. He commanded Captain Delgadillo to take possession of the captured vessels, and keep the pumps working lest they sank at their moorings. At the Viceroy's instructions Delgadillo made ready for an immediate public auction of all the ships, together with their anchors, rigging and sails. The ordnance, in many ways the most valuable part of the booty, was not included. It was intended that the guns should be landed and used to augment the defences of the island.

As he was impatient to depart for Mexico Don Martin allowed

little time for the news of the sale to be spread. Vice-Admiral Ubilla was ordered to strike his flag only three days after he had raised it in the *Swallow*, for this vessel was to be sold along with the three others that remained afloat. Only one ship wrested from the English escaped the hammer. The *Angel* lay, valueless, beneath the waters of the harbour.

The first auction, held on Sunday, September 26th, at the House of Lies in full view of the scene of battle, was ill-attended and drew no bids. A second was arranged next day, but again the response from the ship-owners and merchants of Vera Cruz was poor. One offer of 300 ducats was made for the *Jesus* and 200 ducats was bid for the Portuguese caravel that Hawkins had brought from Africa—a handy vessel for coastal trade and relatively unscarred by the fighting.

The Viceroy was dissatisfied and ordered Delgadillo to withdraw the ships. An accountant in the government, service was appointed to prepare a comprehensive inventory, and two experienced seamen were given the task of surveying the *Jesus*. In particular the Viceroy wished to make sure that Hawkins' flagship was indeed beyond repair. Although dismasted, leaking, and riddled with shot she still bore the appearance of a noble and powerful fighting ship. Many who observed her as she lay offshore, not least the disgruntled Spanish vice-admiral, declared that she should be made serviceable and sent back to join the royal armadas of Spain. The two surveyors reported otherwise. The English flagship could, they said, be patched up, but only at a cost of four thousand ducats, which was more than she was worth.

Strengthened by their opinion, the Viceroy for the third time authorized Delgadillo to sell the ships by auction. October 1st was the chosen day, and there were to be no reserve prices. News of the sale had spread and more bids were registered. In the end the *Jesus* was knocked down for 300 ducats, the *Grace of God* for 200 ducats, the *Swallow* for 300 ducats and the Portuguese caravel for 400 ducats. After the proceedings were over a latecomer arrived who declared himself willing to increase the bid for the *Jesus*. Twice more the auction was reopened, and eventually Hawkins' old flagship was sold for 601 ducats. Her value undoubtedly lay in her parts and her equipment. Although history does not record her end it is easy to imagine her, stripped of all gear, waterlogged and cavernous, abandoned like Diego Felipe's hulk at the moorings of San Juan. The guns she carried had more various fates, and became in time scattered throughout the Indies. Four years later the embossed Tudor rose that adorned one of them was recognized on a demi-culverin that had been carried 100 leagues overland to Tecoantepec on the Pacific coast.

The disposal of the relics of battle was only one of the occupations that busied those in authority at San Juan during the last days of September. It was necessary, in view of the gravity of the incident, to establish by legal deposition a precise account of the battle and all that led to it. The Viceroy summoned the notary from Vera Cruz and for four days, while events were fresh in the mind, he conducted a court of enquiry before which all those principally concerned gave evidence and were interrogated. Don Martin himself opened the proceedings, and from his statement and the slant of subsequent examinations his purpose became clear. If there was blame to be allotted, either for the incompleteness of the victory or for the disastrous casualties in ships and men that the power of Spain had suffered, Vice-Admiral Ubilla stood responsible. Every deponent took his colour from the Viceroy; only Ubilla himself protested that he acted within his authority in giving the signal to attack which, though premature, was better than inaction.

Enraged, but helpless under injustice, Ubilla had to content himself with writing a personal letter to his Sovereign setting forth his version of the story, and implying by innuendo the incompetent, high-handed and corrupt practices of his august superior. But there was no ship available to carry either the official report or the vice-admiral's complaint across the western ocean to the Castilian Court. For several months north winds in the Gulf and Atlantic gales cut off all means of communication. When the weather relented enough to allow ships to sail Don Martin was firmly established as proconsul in Mexico, and the passage of time had softened the urgency of recrimination.

The Viceroy made haste, as soon as his investigations were

completed, to leave the coastal settlements and start the long overland ride to his capital. He was met at the outset by a band of
two hundred levies sent down by the authorities in Mexico to
render aid should any prove necessary. A larger force, with
artillery drawn laboriously on carts, had been prepared, but was
disbanded as soon as news of the arrival of the *flota* reached the
city. The token force, although it arrived too late for the fighting,
served as a useful escort on the return journey.

As an earnest of his coming Don Martin had sent ahead, under
strict guard, the contingent of Englishmen captured at San Juan.
They travelled slowly on foot, a ragged, pathetic group of men.
The Viceroy with his mounted escort overtook them at Jalapa,
the first inland settlement on the road, at the edge of the hills.
Here, before hastening forward, Don Martin paused to complete
his official records by interrogating Robert Barrett, the leader of
the captive party.

The halt was providential, for the hard road to Mexico was
taking its toll of the English sailors. All articles of value had
been stripped from them, and their clothes were pitifully inadequate against the extremes of climate that they encountered.
The track led from the humid, fever-ridden coast, through
jungle, over snow-swept passes and along barren plains of cactus
and stone. Many of the men were wounded and could scarcely
walk; others had endured ill-treatment and even torture from captors
made cruel in the flush of victory. Those who fell by the wayside
from exhaustion or wounds were never seen again.

Robert Barrett, young as he was, assumed the burden of leadership. He endured with them, rallied them when they flagged and
interceded with the guards on their behalf. He kept them alive
as best he could and tried not to contemplate what the future held
in store. Rescue or escape were chances too remote to dwell upon,
but time and again the captives drew courage from a single fact,
Hawkins and the *Minion* had escaped, and their captain never
forgot his shipmates. Throughout the long march, and the
captivity that followed, each prisoner nourished that small hope;
and was sustained by imagining Hawkins, devious and determined
as ever, working to set him free.

For many days after his escape from the harbour of San Juan Hawkins was far too preoccupied with the fate of the *Minion* to give much attention to those who were already past his help. For twenty-four hours he lay at anchor under the lee of the Isla Sacrificios. If the harbour of San Juan had seemed to offer a perilous security against the fury of the north wind, this isolated off-shore reef, almost invisible under the fume of the driven sea, scarcely afforded any protection from the elements.

In the previous day's fighting the *Minion* had lost three hawsers and two anchors. To ride out the norther Hawkins had no more than two anchors remaining. He veered them as far as their cables would permit and prayed that they would hold fast. All that day, and most of the night that followed, Hawkins stood beside the anchor watch while the wind screamed at them and the ship bucketed at her moorings. The two thin strands that held the *Minion* steadfast were stretched almost to breaking point. The hawsers quivered and sang, and streams of water were wrung out of the taut fibres.

The pumps were never silent, for the storm searched diligently to enlarge the ill-repaired ravages of battle. There were shot-holes leaking water, and timbers wrenched apart by the strain of gun-fire, in every quarter of the ship. The men on board were wet, overcrowded and hungry; but mercifully their vigil did not last long. By Saturday morning the north wind had blown itself out and a gentle breeze from the south-east replaced it. The *Minion* weighed anchor and fled, carrying with her two hundred souls and the grievous tale of the foundering of a great enterprise.

She fled from peril into peril. Although Hawkins shaped a confident northerly course, he was sailing an unseaworthy ship through unknown waters in a season of treacherous winds. He carried twice his normal complement and had almost no food or water to keep them alive. There were no harbours nearby where he could seek provisions or security, and none in the whole Indies where his weakness would not be immediately apparent.

Fourteen days they spent at sea; comfortless desperate and hungry days during which they made little progress. The men had no spirit left to endure privation. The crew of the *Minion* began to resent the presence of the men from the *Jesus* and the Frenchmen from the *Grace of God*. Quarrels sprang up, and from them grew the seeds of mutiny. Hawkins watched these developments helplessly. The provisions were almost consumed—two ounces of bread was the daily ration and even with frugal use water would not last much longer. In their extremity they broke into the cargo of hides purchased in Curaçao, cut them up and boiled them until they were soft enough to chew. Rats and mice were hunted and trapped for food. Dogs and cats, parrots and monkeys, once prized as pets, were now killed and eaten. The tyranny of starvation gripped all men alike. They obeyed orders sullenly, and spent their time combing the ship for anything that could assuage the cramps of hunger, quarrelling fiercely over the division of spoils. 'To be short,' wrote one of the survivors, recollecting the misery of those two long weeks, 'our hunger was so great, that wee thought it savourie and sweete whatsoever wee could get to eate.'

As the days dragged by it became evident that they would never reach the islands unless they could first get water. The mutterings of the seamen reinforced Hawkins' decision to turn westward and strike the Mexican coast again, where there was a chance of filling their empty barrels. A faction amongst the crew now spoke openly, saying that it would be better to give themselves up to the Spaniards rather than die of hunger and thirst in freedom. Others declared that they would trust their fortune among the Indian tribes ashore. Reluctantly Hawkins did nothing to dissuade them. With a normal complement and a measure of good luck he believed he could nurse the *Minion* back to England. But with two hundred mouths to feed death and disease would turn the voyage into a catastrophe.

When, on October 8th, the low-lying, unprotected coast was sighted Hawkins brought the *Minion* as near inshore as was prudent. The land shelved gradually, making it impossible to approach closer than a mile or two to the beach. A pinnace was lowered into the water and the haggard, hunger-pinched company were summoned on deck. They gathered in the waist around the mainmast, and Hawkins spoke to them with the blunt authority that he could command at moments of crisis. He told them that, by his reckoning, they were near the River Panuco at the mouth of which there was a Spanish settlement. If any men wished to go ashore he would not deter them. He, and those who chose to stay with him, would sail on. If they succeeded in making an English landfall he promised to return the following year and rescue those who had remained behind. The choice was free, and the alternatives equally perilous and honourable. A few men whom it was essential to retain on board were excluded; the rest were told to divide. Those who wished to stay were to assemble aft; those who intended to land should group themselves round the foremast.

It was a hard choice. Many of those who had been most vocal in demanding to be set ashore stood irresolute and confused. There was a rising clamour of voices; groups of friends argued between themselves, others watched eagerly to see who moved one way, who the other. Gradually the knot of men amidships drifted apart. When a muster-roll was taken it was found that the numbers were almost equally divided.

There was no time for lengthy farewells. Hawkins went on to the forecastle, embraced each man and commended the party to God's care. He offered money to those who desired it, and a length of coloured cloth for trading with any Indians they might encounter. There was little more that he could give. He advised them to leave behind all books and papers as they would certainly fall under suspicion if they were captured, and because their weakness was so apparent he recommended that they should go unarmed, as even a show of force might undo them. One gun for hunting and two swords was all the equipment that they took; they had the clothes they stood up in and no food or water whatsoever. As no officers had chosen, or been allowed, to accompany them they appointed one Anthony Goddard, an experienced west-country sailor with a knowledge of the Spanish tongue, to be their leader.

Two boat-trips were needed to ferry the men ashore. It was a hazardous landing through the surf. The first contingent was beached safely, but the wind had risen by the time the second boatload embarked. John Hampton, the captain of the *Minion* who was piloting the pinnace, decided that he could not risk taking his craft through the surf, and ordered the men to jump out and swim ashore as best they could. They protested, but Hampton was in no mood to be gentle. At his command the boatswain and his mate flogged overboard those who did not obey, and while the fifty men were floundering through the breakers the pinnace turned about and rowed back to the *Minion*. Two men, French sailors from the *Grace of God*, were drowned; the rest struggled ashore and joined their companions who had already landed.

They found little comfort that night. There was water to be had in plenty. Some drank so intemperately that they lost consciousness; others who gorged themselves upon wild fruits writhed and vomited in distended agonies. Meanwhile the rising wind brought with it torrential rain, and those who had escaped a wetting from the sea were soon soaked to the skin. Chilled and faint from the deprivations they had endured on board, the hundred voluntary castaways huddled together in the best shelter they could find upon a little hill overlooking the sea.

They slept fitfully and rose at first light scarcely refreshed. Although they did not know what they sought or how to seek it they were loath to remain where they were. Goddard brought them together and, by consent, they agreed to follow the coast in a southerly direction. They travelled slowly, gathering shellfish and fruit as they went, forcing their way through the rank, luxuriant stretches of reed and flowering grasses that bordered the sea.

Forlorn as they were they did not often look back, and before long the *Minion*, still anchored offshore, was lost from view. In choosing to leave the narrow confinement of their ship they were not actuated by any hope of escape. On every side a hostile land constricted and imprisoned them afresh. By walking blindly forward they could at least enlarge the horizon of their despair and, flattering an irrational vanity, convince themselves that through action they helped to keep alive.

An hour or two after Anthony Goddard had led his men down the coast Hawkins took a boat ashore to fetch water for those who

+ it is a curious reflection that, following Paschal's dict ot Cleopatra's nose, if the cables had been a little weaker

remained on board. He took with him fifty men and all the empty casks he could find. The weather showed no signs of improving and he was anxious to set sail, for every day's delay weakened his chances of survival. Water was easy to find, and before long the barrels were full and they were ready to re-embark. But the surf had grown so boisterous that they dared not launch the boats. In prudence they were obliged to remain ashore where, for three days, they watched the *Minion* riding out yet another storm. This time she had no shelter whatsover, and if her anchors had dragged or the cables parted she would inevitably have been driven ashore. Hawkins fretted impotently, but the baleful streak of good fortune that preserved the *Minion* at the most desperate hour did not desert her now. The storm died down, Hawkins and his precious cargo of water regained the ship, and they risked a further few days' sojourn during which time they foraged ashore for food. On October 16th, the wind being favourable, the *Minion* set sail and headed east.

The three months at sea that ensued would, in normal circumstances, have been accounted an uneventful passage home. But so weakened and ill-equipped for an ocean voyage were both the vessel and her crew that every day seemed unendurable. Only Hawkins, the most reticent of men, has left any account of the prolonged nightmare that he and his hundred men suffered. By the middle of November they had cleared the Florida Channel, having experienced fair weather. But as they reached the Atlantic and beat their course northwards, the mild climate under which they had lived for the past year gave place to more wintery conditions. At the same time the baneful effects of their prolonged starvation began to spread. A profound lassitude engulfed them, and many men complained of swollen limbs and a thirst that the meagre rations of water could not quench. At first they were set to work, for scurvy was considered to breed in idleness; but many of the victims proved incapable of cure by vigorous methods. Old scars reopened, gums rotted, and teeth fell out. The worst cases lay apathetically on their mattresses, with blotched and swollen limbs, freed at last from the desire for food that for so many weeks had obsessed them. Every day or two there were deaths,

[handwritten annotation at top: Hawkins would have been cast away. Had this happened he would have been very lucky to see England again.]

and each time fewer fit men to prepare the body for its sea-grave. Those who were less severely stricken doctored themselves as best they could. They rubbed vinegar on their purulent gums, were bled, purged and scarified, but received little relief. The only cure in which every man had faith lay in the uncorrupt air that blew over the land. There were many weeks to pass before the fortunate survivors would feel its benison.

Not only scurvy but fluxes and burning fevers attacked the defenceless crew of the *Minion*. However much Hawkins tried to raise the men's spirits he found them preoccupied with disease and death. Even the fishing and bird-snaring, undertaken daily to provide a little food, became a burden. Continual starvation had numbed the desire to eat, and life itelf seemed scarcely worth preserving.

Among the ship's company were some to whom even the prospect of reaching England brought no consolation. There had been a dozen negroes on board the *Minion* when she fled from San Juan de Ulua. With the thought that they might yet prove useful in trade Hawkins did not let them ashore near Panuco. They remained on board, where they had been confined for the past year, and endured as best they could. Five of them died, and the fate of only one of the unhappy survivors is recorded.

Had a storm blown up the *Minion* could hardly have resisted the onslaught. There were too few men fit enough to work the sails, and the damage of battle was still unrepaired. But the weather was not extreme, though the wind hampered them in their progress towards England. As a landfall became daily more imperative Hawkins felt obliged to make for the nearest shore rather than risk any extra days at sea. Turning the ship's head away from their homeland, the dwindling band of survivors sought succour where they could expect to be least welcome— the Atlantic coast of Spain. That Hawkins, the most cautious and calculating of sailors, should be so desperate as to expose his weakness in the stronghold of acknowledged enemies in itself testifies to the extremity of his need.

On the last day of the year the gaunt remnant of crew who possessed the strength to come on deck saw before them the grey line of land that they had strained so long to reach. They were weary beyond exaltation; hope had dwindled almost away, and the joy of a landfall was galled by the experience of sufferings endured and comrades dead. Grimly the *Minion* held her course: there was to be no choosing of an anchorage; the first haven that opened before her would serve, and not all the Armadas of Spain would turn her away.

The rocky, indented coast of Galicia yielded her Pontevedra, an isolated seaport, well garrisoned and with a natural anchorage. The *Minion*, arriving in mid-winter from the open sea with patched, weather-stained sails and an unconcealed air of delapidation, must have caused a stir of excitement and speculation ashore. She fired her guns to indicate that she needed assistance, and anchored slowly and clumsily well clear of other ships. Of the many boats that came out to aid her only a few, containing Spanish officials, were allowed alongside, and no man was permitted to come aboard armed. One of the first, and most welcome of visitors, was an English factor, Edward Boronel. He was immediately introduced to Hawkins—a striking, well-dressed man, full-bearded and with a haggard face. Despite protestations that he only travelled as a passenger on the *Minion*, Boronel rightly judged from the respect and honour in which he was held that he exercised complete command.

Food and water were the first essentials for which Hawkins asked, offering ample payment and urging that they be delivered with haste. Glancing around the half-deserted decks Boronel began to appreciate the urgency. Such men as he could see were ill and emaciated, with swollen stomachs and all the symptoms of starvation and scurvy. Others still bore the scars of battle. One of the Spaniards who came aboard reported seeing 'one man who had lost his leg close to the knee, and two more with their heads bandaged'.

Various estimates put the number of observed survivors at between forty and sixty—only about half of those who chose to stay on board and risk the ocean passage from Mexico. Others presumably lay below, too sick to come on deck. A few of these men were landed and taken to Boronel's own house where they

The *Minion*

Actus fidei promet in Hispania celebrator

A Spanish *auto de fe*

could receive better care, and for his pains Hawkins presented him with a negress, one of the poor remnant of his slaves.

Hawkins himself does not seem to have gone ashore, but the dignity of his presence so impressed the Spaniards who visited the *Minion* that they were able to recollect his appearance in some detail when called to do so at a later enquiry. He was, one said, 'youthful, well-dressed with velvet trunk-hose, knitted stockings, and a scarlet leather jacket embellished with silver trimmings, of medium height and of a somewhat dark complexion'. Another added that against the inclemencies of the winter weather he wore 'a pelisse lined with martin's fur, and a large gold chain'. Quite evidently before a man of such nobility the simple Pontevedrans were in awe.

By limiting the number of visitors and dressing his men elegantly Hawkins may have hoped to conceal utter weakness and dire need. But the feverish excitement with which the provision-tenders were greeted and the frantic, fumbling efforts that the sailors made to haul long-dreamt of delicacies aboard, must quickly have betrayed their plight to the curiosity of folk ashore. With victuals at hand all caution was thrown aside. The galley range was lit, the unpalatable broth of stewed hides was thrown aside, and such food as they had not tasted in months was immediately prepared.

Hawkins had not the spirit or the authority to enforce moderation. Certainly neither he nor they realized what ghastly consequences would pursue their intemperate feast. Racking pains or insensibility seized them. Some vomited and survived, but many, weakened past endurance, were destroyed by the bounty of the land. How many of Hawkins' men died in the harbour of Pontevedra it is difficult to say. One report gave the almost incredible number of forty-five, leaving only fifteen who were fated to walk ashore at the journey's end.

Death was a common visitor on shipboard in Hawkins' time. A wastage of men on a long voyage was expected. But the *Minion*, true to her tradition, seemed to have brought almost total disaster to her crew. To Hawkins, a living wraith aboard a ship largely peopled by the dead, the end must have seemed squalid and at hand. At the anchorage, as he nursed his survivors into health, he heard rumours that, their weakness being detected, his ship was likely to be seized at any moment. The peace that prevailed between the two countries did not extend to friendship. Suspicion grew with every day the *Minion* tarried, and only from lack of authority did the Spaniards hesitate to impound her.

With barely a dozen men fit enough to work the ship Hawkins could not go far. But an instinct for preservation urged him to depart. Secretly he weighed anchor and fled with the prevailing wind to Vigo, a few hours sailing round the coast. Here he had hopes that his presence might not yet have been reported.

The wide and deep-set Bay of Vigo was full of shipping. As he anchored Hawkins was gratified to find a few English merchant vessels amongst them. Once again he refrained from letting his men ashore, where their condition might be judged by those whose eyes would be hardened by the sight of want and helplessness. How well he succeeded in his brave deception may be gathered from yet more Spanish accounts of his courtesy and charm. He asked permission to pause and re-equip his ship, and it was granted.

No sooner had Hawkins gained this respite than he turned to the captains of the English merchantmen. To them he was frank and open. He needed a few fit men to supplement his crew and bring the *Minion* back through wintry seas to England. He had the power to enforce his request, but it is doubtful if he used it. A dozen seamen were seconded to his command, and within a day or two Hawkins felt able to undertake the last lap of his ill-fated voyage. On January 20, 1569, the *Minion* cleared the bay of Vigo and set sail for Cornwall.

Two day later, unknown to him, Drake entered Plymouth Sound with the *Judith*, after a voyage from San Juan de Ulua that must have taxed his untried skill in seamanship and command over men to the uttermost. Not a single incident has been recorded of that adventure. Neither the casualties his crew suffered nor the storms that must surely have delayed the progress of the swift-sailing *Judith* are mentioned in any chronicle. Hawkins for his part believed that he had been betrayed and deserted by his kinsman when the *Judith* slipped her anchor and departed from San Juan by night. But if he felt rancour he did not betray it publicly. He realized that whether Drake had stood by him or not the presence of the *Judith* would not have eased the agony of the voyage home.

It was a struggle, even with the help of the reinforcements from Vigo, for the *Minion* to make a landfall. On January 25th she crept unannounced into Mount's Bay, the most westerly haven on the coast. Even if he had wanted Hawkins could not have persuaded his men to sail her further. They had developed a loathing for the ship and desired only to be set ashore.

In the belief that the *Minion* alone had escaped Hawkins wrote on the day of his arrival to his brother in Plymouth, asking him to arrange for a fresh crew to bring the vessel into port. He also wrote to Cecil, stating briefly the misfortunes that had overtaken him and promising a lengthier report as soon as he could come to London. The news of his return was fortunate for rumours of disaster were abroad. Hawkins, it was said, had been attacked and killed in the Indies, and already his brother was urging reprisals against the Spaniards.

But one Spaniard, who found himself the following month a suppliant for Cecil's mercy, proved, ironically enough, to have been a good friend to the expedition. Since the middle of August, when in heavy seas at the mouth of the Florida Channel Hawkins had led his ships northward, nothing had been seen or heard of the *William and John*. Having neglected to change course it was presumed that she had subsequently foundered with all hands. In fact she survived; but once again no account of her movements has been preserved. Presumably she sought shelter after the storm was over, and spent some weeks in a secluded anchorage while her crew busied themselves making her seaworthy and building up a store of provisions. There is a single reference by one of the supercargoes to buying meal at some settlement in the islands, but nothing more.

That her passage back across the ocean was arduous we may judge from the fact that she was found, short of food and far from her intended course, by a Spanish vessel under the command of one Juan de Mendoza. The Spaniard not only furnished the *William and John* with necessities but bore her company to the Azores, where he sheltered the Englishmen from the hostility of the Portuguese by telling a false tale to account for their presence. The two ships continued in company, but a storm engulfed them and drove them relentlessly to the north-east. Off the coast of Ireland Mendoza's ship foundered, and when at length the *William and John* found shelter in an Irish port she carried on board the shipwrecked and penniless crew of her unfortunate escort.

Three of the six original vessels had returned to England, carrying with them a tithe of their crews. The voyage was over and the ships' companies were paid off. When the better weather came the *Minion* was taken to the Medway dockyards, but neither she nor the *William and John* are heard of again. Each vessel had been strained to the uttermost by storm and shot and the insidious boring of the teredo worm. Unlike the men who sailed in them their part in the story was accomplished. Only the *Judith* remained serviceable and retained her place in Hawkins' fleet.

The undertaking itself had not been wholly vain. The trading profits, more than 25,000 gold pesos in all, were carried to London on four laden pack-horses—a galling sight for the Spanish Ambassador who witnessed its arrival.

But for those who studied the diplomatic and military aspects of the expedition there were lessons to be learned and conclusions to be drawn far more valuable to the realm of England than the treasure Hawkins had amassed. The mask of peace and friendship had been stripped from the imperial and Catholic face of Spain. There was to be no tolerance of the Protestant heresy, no freedom of trade within the arrogant boundaries of empire that the Iberian powers had established. With England, to whom trade and seapower were twin arteries for survival, a clash was inevitable. Not, perhaps, for many years, but sooner or later war would grow out of the bitter skirmishes in distant seas. The fight at San Juan gave the policy-makers in Elizabeth's court a warning of what was to come, and a breathing space to prepare for it.

The day-long battle between Hawkins' ships and the fleet of

Don Martin Enriquez had taught the English many vital lessons about Spanish fighting techniques and the strengths and weaknesses of their respective vessels. When, in 1588, Hawkins and Drake harried the Great Armada along the Channel coast, they knew the quality of their opponents and could face them without trepidation. Even the fireships that flushed the Spaniards from their anchorage at Gravelines seemed an echo of the final act in Hawkins' earlier engagement. By the English at least the lessons of San Juan had been taken, in order, twenty years later, to be applied.

Such thoughts were far from Hawkins' mind immediately after the return of the *Minion*. His official reports, his private affairs, and the winding up of the syndicate kept him well occupied. In particular he spent much time preparing for the Court of Enquiry that was held two months after he landed in England. By compiling a detailed valuation of the ships and their contents a sum was agreed that represented the estimated amount of damage that the Spaniards had inflicted on the syndicate. It was a grossly exaggerated figure, but it reflected the seriousness of the loss that Hawkins and his companions considered they had undergone. To have established a claim for £28,000 by agreement with the Admiralty Court was, Hawkins obviously felt, worth while. Legally and morally the wrong he had suffered was officially recognized. And on a more practical basis he was better placed, if the occasion should arise, to make good the depredations of Spain by reprisals of his own.

But for all his business and affairs at home Hawkins' greatest concern was for the men whom he had lost into captivity or exile along the shores of Mexico. They had all of them been under his charge, and if he failed to help them now he would be much to blame. Long and deviously he laboured on their behalf, and in small measure he achieved success; but while their fate remained obscure the chronicles of the voyage could not finally be closed. Like human flotsam the boys and men from his fleet became scattered throughout New Spain and Old. Some disappeared without trace; others, many years later, struggled home, matured by hardship.

As if to commemorate their long sufferings Hawkins chose as

an addition to his coat of arms the staves and scallop-shell of a pilgrim. It is possible to imagine that he accepted these tokens as a symbol of his dogged resolve never to abandon to an obscure fate those men that the companionship of the sea had bound together.

The pilgrims' road had many endings, from the seven cities of Cibola to the stake in the market place of Seville. Secretly Hawkins strove to trace each man and solicit his release; but he kept his counsel well, and only from Spanish documents and the accounts written after their return by three survivors can a picture be established of the strange destiny that overtook a third part of his crew. For his own part Hawkins was not willing to dwell publicly upon misfortune.

'If all the miseries and troublesome affaires of this sorrowfull voyage should be perfectly and throughly written,' he declared in a bitter epitaph to the ill-fated venture, 'there should neede a painefull man with his pen, and as great a time as he had that wrote the lives and deathes of the Martyrs.'

CHAPTER 13

The Overlanders

FOR those who survived, and landed in England from one of the three ships that returned, the adventure was over. But for the hundred castaways who had chosen to chance their luck on the Mexican coast the road home was far from clear. Anthony Goddard had led them on the bleak and rain-drenched morning of October 9th, down the coast towards Panuco. They had forty or fifty miles to walk according to Hawkins' calculations, and at the end they would find a Spanish settlement, which meant internment and an unknown fate. When they set out no one questioned very seriously that this should be their objective. They were hungry, exhausted and bowed down in spirit by their afflictions. Hawkins' cheerful promise to come back in a year's time to pick them up was silently dismissed. The desolate Gulf coast offered them no means of life, and they had neither the tools nor the energy to form a settlement.

As he formed his ragged band of men into marching order and led them forward, three abreast, Goddard must have wondered how many would survive even as far as the river Panuco. It was not easy country to traverse. The shoreline was low and broken with extensive salt-pans and brackish marshes that forced the English sailors to make long detours inland. Where the earth was firm underfoot coarse reeds and grasses engulfed them. At times they used the two swords they had with them to hew a path towards more open ground They marched without caution, for they knew they were defenceless. At times they scattered in the all-absorbing quest for food. Privation had already made them reckless in what they ate—crabs, berries, the pith of reeds were seized upon, but failed to satisfy the ache of hunger.

Even before they broke camp the more observant members of the party realized that they were being watched. As they trudged wearily round the saltines and through the wind-ruffled fields of rushes they knew that at any moment they might be attacked and massacred. When it came the assault was almost a relief.

It found them in a glade at the edge of a wood. The Indians broke from cover on all sides, screaming their battle-cries, and firing a fierce rain of arrows at the undefended sailors. Eight men fell at the first assault and many others were wounded. In the pandemonium that ensued some of the Englishmen started to run, some threw themselves to the ground, while others, dulled by the hopelessness of their plight, stopped in their tracks and waited.

When it was evident that there would be no resistance the Indians held their fire and advanced in silence. In appearance they were hideous. Squat and nearly naked, they had daubed their faces with lines of coloured dye that from a distance almost obscured their features. Their long black hair hung in disordered skeins. As the chieftain of the band came forward Anthony Goddard and John Cornish went to meet him, making gestures of submission.

The Indian spoke a few words of Spanish, and when he learned that Hawkins' men were not of that nation seemed more disposed to parley. His tribe, he informed them, was the Chichimeca, between whom and the Spaniards there was bitter war. By signs he told the Englishmen to sit down; then, pointing at the coloured shirts that several of the men wore, indicated that these should be given to him. There was no option except to agree with good grace; but when some of the Indians made an attempt to strip the men completely John Cornish turned swiftly to remonstrate.

In a flash an Indian boy at the chieftain's side drew his bow. The arrow struck Cornish and killed him instantly. There was a gasp and a movement of men on both sides, but the Indian chief halted them with a word, and, turning to the boy, felled him to the ground with a stroke from his bow. With no sign of emotion he continued the parley with Goddard alone.

It was now evident that apart from robbing them of their coloured clothes the Indians were proposing to let the English party go free. Pointing to the south-west the chief, and several of those around him, repeated 'Tampice, Christiano; Tampice, Christiano', indicating, as far as could be told, that at Tampico, the settlement five miles up the River Panuco, there were Christians who might give them succour. The Indians then led the Englishmen to a nearby clearing where there was a pond of fresh water, and ordered them to remain there. As they understood him the chieftain said that he would go hunting for them and return before long with five or six deer. Or perhaps that was what they hoped he said, for in fact he never came back. A short while later five of the English party strayed outside the clearing, were set upon by the Indians who still secretly kept watch over them, and were stripped naked. But that was the last they saw of these particular Chichimecas. At three o'clock in the afternoon, having grown tired of waiting, Goddard led his men cautiously out of the clearing and resumed the march to the south-west.

To have survived their first encounter with the Indians encouraged some of the braver men to believe that they might yet escape without falling into the hands of their acknowledged enemies the Spaniards. The Frenchmen from the *Grace of God* had probably talked about René de Laudonnière and his Huguenot settlement near the River of May, far to the north on the coast of Florida. Here they might expect to find hospitality without fear of persecution. Any of the English sailors who had been on Hawkins' previous voyage would have remembered calling there, and have witnessed the amity and gratitude that the French garrison displayed; for Hawkins had given them victuals, and sold them a small craft from his own fleet, when their need was dire.

What they might not have realized, for news, even of disaster, travelled slowly across the ocean, was that soon after Hawkins' visit a Spanish fleet had descended on Laudonnière's settlement and wiped it out. There would be no welcome awaiting any overland travellers that succeeded in reaching the River of May, or, for that matter, any other point on the North Atlantic seaboard.

Nonetheless, whether they knew of Laudonnière's fate or not, Goddard was soon aware that a number of the men he was leading had no desire to march any further towards captivity. He called a halt and agreed that the party should divide. He himself would continue on a south-westerly course, taking with him the wounded, the weak and the less adventurous. But about fifty men elected to strike north under the leadership of John Hooper.

Not all the northern party were equally resolute or determined in their course. Two days after they had left their companions they were ambushed by a band of Indians, and before they could demonstrate their peaceful intentions Hooper and two of their number were killed. Leaderless, and appalled by the lonely peril of their situation, they again resolved to separate. James Collier retreated with half the northern party, who had become convinced that only with the Spaniards at Tampico lay any hope of survival, and made to rejoin Anthony Goddard's group. Between twenty and thirty men were undeterred and resumed their northerly course. As leader they chose David Ingram, a common sailor whose gifts of fortitude and resolution were only exceeded by his erratic imagination.

Four days after their first encounter with the Chichimecas Anthony Goddard and his men were set upon by Indians as they were on the point of fording one of the rivers that lay across their route. They offered no resistance and suffered no casualities, but most of the few remaining clothes that they possessed were stripped from them. Having crossed the river they spent the night disconsolately on a nearby stony mound. Owing to the wounded and sick who travelled with them their progress had been slow and for many painful.

Before night fell they heard, a little upstream, a repetition of the blood-chilling sounds of assault that had engulfed them only a few hours previously. Curiosity and fear led them to keep a sharp look-out, and before long they recognized James Collier's group who were seeking to rejoin the main party. They also had been robbed as they approached the river, and lost one man in the attack. The two groups came together and passed the night on the barren hill.

During the hours of darkness they slept fitfully and at first light saw around them a land of flat savannahs and dense woods; an ordeal that seemed to have no end. With their backs to the sun they trudged forward, taking turns to beat a path through thickets, and enduring the lacerations of thorns and sword-sharp grasses against their naked skin.

In a clumsy attempt to protect themselves from these discomforts and from the burning sun, they fashioned garments out of leaves and plaited grass. But the protection was flimsy and in no way deterred their most persistent enemies, the mosquitos and venemous flies that sucked blood and settled in black clouds upon the running sores and cuts that disfigured every limb.

The constant irritation and swellings caused by these bites drove most of the men nearly mad, and exhausted them in vain efforts to protect their nakedness. Only at night did they obtain respite, when they lay, supperless, under the stars, brooding upon their pain and listening fearfully to the small noises that came to them out of the surrounding darkness. Wild guavas and a few roots kept them alive. Water they found from time to time, but often they suffered intolerable thirst because they lacked all means of storing it, and the sun burnt over them with torrid heat.

Not a day went by without an encounter with the Indians. At no time were they free from observation. Often shadowy, quickly-moving shapes could be seen passing from tree to tree a bowshot or more away. The signals and calls these scouts made to one another became at length as natural as the warning cries of the birds and the rustle of animals and snakes in the dry grass on either side of their path. But now and again, without warning, there would be the whine of arrows, and the shrill, inhuman war-cries that heralded an attack. The Englishmen would throw themselves to the ground, counting themselves lucky if no one was hurt, and await the appearance of their tormentors. Usually they were released from their submission with the sacrifice of a few rags of clothing. One group of Indians was even friendly enough to point them on their way to Panuco. After this last encounter they crossed a river and travelled without molestation.

Whenever they came to a particularly high tree Goddard made one of the boys climb aloft and scout out the land. Usually this was a dispiriting occasion, but on the seventh day the boy cried out that there was a great river ahead, flowing from the north-west into the open sea. Very shortly afterwards they heard the report of a gun and realized that they must be near a Spanish settlement. Quickening their pace Goddard and his men pushed forward. An hour later they heard a cock crow, and at last stumbled down the bank to quench their thirst in the Rio Panuco.

Before they could determine whether the Spanish settlement that they were seeking lay up-stream or down, a group of horsemen appeared on the further bank. There was no need to attract their attention for the Englishmen could see that their arrival was already the subject of discussion. Some of the riders turned about and galloped out of sight. A little while later a canoe, paddled by two Indians under the direction of a single Spaniard, came into view and cautiously reconnoitred from mid-stream: then it retreated to where the horsemen were assembled. The Spaniards on the bank now seemed to have decided on their next move. About twenty of them dismounted and embarked in several canoes that were moored nearby. The horses swam behind, guided from the canoes by their reins. The riders landed a little distance from the English party, mounted swiftly, and bore down upon them with lances couched.

Goddard never thought, until he saw them break into a gallop, that their approach was likely to be hostile. None of them realized that their nakedness and unkempt appearance made them almost indistinguishable from Indians. Immediately he saw the danger in which his defenceless men stood, Goddard ran forward, shouting at the Spanish horsemen in their own tongue. The horses were pulled up before any damage was done, and the Englishmen surrendered. Once their nationality had been established Goddard had little need to explain more. The news of the fight at San Juan had spread swiftly through the garrisons of New Spain. At San Luis de Tampico which lay, they now gathered, only a mile away on the further bank of the river, the two hundred Spanish inhabitants had talked about little else for the past few days.

Tampico was a fever-ridden, unhealthy community; a backwater in the main stream of Spanish settlement. It existed not because of its river, navigable only to the smallest of coastal craft, but on account of the salt workings on the western bank. There were no other riches. Some fruit was grown, and the Indians sold maize for making bread. Thus the staples of life were reasonably plentiful, but no Spaniard regarded Tampico as agreeable, and none wished to remain there long.

The seventy-odd English survivors were less disposed to be critical. After the hardships they had undergone even the half loaf of plain bread, that each man had been given when the canoes had ferried them, four at a time, across the river Panuco, seemed a bountiful taste of luxury. It was difficult to realize that after so much endurance they had achieved not liberty but captivity. Yet it was evident that their captors regarded them as desperate and dangerous men. The worst wounded, and some of the boys who were incapable of walking further, were ridden to Tampico, but the majority of the men were marched to the town under close guard. Almost every inhabitant turned out to watch them arrive.

They were assembled in the central square to await the arrival of the Governor, Don Luis de Carabajal. When he came Anthony Goddard was brought before him and harrangued in Spanish. There was no misunderstanding the tone of his speech. Goddard looked grim as he returned to his men and reported that the Governor was threatening to hang them all as pirates.

Throughout the interview Goddard seems to have succeeded in passing himself as a Portuguese national called Antonio Texeda, but to what purpose is not clear, except that it was not him but another, unidentifiable Englishman whom the Governor chose to torture in an attempt to extract more information. All too little is known about Goddard. One unsubstantiated report suggests that, earlier, he had acted as servant to the renegades, Luis and Homem, and was partly responsible for their flight.

Whatever the reason for his present subterfuge, Goddard evidently succeeded in deflecting the irrascible Governor from his original purpose. Instead of hanging them out of hand Don Luis ordered a list to be compiled of the prisoners' names, and told Goddard to collect whatever money they had amongst them. It amounted to some five hundred pesos, for gold coins were commodities in which the Indians had shown no interest. In the hope that it might help to soften the Governor's wrath Goddard himself added a gold chain, a gift from the haughty Governor of Cartagena to whom he had delivered Hawkins' letter three months before.

The money and the chain were received without comment, and the order given to secure the prisoners in the town gaol.

For so large a number of men the accommodation was totally inadequate. They were herded in with no sympathy on the part of their captors, and to assuage their hunger were offered nothing better than bowls of sodden maize fit only for pigs to eat. When they asked for a doctor to look after the wounded, the gaolers answered them roughly, saying that the only doctor they could expect was the hangman, who would certainly cure their moaning. After that, whenever Goddard or any of his men tried to speak, they were reviled as pirates, English dogs and Lutheran heretics.

For three days they lay in prison, half suffocated and half starved. They were frightened by the threats they had received, and fully expected, every time the door was unbolted, that their last hour had come. On the fourth day they were ordered out and saw, waiting to receive them, a crowd of Spaniards and Indians, all armed. One of them carried several lengths of newly-made rope fashioned into nooses. Seeing these the Englishmen cried out to each other in alarm, for they reckoned that the Governor was intending to make good his threat and hang them all. While they were hastily commending themselves to God and lamenting their fate, the Spaniards seized them roughly and, using the halters for quite another purpose, bound them in fours with their hands behind their backs, and set them marching through the town into the open country beyond. They were going to Mexico City, they were told, where their punishment would be determined. When they enquired how long they would be on the road their spirits sank. Already exhausted, they faced a march of three hundred miles.

As soon as they had cleared the town of Tampico most of the Spaniards turned back. The permanent escort for the English captives turned out to consist of two Spaniards only, and a numerous band of Indian levies, armed with bows and arrows, with whom communication was impossible, and whose stony faces showed no feeling of sympathy or human kindness. Probably not many of the Englishmen would have survived the hardships of the road had it not been for occasional acts of compassion on the part of one of their guards and the consideration with which they were treated at the various religious houses that marked the stages of their way.

They had not travelled far before they realized that their senior escort, the Commander of the Watch, bore no animosity against them. He spoke courteously and took some care to see that they were as well provided for as conditions along the road allowed. When they approached a settlement he would ride ahead, and invariably they would find food and shelter arranged for them when they arrived. The younger of the two Spaniards was of a very different disposition. He seemed to take a cruel delight in the exercise of his power over the prisoners. In particular he vented his spite upon the stragglers, and these became numerous as the journey progressed. If they did not march as fast as he desired he would beat them over the shoulders with the shaft of the short spear that he carried, crying out in Spanish the wearisome refrain that grew to haunt those at the end of the line. 'Keep marching, you English dogs.' As he belaboured and abused them the stragglers would stumble forward, one man dragging the companions to whom he was bound, pursued by the hated voice of their tormentor denouncing them all as Lutherans and enemies of God.

The Carmelites at Santa Maria, the first habitation at which they stopped, acted more charitably. The older Spaniard had gone ahead to make arrangements, and when, as light began to fail, the prisoners reached the little settlement, they were shown into the courtyard of the monastery and greeted with a hot meal and clothes to cover their nakedness. So many days had passed since the Englishmen had eaten enough to satisfy their hunger that they gorged themselves and later suffered for their greed. But their spirits revived under the kindly treatment; and as they put on the white, monastic cloaks that the Carmelites had provided, they felt encouraged to believe that having survived the first two days of the march they might endure the rest.

For one of their company, however, the relief came too late. Thomas Baker, who received an arrow-wound in the throat at the time of the first encounter with the Chichimecas, had struggled to keep going; but for the past few days he had been half-delirious and was sinking fast. His friends had supported him as best they could, but in the night, despite the care that the white friars bestowed on him, he died.

At ten o'clock next morning the Englishmen were bound together as before and the march to Mexico was resumed. It cannot be doubted that it was a gruelling trek; even worse, on account of their weakened state, than it had been for Robert Barrett and his band of captives. But neither Miles Philips, a boy in his early teens, nor Job Hortop, the tall, spare, gunner from Lincolnshire, who wrote down, many years later, their remembrances of captivity, dwell upon this journey. Philips mentions a few of the habitations they passed through and marvels at the digestive peculiarities of several of the local fruits that he found to eat. Hortop is even less informative: his recollections are almost entirely of strange foods. Perhaps hunger drove out all other curiosity. He says nothing of the climb from the tropical coast to the high central plateau; nothing of the hardships of the road. His memory recalls the white crabs that he found and ate sixty miles distant from the sea, and the many uses that the Indians found for the agave, a spiney, unfriendly plant that alone prospered in the barren uplands. Indeed Hortop always seems to have been a phlegmatic traveller. Even at Tampico, where the Englishmen lay in prison, fearful for their lives, he simply records the habits of the great, browsing manatees that swam in the river, whose flesh, he declared, was not unlike bacon in taste.

Half way along their road, at Metztitlan, the Englishmen were treated with courtesy by the Dominican friars and by the local Spanish population. Cooked food was sent to them, and some of those whose clothing was most insufficient were given shirts and other garments that were to prove most necessary in the days to come; for the track was beginning to wind its way upward to regions exposed to the wind; where nights were crystalline and cold.

Pachuca was the next place at which they paused, a prosperous town with silver mines sunk into the hillsides a few miles away to the north-east. Here the older of their guards overruled his companion who wished to press on, and gave the Englishmen two days' rest—the first that they had had since leaving Tampico. Without question they needed it. All of them had untended ailments and many were on the point of collapse.

After leaving Pachuca the road became a little easier. The surrounding country was still mountainous, and the volcanic rock intolerably hard under foot; but the main climb was over, and more settlements along the route gave the slowly-moving procession of bound and limping men chances to pause for succour and refreshment. Only seventy miles lay between Pachuca and Mexico, but however hard the younger guard drove them they could stumble little more than ten miles a day. Five days later they rested for another whole day at Cuautitlan, only fifteen miles from their objective. Whatever fate was in store for them at Mexico seemed welcome. To be freed, even by death, from the interminable exhaustion and degradation to which they had been submitted, was the one hope that sustained them and urged them forward.

Somewhat revived by their rest the prisoners started early on the last day's march. By midday they arrived at an ornate and richly decorated church, round which was gathered a crowd of elegantly-dressed Spanish horsemen, who seemed to be awaiting their arrival with curiosity. They were, as it turned out, gentlemen from the city. They had ridden as far as the Church of Our Lady of Guadaloupe in order to have the first sight of the notable band of prisoners who were known by the authorities to be approaching. The Englishmen, almost too tired to be embarrassed, were stared at and commented upon, but not molested. Their gaunt faces and travel-stained rags contrasted strangely with the sleek well-being of the Spanish gentlemen and their gaily caparisoned horses. But the guards allowed the prisoners little time to brood upon their condition. They were hustled on their way, and the Spaniards departed for the city to spread the news.

One custom, however, was scrupulously observed. No one, the

Englishmen observed, passed by the church without dismounting and passing inside to murmur a brief prayer before the image of Christ's mother that stood, splendid in gold and silver, above the altar. The Englishmen, so long upbraided as Lutheran heretics, were wise enough to follow their escorts' example without hesitation. They knelt before the Madonna, and said their prayers in good faith, well aware that under the power of Spain the only hope of freedom lay in an acceptance of the Catholic Church. To many of them this was no conscious dissimulation. Memories of the old manner of worship still remained. The new doctrine of Protestantism had not yet struck deep roots into the soil of patriotism. Over matters of dogma men and boys alike were content to trim their sails to whatever wind might blow, and reconcile their God to the prevailing system.

Since Cortes wrested it from Montezuma forty-seven years before, a new city had extinguished and engulfed the old in the valley of Anahuac. A city of wide streets and substantial buildings that proudly reflected the glory of Spain, and the wealth that her conquest had acquired. The great temples had been pulled down, and in their place churches and monasteries, friaries and hospitals arose, rivalling each other in wealth of decoration and beauty of design. So earnestly and so vigorously was the building of religious houses undertaken that already Mexico rivalled in piety and magnificence the great cities of Toledo and Seville from which it drew its inspiration. Nor were the masons and sculptors devoted exclusively to the glory of God. There were more than fifteen hundred Spanish householders dwelling in the city, all of whom demanded houses or palaces of a splendour that they could certainly not have afforded at home.

The grandeur and opulence of Mexico City was made possible by the labour of the subject Indians. A few of the Aztec princes and nobles preserved a little dignity by living amongst their conquerors in the water-borne inner town. But the great mass of the population, not far short of half a million souls, was crowded in reed and adobe huts on the outskirts. They worked for their new masters, the Spaniards, with the same passive obedience that they had devoted to the tyrants of the previous age. Their labour was exploited; they suffered hardship and cruelty; but they accepted and endured abuses as the natural order of things, against which their imagination had not taught them to rebel. The Spaniards did not scruple to use this vast, inert fund of labour to advance their own designs. If the Indians were, as they believed, too low in the scale of humanity to be capable of the Faith, it was not reasonable to treat them with more consideration than labouring animals. They could be used on manual tasks in return for which little or no payment needed to be given. Food they seemed capable of providing for themselves; and as their masters were taking pains to teach them, unworthy though they were, the means of Salvation, the least they could do to show their earnestness was to provide the building materials for the churches themselves. Thus by exploiting the already exploited, by the use of forced labour, and by an unimaginative disregard for human dignity, the city of Mexico grew and prospered.

Wearily, but with a renewed interest in things around them, the English captives trudged towards the town. They passed through fertile orchard-lands with Indian settlements lining the road. On all sides they met the expressionless gaze of an apathetic, down-trodden race, and occasionally the haughty stare of a Spanish horseman who had ridden out to observe them. By mid-afternoon the procession reached the causeway that led over the shallow lagoon to the inner city. The waterways hereabouts were crowded with canoes and small craft, many of them laden with fruit and vegetables, making their way through narrow channels right into the centre of the town. There were fishermen too, squatting motionless in their shell-like boats on the open water, and barges, laden with building stones, being laboriously ferried into the ever-growing metropolis.

Once they had crossed the causeway the road widened and the Englishmen found themselves marching down the Calle Santa Caterina, a road broad enough for two carts to pass each other, and flanked on either side by merchants' houses, solidly built in stone. They crossed as many canals as roads, and observed at every turn the busy commerce taking place around them. After long absence the life of a big city filled the Englishmen with awe and excitement. The medley of smells, the jostling crowd of onlookers and the atmosphere of comfort and well-being, so bemused them that they stumbled as they walked, though the road was smoother under foot than any they had traversed since they came to land.

Their guards did not let them halt until they came to the central square, an open space, fully a bow-shot across, lying in the very heart of the town. It was here that the Aztecs held their market every fifth day; a market so bewildering in its variety and splendour that it out-did the greatest concourses in Spain itself. Nearby had stood the great *teocalli*, from the summit of which Cortes, with Montezuma at his side, had surveyed the well-ordered city and the rich valley of Anahuac. Of that enormous temple nothing but an earth-mound now remained. The blood-encrusted block, and the sanctuaries with their fearsome images of strange gods, had long ago been destroyed; and the facing-stones of the pyramid torn down and used for other buildings. The little cathedral-church that the early settlers had built in the market-place next to the enclosure of the temple had as bases for its columns some of the stone idols that were cast down from the *teocalli*—a useful and symbolic foundation for the establishment of the Faith in Mexico.

The cathedral was not the most impressive building in the market square. It was far too small and meanly designed to serve so rich a city. On one side the viceregal palace had recently been completed, a solid, dignified frontage of faced stone, with twin towers, carved architraves, and massive doors. Opposite, above the long arcade that sheltered the stall-holders, stood the palaces of the Governor and the Archbishop.

In the shadow of these buildings the Englishmen were halted, their long march over.

Not many minutes passed before a crowd of friendly and curious folk gathered round them. Some of the Spaniards, seeing their need, brought gifts of food and clothing from the market for the exhausted prisoners. Others gave money, and soon, so kind-hearted and generous were the onlookers, they had more food than they could consume, and a strange but welcome assortment of garments to wear. Enured as they were to ill-treatment, they were surprised to find their condition pitied. Goddard, and a few others who spoke a little Spanish, were eagerly questioned, in particular by some priests who enquired if they were Christians. 'Praise God, we are as good Christians as you are', Goddard replied.

Two hours later, at sundown, their final destination was decided upon. The main hospital, they learnt, was already full with fellow Englishmen who had been captured at San Juan, but they were allowed no opportunity to meet them. Instead they were transported in two large canoes to a tannery, where they spent the night. In the morning the sick and ailing were taken to hospital, after a delegation of priests and friars had briefly catechized them and heard them recite the Lord's Prayer in Latin.

On the strength of this examination and the favourable report that the priests delivered to the Governor, considerable humanity was shown to the English sailors. Miles Philips, who was amongst the sick, found a number of his friends from the *Jesus* already installed. A fortnight later, when he and his shipmates were moved to the Hospital of Our Lady in the middle of the town, they met still more of their companions. But a number of sailors never recovered from the rigours of the march and died soon after arrival. Even Philips, who was young, resilient and uninjured, took six months to regain his health. Only then was he judged strong enough to undergo the corrective punishment that it was considered he had earned.

Job Hortop and the survivors who had no need of medical care were taken to a house on the outskirts of the town. Here, while the Viceroy and his Council debated their fate, the Englishmen idled away the time, and became the object of many visits from charitable or curious citizens. They were forbidden to leave their quarters, but rumours constantly reached them of how Don Martin Enriquez purposed to hang every man, of intercessions from less choleric advisors, of gallows being erected and of the legal doubts that hindered their use. Before long a different place of confinement was chosen for them, on an island in the lagoon. Here the Englishmen were again examined by priests, and their confessions heard. No taint of heresy was discovered, and the

Viceroy was assured by the bishop that his prisoners had offended only against the state, and not against the church.

As simple prisoners of war the Englishmen were easily dealt with. The officers and gentlemen who had been captured at San Juan were confined in tolerable comfort at the viceregal palace; all the sailors who were fit for work were sent to Texcoco, a town twenty miles to the east, and given the menial task of carding wool amongst the Indian slaves. A month or two of rest and regular prison food had done much to revive the spirit and self-respect of the captives. They considered the work they had been given degrading, and the discipline overbearing and intolerable. Job Hortop, in a terse phrase, tells how the entire English contingent decided to rebel 'and concluded to beat our masters, and so wee did'.

The Spaniards, chastened by their unruly labourers, appealed to the Viceroy, and the Englishmen were marched back to house-arrest in Mexico. Anthony Goddard, identified as a ringleader, was singled out and sent down to the coast, under suitable escort, to stand trial in Spain. With him went George Fitzwilliam and all the other English hostages and well-born prisoners captured at San Juan. In all twenty-nine Englishmen and two Frenchmen marched back to that fateful anchorage, where General Luxan, his fleet repaired and seaworthy once again, was on the point of sailing for Seville.

At least one of the hostages went to Spain under grave suspicion of being a heretic. He was a young man called William de Orlando, formerly a page to Queen Elizabeth. Once, during his confinement in the viceregal palace, he had been incautious enough to declare in public that, although he was a good Catholic, Elizabeth was his Queen, and he would die for her. His brag of loyalty proved his undoing. The ecclesiastical authorities in Mexico sent him under suspicion to Seville, where, within a year of his arrival, he died in gaol.

But most of the English sailors remained behind. They paced the inner courtyard of their prison for exercise, ate the daily ration of mutton and maize-bread that was given them, and speculated endlessly about the future. Months crept by: it would be springtime in England they reckoned, and in Mexico the first showers of the year were laying the dust and bringing a freshness to the air that reminded them of their homes, and the families they might never see again. In their crowded quarters the captives quarrelled half-heartedly, grew bored, and began to suspect that they had been entirely forgotten.

Later that summer they were joined in their confinement by Miles Philips and those with him who had spent six months in hospital. They had a lively story to tell, for, after their discharge from hospital, they too had been sent to Texcoco. Instead of being set to work they had languished for two months in the town gaol, from which, they soon learnt, Indian petty offenders were sold off into slavery. There was every reason to believe that they were destined for a similar fate. More immediate than the fear of slavery was the prospect of starvation. Almost no food was provided by the authorities, and the Englishmen had no money to buy provisions from outside. They were sustained, they said, only through the help rendered by a certain Robert Sweeting, the son of an English father and a Spanish mother, who lived in the town and heard of their plight. By his influence and command of language enough victuals were procured from the Indians to keep them alive. But he had no power to do more.

At length, in desperation, the Englishmen agreed to make a united effort to escape. Plans were carefully made, and complete success achieved. In the middle of a dark and rain-swept night they broke out, and started to walk in whatever direction seemed to offer most hope of freedom. It was a forlorn attempt. Within minutes they were drenched and chilled. A vast, unfriendly country surrounded them on all sides, from which there was no escape or means of support. As soon as the exhilaration of gaol-breaking had passed they realized that they were lost and lonely. They trudged forward in scattered bands, keeping moving in order to keep warm. When day dawned Miles Philips found himself within sight of Mexico, and before very long a search party of mounted Spaniards rounded up him and his companions and brought them, hungry and bedraggled, before the Viceroy and the justices. They were stormed at, abused, threatened with hanging, but not sent back to Texcoco. Instead they were re-united at last with their shipmates in the inner courtyard and prison of the Viceroy's palace.

To guard and support a hundred prisoners, who had proved too unruly to be employed as a group, was a burden that the Viceroy was not prepared to support any longer. Robert Barrett had been ill for several months after his arrival in Mexico and could not be sent back to Spain with the plate fleet. He was still detained in captivity; but all the others, it was decided, should be given away separately as servants to any Spanish gentleman wishing to engage them. On a proclaimed day the English men and boys were paraded in the courtyard and inspected by a variety of employers. Although there was no shortage of labour in Mexico there were very few men who had the skill to direct it, or who were trained in a craft. Every Spaniard wished to be his own master, and only the most unenterprising was content with stewardship when wealth and independence could be seized. An English prisoner was admirably fitted to stand between an Indian slave and his master; an intelligent servant whose ambition would always be controlled by his captive state. Before the day was over every one of the sailors had been bespoken, and carried off to some new employment.

The boys, who had no particular skill, were mostly kept in a domestic capacity. They waited at table, attended to their masters' wants at home, and escorted them when they paid calls within the city. To some the tasks were familiar, for they had been pages or servants at sea. Before long they mastered the Spanish tongue, and found their employment more congenial. They were given good clothes and a little money to spend, and as the months passed some of the boys grew accustomed to their new conditions and yearned less passionately for their homeland. Others, like Miles Philips, kept the prospect of escape ever before them.

The men were more variously employed. Some were apprenticed to craftsmen in the city. John Lee, whose father, Hawkins' chief gunner, had been killed at San Juan, was put to the hosiery trade. John Martin, a young Irishman from Cork, began to learn the craft of barber-surgeon, and Job Hortop was able to practise his old trade of tinsmith and powder-maker in the Calle de Tacuba. But many more were sent into the provinces to act as overseers at the silver mines. John Farenton, George Rively and others found it a profitable task. As soon as they had gained their master's confidence they were given a large measure of freedom and responsibility. Unsupervised, they were left in control of the negro and Indian labourers who worked the mines. Very often they could supplement their wages by employing the workmen themselves on rest-days and after hours. All the silver that was extracted at these times was retained by the English supervisor. In a year or two many of the sailors had become men of substance with private fortunes worth many hundreds of pounds.

Not many details are recorded of the daily lives of the Englishmen after they had scattered to their various employments. Some, doubtless, were luckier than others; but for the most part they prospered, and made no serious attempts to escape from their mild bondage. Outwardly they became good Catholics and good citizens. Job Hortop, by now a tall, thin, slightly-bearded man of twenty years, was well remembered by the friars at Texcoco for the fireworks and set-pieces he made for them to celebrate their holy days. His work also took him back to Pachuca, the mining town where he and his companions had rested for two days on their way to Mexico. Here he met a shipmate, William Collins, and was seen conversing with Don Juan, the principal Indian caicique. However, Hortop did not entirely avoid the displeasure of the authorities. For some unspecified minor offence he suffered a short return to prison in the viceregal palace.

Whether arising from this incident or for other reasons, Hortop was not allowed to follow his trade for much more than a year. In 1571, when the plate fleet was preparing once again to depart for Spain, Hortop was sent on board, together with Robert Barrett and about ten other Englishmen. They could not have been unaware that in Seville they would experience less tolerant treatment from their captors than in Mexico; yet the voyage seemed to bring them nearer home, and was a welcome change.

To Hortop it was a privilege to travel with such strange cargo

as Don Martin Enriquez had elected to present to the King of
Spain. Far more wonderful than the annual tribute of gold and
silver were the earth-filled chests of living ginger-roots that had
come from China, and the skeleton of a giant from the same
fabulous land. 'It did appere by the anatomie, that he was of a
monstrous size, the skull of his head was neere as bigge as halfe a
bushel, his neckebones, shoulder-plates, arme-bones, and all other
lineaments of his other partes, were huge and monstrous to be-
hold, the shanke of his legge from the ankle to the knee was as
long as from any mans ankle up to his wast, and of bignesse
accordingly.'

CHAPTER 14

The Prisoners in Spain

NOT long before Barrett, Hortop and the skeleton of the Chinese giant sailed up the river Guadalquivir and ended their ocean voyage alongside the Torre del Oro in Seville, the first English prisoner to escape from captivity had made his way home.

George Fitzwilliam, with thirty others, had left Mexico in 1569 on board the very fleet that they had come so near to destroying. Apart from Anthony Goddard, who was regarded as a man of influence, and two Frenchmen from the *Grace of God*, the captives were all Englishmen of quality. But any hopes that they would be treated with respect were quickly dashed. As soon as they arrived at Seville they were put in prison, and remained in a dungeon under appalling conditions for many months. All attempts to make contact with the outside world failed, though between them they had many friends in Spain. Above all they wished to get news of their whereabouts to England, where, they felt sure, some influence could be brought to bear on their behalf. Meanwhile virtually no food reached them, and they lacked the means to procure any by bribery. Their clothes were in rags, and the endemic sicknesses of prisons began to undermine their health. As they themselves put it, 'since the ayre is so evell in this pestered place pryson, er the summer passe most of us shall perishe continuing here'.

When, at last, they succeeded in passing a message to Hugh Tipton, an English merchant who lived and worked in Seville, four of their number had succumbed and six others were on the point of death.

To Tipton's efforts the remainder owed their lives. His own position could not have been easy, but he disregarded all the personal danger of contamination with pirates and suspected heretics, in order to bring succour to his fellow-countrymen. First of all he brought them food, and, in time, persuaded the prison authorities to provide adequate sustenance to keep the starving men alive. More perilous still, he introduced paper and ink, so that Fitzwilliam was able to write to Cecil, to Hawkins, and to the Duke of Feria. Tipton smuggled these letters out of the dungeon in Seville and saw that they were delivered.

To Hawkins in England, who had been chafing for news, Fitzwilliam's letter was a signal for immediate action. The full story of the skilful and unscrupulous plotting and counter-plotting that he engaged in will probably never be told. Hawkins had good cause for reticence and cunning. Even at the beginning, when he dissimulated his allegiance to the Crown in order to persuade the Spanish ambassador, as an earnest of good faith, to recommend the release of the English prisoners, Hawkins could afford to disclose his negotiations to no one except, perhaps, Cecil. Later, as his intricate net of double-dealing involved him in the unravelling of the treasonous Ridolfi plot, he appears from the State Papers, that alone disclose some facets of his diplomatic activity, as a man of many masks. But to one objective he was always constant: his desire to obtain the release of the members of his ships' companies whom he now knew to be languishing in prison at Seville. He must also have wished to intercede for those in Mexico. Indeed there are rumours of an abortive attempt to sail on an expedition to their relief. More probably he dismissed such a scheme, albeit reluctantly, in the realization that they were beyond his capacity for help.

The first prisoner to escape from Seville, George Fitzwilliam, owed his good fortune, in all probability, less to Hawkins' diplomacy than to his own family connections. As soon as he was able he had got into touch with the Duke of Feria, a nobleman of some influence at the Spanish Court, who had accompanied his Sovereign to England when the marriage to Mary Tudor had temporarily united the two royal houses. The Duke had himself married an English wife, a kinswoman of Fitzwilliam's, Jane Dormer. Through this happy connection Fitzwilliam, and only he, obtained his release.

Fitzwilliam, who always had Hawkins' confidence, was no sooner back in England than he became involved in the web of intrigue that had drawn the fate of the Ridolfi plotters and the remaining prisoners together. As Hawkins' personal representative he returned twice to Spain and held secret audience with the King whose dungeon he had so recently inhabited. On the second occasion, in the summer of 1571, he achieved what he desired. In return for certain treasonable promises of aid in an attempt to usurp Queen Elizabeth and place Mary Stuart on the throne, King Philip ordered the release of the remaining English prisoners. There were, perhaps, two dozen of them, and one at least, Anthony Goddard, was known to be alive and well in Plymouth many years later. The deceitful undertaking that Hawkins and Fitzwilliam had given to aid the overthrow of the Queen, the government and the Protestant faith was quickly forgotten, and Cecil, who had watched and waited until all the plotters had been revealed to him, quietly suppressed the insurrection.

There was only one flaw in a perfect scheme. Unknown to Hawkins or Fitzwilliam, the plate fleet returning from Mexico in the summer of 1571 was bringing Robert Barrett and a further band of prisoners to Seville just at the time that the repatriation of the first contingent was being negotiated. The Spanish authorities never mentioned them, and as they were not included in King Philip's amnesty it was never considered that they too should be released. Worst of all, the second party never succeeded in drawing attention to their plight, and once the intransigence of Fitzwilliam had become plain there was little chance that the Spaniards would let themselves be tricked again.

Barrett and his companions had had an exciting and, at first, not uncomfortable voyage. They were scattered among the principal ships of the fleet, and before casting off the seven men who had been allotted to sail in the flagship were summoned before the General, Don Juan de Velasco de Varre. He asked them what conduct he could expect from them if the fleet was attacked during the voyage by English ships. Robert Barrett, acting as spokesman, replied without hesitation that they would not fight against their own nation, but that they would help as best they might to resist an attack by any other country's ships. Barrett's frank response pleased the Spaniard. He confessed that he would not have believed them if they had said otherwise, and would repay their honesty by treating them throughout the voyage on an equality with his own crew. Accordingly he allotted each Englishman to the charge of an appropriate mess where he kept watch, and performed the duties to which he had been accustomed under Hawkins' command.

They had a slow but uneventful passage of twenty-six days to Havana, where they anchored, took on water, and waited for over a fortnight for the other half of the plate fleet to join them. These ships, under the command of an admiral of equal seniority but less volatile disposition, Don Diego Flores de Valdes, had collected the year's treasure from Peru at Nombre de Dios. United and strong, the combined fleet prepared to brave the dangers of the ocean sea together.

The two admirals commanded the fleet by turns. During the first two-week spell under Don Juan, Robert Barrett and Job Hortop repaid the good opinion and trust of the Spanish admiral by averting the shipwreck of the entire fleet. They had passed through the Florida channel, leaving the Bahamas on the starboard hand, and were following a course parallel to the mainland coast, when Hortop, whose turn it was to keep the middle watch on deck, noticed a low shoreline looming almost straight ahead in the darkness. He called out to Barrett, who was nearby, that they were standing into danger. Barrett confirmed in a glance that the fleet was entering shoal water, and that the pilot had not kept sufficiently clear of Cape Canaveral. Without considering his right to give such an order he cried out in Spanish to the boatswain, telling him to let fly the foresheet and bear down with the helm.

A few moments later, as the ships that followed their admiral's stern lantern were turning hastily out to sea, a leadsman in the chains reported soundings in seven fathoms. Don Juan and his principal officers, disturbed from their sleep, hastened on deck to investigate the commotion. Very little explanation was necessary. The line of surf and shore was perfectly visible, and the soundings spoke eloquently of the peril they had so closely avoided. Don Juan alternated between rage at his pilot, who had set so inaccurate a course, and praise for the vigilance of the two Englishmen. At daybreak he fired a gun to summon a council, and Don Diego was rowed across to the flagship. Before he retired to the privacy of his day-cabin Don Juan was heard threatening to hang the pilot, and asserting that this was not the first time that he had found him incompetent. But moderation prevailed; the unfortunate pilot survived his general's anger, and the fleet resumed its leisurely progress up the coast until, having gained sufficient northerly latitude, it struck east across the open sea.

The only noteworthy event was the sighting of a merman. He appeared, Hortop declared, in the sea off Bermuda, and 'shewed himselfe three times unto us from the middle upwards, in which parts hee was proportioned like a man, of the complection of a Mulato, or tawny Indian'. Don Juan was as impressed by the apparition as Hortop, and recorded a description of the monster for the benefit of the King when he reached home.

Soon afterwards the weather grew boisterous, and for a fortnight the fleet wallowed through heavy seas and squalls. Later on it became calmer, and continued fair until they sighted the island of Fayal in the Portuguese-owned Azores.

On St James' day at the end of July, Hortop was able to exercise his craft as a maker of fireworks. That night he entertained the Spanish sailors with rockets, fiery wheels and set-pieces that threw their golden sparks into the surrounding darkness and cast a sudden, transitory light upon the moon-white sails and the oily blackness of the sea.

Robert Barrett, who shared the pilot's cabin, had no difficulty in learning that the fleet was scheduled to pause in the Azores at Terceira before proceeding to Seville. It seemed to him that this offered a possible opportunity of escape. In the greatest secrecy Barrett and the six fellow-countrymen, in whom he confided, began to collect ships' biscuits, and stole a large goatskin water-bottle which would give them enough food and drink for nine days if they rationed themselves strictly. They planned to slip away in the pinnace that their flagship, alone amongst the vessels of the fleet, towed astern. If they departed before the ships came to anchor Barrett hoped to land at some deserted place on one of the less-frequented islands, and stay in hiding until the Spanish fleet had sailed. In order to be sure of making a landfall they needed a compass, and this proved their undoing. Barrett borrowed one on some pretext, but unknown to him aroused suspicion and watchfulness on the part of his captors. A trap was set, and the Englishmen were caught red-handed.

All seven were immediately placed in the stocks on deck, and observed with growing apprehension the fury that their attempted escape had roused in Don Juan. At his command pulleys were fixed at the main yard-arm, and seven nooses prepared. A gun was fired to summon a council, and while Don Diego was, for the second time, being rowed across to join his fellow-admiral, the Englishmen were told to confess themselves quickly before they were hanged.

Just as before, when he calmed the impetuous wrath of Don Juan off Cape Canaveral, Don Diego proved himself a peacemaker. He heard of the plot and its discovery, and learnt the manner in which Don Juan proposed dealing with the offenders. Mildly he remarked that had he been in the same circumstances as the Englishmen he too would have attempted to escape. It was no part of their duty to pass sentence. That would be done if necessary at the Contratacion House in Seville. Until they could be delivered there Don Diego counselled that the prisoners should be kept in close confinement, but be otherwise unharmed. As was evident from this and the subsequent opinions that were voiced at the council table, Don Juan's idea of summary justice found no support.

After the meeting had disbanded, the participants returned to their ships and the voyage was resumed. But for Barrett, Hortop and their five companions, the last sixteen days before the fleet anchored in the roads of San Lucar were disagreeable in the extreme. They remained in the stocks the whole time, exposed to the weather, the occasional jibes of the crew, and the discomfort of cramped limbs. Even at San Lucar, the port at the mouth of the river upon which, fifty miles upstream, lay Seville, they were allowed no opportunity to stretch their legs. Instead they were transferred, stocks and all, into a pinnace, and conveyed up the sluggish, marsh-fringed Guadalquivir. Not until they were within the walls of the Contratacion House were the stocks opened, and the seven Englishmen allowed the unfettered walking space of a narrow cell.

Life in a Spanish prison was no easier for Barrett and his companions than it had been for Fitzwilliam's party the year before. They were not lucky enough to attract the attention of Hugh Tipton; they had no influential friends in Court circles. But Robert Barrett was content to rely upon his own resources. He was a determined man, and could not tolerate the thought of languishing in gaol without attempting to escape. His chance came the day after their first Christmas in Spain. He and six others broke out of the Contratacion House and scattered in the winding lanes and busy thoroughfares of the city. For Barrett, Hortop and three others, the hours of liberty were few. They found themselves conspicuous and friendless. Very soon they were cornered and recaptured. Two men managed to get away, but of their eventual fate there is no record.

The guards at the Contratacion House, evidently unused to rebellious conduct amongst their charges, petitioned to have the Englishmen moved to the main city gaol where more precautions could be taken to prevent escape. Meanwhile the five recaptured men were secured in the stocks until the Christmas festivities were over, and an order committing them to the central prison could be made out.

They did not stay long in their new place of confinement. After barely a month they were transferred, under close escort, across the solitary bridge that spanned the river, to a turreted castle, whose windowless outer walls guarded the approaches to the city from the Triana side. Over the arch through which they entered was a simple cross: the Englishmen had passed from the neglectful custody of the secular authorities to the dangerously solicitous charge of the Holy Office.

R

THE DEFEAT OF JOHN HAWKINS

Whether their abortive attempt to escape had attracted the attention of the Inquisition, or whether the slow but scrupulous machinery of spiritual justice had chosen its own good time to start interrogation, no one can say. Nor is it clear how aware the Englishmen were of the nature of the dangers they now faced. There are some indications that Barrett, for one, was foolhardy in his disregard for the high seriousness of the tribunal before which he was to be arraigned. For a whole year they were subject to examination: sometimes singly, sometimes in groups. For long periods they would lie, seemingly forgotten, in their cells; then, unaccountably, would be summoned to testify before the officers and clerks of the Holy Office. Questions were asked and answered in a grave, endless succession. The Englishmen were catechized on the nature of their Faith, their manner of worship, their customs at home, and the habits of their friends. Some of the questions were so innocent and irrelevant that they answered them eagerly; others, subtle beyond their experience, concerned dogma and belief. At the end of each examination the clerks, who had recorded every word that passed, read over the deposition. As month succeeded month the pile of evidence grew, and with it the inevitable contradictions, misconstructions and innocent betrayals.

When, one Sunday in 1573, the time was considered ripe for an *auto de fe*, eight bewildered and frightened Englishmen were taken from the darkness and solitude of their cells, clothed in sanbenitos— saffron-coloured tabards with red crosses on the front and back— and led in procession over the bridge and through the hot, teeming streets to the Plaza de San Francisco.

In their hands they held long green candles, and they walked barefooted, guarded on either side both from escape and from the violence of the great crowd that was gathered along the roadside. Surrounded by a hostile throng upbraiding them as Lutherans and threatening them with the stake, the Englishmen came to a square with a little fountain in the middle, and mounted a wooden scaffold facing a half-circle of raised benches. Here, under the shadow of the enormous Giralda Tower that rose high above the houses to the east, the dignitaries of the Holy Office

sat in the habits of their order, to accuse, to judge and to reconcile those who had stumbled into heresy.

For two hours the Inquisitor spoke before the assembly, telling
of the subtle perils of unchecked heresy and of the merciful
operation of those who were skilled to detect and root it out.
The Englishmen must already have realized how unlikely it was
that they would be acquitted, but they could not have failed to
be appalled by the savageness of the doom that was now pronounced upon them. Two at a time the prisoners were called
forward and asked if they were truly repentant. When they
replied that they were, and a form of abjuration had been read
and repeated back word for word, the mercy of the Inquisition
was extended to the penitents and the sentence read.

The first pair of Englishmen were condemned to the galleys
for five years, the second pair for eight years, and Hortop who,
with one companion, was the next to be called forward received a
sentence of ten years in the galleys followed by life imprisonment.
John Gilbert and Robert Barrett were the last to hear their fate.
But impenitent heresy such as theirs was beyond the ability of
the Inquisition to correct. With a formal exhortation that no
drop of blood should be spilt and no hair injured, the two
unfortunates were given into the charge of the lay authorities.
Their companions never saw them again. The following day,
in order not to pollute the Sabbath, they were taken to the
quemadero outside the city walls and burnt at the stake.

By the death of Robert Barrett, Hawkins and Drake lost a
kinsman, and England was the poorer by a sea-officer already
notable for his skill in handling ships and men. He was barely
thirty years old, and there is little doubt that, had he survived,
his name would have been illustrious for his service to his
country. Although there is little evidence to show why Gilbert
incurred his ~~most grievous~~ sentence, it is clear from the de-
positions extracted from several of his shipmates that Barrett had,
in the eyes of the Holy Office, fallen consciously and irremediably
into the pit of heresy. A Portuguese who had talked and dined
with him off the Coast of Guinea affirmed that he neither crossed
himself nor asked a blessing on sitting down or rising from table

and had mocked those who did. He and several of his companions had thrown rosaries into the sea and denounced the Catholic faith, saying that they had found a better path to salvation. William Collins, a sailor from the *Jesus*, confessed that he believed Barrett to be a Lutheran because he had torn down and kicked aside a wooden cross from the wall of his prison in the viceregal palace, 'and many times both on the vessel and on land he had seen him eat flesh on Fridays and Saturdays'. Most damning of all were several accounts of how, while still in Mexico, Barrett had been called upon to translate a sermon that was being preached to his fellow-prisoners. He performed the task, but interpolated his own commentary, declaring the doctrine to be false and the Pope to be 'a rascally Jew Swindler'. The Holy Office, to whom these indictments were revealed, was not lightly mocked, and Barrett's impetuous and irreverent conduct in their eyes sealed his doom.✷

Of the six men who served in the galleys, only Hortop returned to England to tell his tale. He and three others were chained together and shared a rowing-bench and a heavy oar. It was a rough and callous life that they were forced to live, and only the sturdiest survived. Two pounds of hard tack was their daily ration of food, and water their only drink. Once a year they received an issue of clothes—two shirts, two pairs of canvas trousers, a poorly-made jacket and a hooded cloak to protect them from the weather. They had no other possessions, and they slept on the bare boards. Many of the galley-slaves were carried off by sickness, and others collapsed under the cruel discipline of their overseers. There was no chance of escape and not all had the endurance to complete their sentence. Hortop gives a brief glimpse of the degrading existence that he suffered for twelve years (for his original sentence was extended, doubtless through some alleged misconduct). 'Our heads and beards were shaven every month, hunger, thirst, cold and stripes we lacked none, til our several times expired.'

In 1585 Hortop returned to the Inquisition House in Seville where he exchanged his haircloth gown for the sanbenito, and prepared to spend the rest of his days in the dungeons. During the four years he was encarcerated, and quite unknown to him, the Great Armada assembled and sailed from Lisbon against his own country. The story of its fate is too well known to need repeating. But while Hawkins and Drake were harrying the Spanish galleons up the Channel, Job Hortop, who sailed in their company twenty years before, had at last discovered a means of escaping from 'everlasting prison remedilesse'.

He did not escape as a free man. But he managed to prevail upon the Inquisitorial authorities to relieve him of the sanbenito and allow him to go into service in a respectable Spanish household. His master, Hernando de Soria, the treasurer of the royal mint, paid fifty duckets to the Holy Office, which he assessed as seven years' wages. Hortop was therefore bound to serve de Soria until the debt was repaid by labour. It was a hard bargain, but it offered Hortop a real chance of escape.

The opportunity came in October 1590. He made his way to San Lucar and managed, without incurring suspicion, to take passage in a coastal craft manned by Flemings, who were allied to the power of Spain, and had aboard a cargo of wine and salt destined for the Low Countries. Once at sea Hortop's luck turned. The Flemish boat had sailed no further than Cape St Vincent when she was intercepted by an English warship, the *Dudley*. It seems likely that this ship was one of twelve galleons, commanded in two squadrons by Hawkins and Frobisher, that were returning from a fruitless patrol of the Azores, where they had hoped to intercept the annual treasure fleet of Spain.

To have rescued a solitary Englishman was not so glorious a feat as had been planned, but Job Hortop deserved his good fortune. On the second of December the *Dudley* brought him to Portsmouth, where the authorities treated him with kindness and curiosity before sending him to London with a letter of introduction to the Earl of Sussex.

He answered many questions and his story was taken down in as much detail as he could recollect. It was flattering, after so many long, grey years of captivity, to be an object of interest and to be received with courtesy by great men. But Hortop was not ambitious. He still had one short journey to undertake before he could truly feel that he was home. On Christmas eve he took his leave of the Earl and came to Redriffe, where he had first learnt and practised his trade. Amongst those friends who were left he purposed to carry on his old life, and forget the long nightmare that had claimed so many of his years.

CHAPTER 15

The Prisoners in Mexico

WHEN Barrett and Hortop left Mexico in 1571, ninety years had passed since the first Tribunal of the Faith in Spain condemned six Jewish heretics to the stake. During those years, inspired by the holy eloquence and persuasive zeal of Torquemada, the Inquisition had reconciled and relaxed many hundreds of souls each year. Purity of Faith was scrupulously guarded at home, but curiously disregarded in the colonies beyond the seas. In Mexico there was a commissary of the Inquisition, but its function was ill-defined and its powers slight. For the most part it confined its activities to cases of blasphemy and bigamy, and only four times since the conquest had the episcopal authorities delivered a sentence that necessitated the shedding of blood. By comparison with Spain religious discipline in Mexico was mild indeed. Even in England the anti-Catholic laws were more sternly enforced. But tolerance in matters of Faith was uncommon in rigidly-established societies, and both England and Spain oppressively defended their conflicting orthodoxies.

In Mexico the pursuit of material wealth and the conversion of the heathen were more urgent occupations. Heresy was certainly abhorred, but to have paused to root it out would have deflected the colony's ebullient progress. There was tacit agreement amongst the authorities, both civil and ecclesiastical, that the time was not ripe to look inward. Even the Viceroy was reluctant to admit that the taint of heresy might already exist within the boundaries of New Spain. In 1575 he wrote to the King declaring that not a Lutheran could be detected. 'Thank God! the country is well in this respect.'

The Inquisitors of Spain were not so confident. In 1570 King Philip was persuaded to appoint the elderly Inquisitor of Murcia, Doctor Moya de Contreras, to a new tribunal that was designed to enquire into the spiritual health of the colonists in Mexico. Not until the following year did he sail to take up his duties. In the late summer of 1571, when Barrett and his companions were on the last, ignominious lap of their voyage to Spain, Contreras was shipwrecked on the coast of Cuba. Another vessel took him to San Juan de Ulua, and eventually, in September, he arrived in Mexico. So exhausting had the journey been that the official welcome to which he was entitled was delayed for two months. It is probable that the summons by drum and trumpet, that drew the whole Christian population of the city together at the appointed time, was the first warning for the remaining English captives of the new danger that confronted them.

For some months the Englishmen, ostensibly good Catholics and orderly citizens, had been scattered throughout the city and the nearby provinces, working under the direction of their Spanish masters. They were ordinary seamen and ship's boys for the most part, and none of them was accustomed to a life of luxury. Their employment was not unpleasant, and some were better off than they had ever been before.

When the call came on November 4th, those that were in reach of the city joined the assembly in the central square, and watched the Viceroy, the members of the *audiencia* and the senior clerics of New Spain escort the Inquisitor to a solemn service of dedication and resolve in the cathedral. Afterwards the royal letter of appointment was read aloud, followed by the Edict of Faith. The assembled Spaniards were exhorted to confess their heresies and faults, and to declare without hesitation those of their families and friends. The operation of the tribunal was merciful, but to harbour heresy was a defiance of its holy and lawful purpose, and a deadly sin.

The splendour and solemnity of the occasion did not fail to make its impression, and before the Inquisitor had completed his tour of the provincial towns, reading the Edict to the populace, a trickle of confession and denunciation became a flood. Depo-

*not, doubtless, through any humanitarian reasons.

sitions were taken, evidence was digested, and gradually, with slow but implacable certainty, the prisons became full of those whom the Holy Office felt impelled to interrogate.

Not only confirmed heretics heard the reading of the Edict with trepidation. There were many who feared denunciation by their enemies, others who were by nature intemperate of speech, and not a few in high places who found in the imposition of an absolute authority, such as Contreras wielded, a diminution of their own power. The Viceroy, Don Martin Enriquez, is known to have openly opposed the entry of the Holy Office into Mexico, and did his best to obstruct the operation of the Inquisitor-General. It may well be that in order to confine the activities of the Inquisition, which he considered harmful to the material prosperity of his province,* he forced upon Contreras' attention those persons that he had least reason to love, the English prisoners. One by one during the ensuing year they were arrested, their small store of wealth was confiscated, and they found themselves once again in the dark confinement of a Mexican prison.

Miles Philips was among the first to be apprehended. He remained in an ill-lit cell, either alone or with a single companion, for eighteen months, and only gradually became aware that all his friends and shipmates had also been rounded up. In another dungeon William Collins first learnt that young Paul Hawkins was also imprisoned nearby when he 'heard a very piping voice which must (have been) that of little Paul'. But none of them was ignored or forgotten. From time to time there would come a summons from above, and the guard would lead a prisoner through the stone corridors and upstairs into the blinding daylight of a Council chamber. Confronting him was a large cross, and below it, flanked by the Inquisitorial guard, the members of the tribunal sat in grave and solemn dignity. They were dressed in the black and white habits of their order, and on the long table that separated them from the prisoner official documents and books were piled in profusion. At first, as though unaware of the prisoner's presence, the notaries sifted their papers and cut their pens, while the Inquisitors sat abstracted in thought.

The first requirement was for the suspected heretic to be

placed on oath. He was made to swear that he would observe the mandates of the Church, that he would answer truthfully all questions asked of him, reveal all heretics known to him and submit to whatever penance or punishment might be imposed upon him. The nature of the oath revealed to the prisoner, if he had any doubts, that the fact of his arrest pre-supposed some measure of guilt. To refuse to swear, or to staunchly profess innocence of the charges, only served to condemn him still further as a defiant and obstinate heretic.

None of the Englishmen was foolhardy enough to refuse entirely to co-operate with the Tribunal, and the first questions put to them were simple, and even vague. They were asked if they knew why they had been arrested, if they had enemies, or if they had knowledge of heresy being practised around them. Such questions could be briefly answered, but the Inquisitors encouraged expansiveness. To men who had been kept in silence for many months it was pleasant to recollect the past, and often they failed to realize the subtle drift of the interrogation. Sometimes, however, they saw the snares that were being laid for them, or else were honestly puzzled by the complexity of the questions. If they hesitated, or became mulish in their answers, the tone of the Inquisitors was quick to change. They spoke harshly of the pains of damnation, and did not hesitate to use torture when they felt it necessary, especially if they detected contradictions in the replies they received.

Frightened and angry from the pains of the rack, the Englishmen stumbled on through the endless catechisms. Questions and answers fell like leaves in autumn, and were carefully garnered by the scriveners. Most of the men were fluent enough to make their responses in Spanish, but when their knowledge of the language failed, Robert Sweeting, who had helped some of them when they were in prison at Texcoco, was called in to interpret. To Sweeting they repeated the prayers that they had learned as children, and he vouched to the Tribunal that they were unexceptional in their English form.

Some days the interrogation continued for hours without a pause, returning again and again to certain key subjects. Miles

Philips tells how, as an eighteen-year-old youth, he was expected to give his views about the doctrine of transubstantiation, and the methods of religious instruction in England.

Each man was encouraged to inform on other members of the crew and gradually the web of indictment touched them all. They were never confronted with each other's evidence: if need arose a prisoner could identify a companion through a secret grating without his presence being known. As the months passed fear of betrayal began to obsess them. George Rively, in the middle of an interrogation, cried out that he was 'afflicted and cannot sleep at night on account of this trial'; and Richard Williams, a youth whose face during those prison years was said to have 'worn a nearly constant look of melancholy', reproved his cell-mate William Collins one day for talking rashly, with the nervous exclamation, 'May the devil fly away with thee, for shouldst thou declare and confess all that stuff, burnt thou wilt certainly be, and I with thee'.

Williams was wise to utter such a warning, for an informer reported their strained and pathetic conversations to the Tribunal. By eavesdropping over four centuries it is possible today to understand a little of the fear and loneliness that engulfed the prisoners in their dark cells and made them malleable to the persistent, earnest questioning of the Holy Office. 'Oh how I wish that I had some dainty to eat!' cried out Williams at one point, and again 'Oh mother of mine, if thou didst only know that I am here'. Collins, an older, rougher man, seems to have become irritated by the boy's weakness and fear. They quarrelled intermittently: after one such argument Collins in a sulk 'did walk to and fro the whole afternoon and afterwards did go to bed where he sleeps with [Williams] and did draw his clothes to one side giving to understand that it was because he caught lice off him'.

There was nothing to occupy them except their own fears and speculations. In bewilderment they brooded upon the injustice of their fate. 'It is now a year that I have lain rotting here and they have only begun to read my deposition', one cried; and another, incapable of understanding why, because his Queen had commanded him to be a Protestant, he should have to suffer for it, complained 'I only did what they all do in that land'.

But to the Inquisitors they declared that they had never accepted the Protestant heresies. If, advertently, they had sinned, they freely repented, and as they had never offended against the laws of Spain, they appealed to the Inquisition for mercy. The Tribunal of the Faith was unmoved by such material objections. It sat not as an earthly court of law, but in anticipation of Divine justice. Deeds were not its concern, except for the light they might throw upon beliefs. Not the actions of the accused but the workings of his mind was on trial.

However confident they may have been that they had not betrayed themselves, the Englishmen furnished Contreras with ample evidence of their heretical tendencies. In particular they soon realized that to satisfy their interrogators they had to incriminate each other. Some, like George Rively, remained taciturn, and were judged impenitent; others, such as Morgan Tillert, confessed under the increasing agony of the rack that Francis Drake had converted him to Lutheranism, knowing as he said it that Drake was beyond the Inquisitor's power. But William Collins and many others were less resolute. They declared of one shipmate that he confessed direct to God without the intercession of the Saints, or of another that he was 'a scoundrelly Lutheran'. In many cases more than fifty charges were preferred against a single man.

Accordingly, early in 1574, the last pages of evidence were taken down and the investigation was considered to be completed. All that remained was a public act of faith at which repentant heretics might acknowledge their sins, and receive the penalties that would bring them, through suffering, to Salvation and a state of Grace.

One day in the middle of February the public criers in Mexico and the neighbouring settlements summoned the populace by trumpet and drum to hear of an *auto de fe* that would take place in a fortnight's time; and a period of indulgence was promised to those who attended. Meanwhile the civic authorities caused stagings to be erected inside the cathedral church and also in the market square.

By the evening of February 27th everything was ready for the
solemn ceremony on the following day. The Englishmen were
warned of the part they were to play and issued with sanbenitos.
When they had dressed themselves they were assembled in an
inner courtyard. In the flickering torchlight they could scarcely
recognize each other with the brilliant yellow sanbenitos, slashed
with the scarlet cross of St Andrew, hanging loosely over their
drab prison clothes. Many months in confinement and the torture
of the rack had left its mark upon their pale faces. As they
shuffled round the courtyard at the direction of some minor
officials of the Holy Office they may have greeted each other in
undertones and exchanged wry comments, but none of them was
without fear of what the next day would bring.

They got no sleep that night. The rehearsals continued without
a pause. Again and again they traced the order of the procession
and were instructed in the nature of the responses that would be
demanded of them. By dawn everyone was worn out and tempers
were short, but the prisoners were thought to have learnt their
lessons. There were more than seventy of them in all, but only
half of them were Hawkins' men and accused of the grievous sin of
Lutheranism. The others were Spaniards who had for various
faults fallen under the displeasure of the Church. Most of them
were bigamists, but others were accused of a miscellany of
failings: wearing prohibited articles, 'propositions', and rashly
asserting that fornication was not a sin. One man, it was alleged,
had made his wife confess to him.

Soon after dawn they were all given breakfast—a cup of wine
and a slice of bread fried in honey—and at eight o'clock a strong
guard came to take the prisoners across the central plaza to the
cathedral. The Chief Constable of the city, who was in charge of
the escort, was familiar to many of the Englishmen. He was
Antonio Delgadillo, now promoted from his former command
over the batteries on the island of San Juan de Ulua.

Barefoot, and carrying an unlit green candle, each of the accused
walked from the prison, flanked on either side by a pikeman of the
guard. They needed protection, for a crowd of several thousand
had gathered overnight, and had been worked into a frenzy of

A penitent wearing the sanbenito

hatred and condemnation. Amid cries of insult and abuse the prisoners threaded their way through the mob, and found sanctuary on a wooden scaffold facing the high altar in the cathedral. They sat in carefully-rehearsed order and awaited the arrival of their spiritual judges.

In strict order of precedence the Viceroy, the Archbishop of Mexico (for Contreras had now been elected to this office), and the various dignitaries of Church and State took their places on an opposing scaffold. There were three hundred of them in all, including a multitude of friars of all orders. As soon as they were settled, silence was called and the ceremonies began.

It seems probable, as the church was so cramped, and the crowds that had been drawn to the city to witness the spectacle were so great, that only the celebration of Mass and the customary sermon took place within the cathedral. There was an additional reason for adjourning the process and reassembling in a public place; some of the sentences were expected to lead to the shedding of blood, and it would have been wrong to pollute the church with such pronouncements.

From the staging in the market-place the oath of obedience was administered, and a general decree of excommunication was fulminated against anyone who might attempt to hinder the workings of the Holy Office. In an awed and respectful silence the crowd listened attentively as a notary read aloud the confessions of each of the accused. One by one the yellow-clad figures were called forward and asked if the statement was true. In each case (for the warning against denial had been unequivocal) the reply was in the affirmative. The prisoner was next asked if he wished to repent, or whether he chose to lose both body and soul by persisting in heresy. In accordance with the instructions he had received the night before the accused man readily agreed on repentance. A form of abjuration was then read and the penitent repeated it word for word.

The Inquisitor was now able to absolve the accused from the automatic excommunication that he would otherwise have incurred, and promised him mercy if he behaved well under the remedial punishment that was imposed upon him. Finally, the long awaited sentences were pronounced, and the true nature of the mercy of the Tribunal became plain.

The first men to be called had reason to be thankful, for according to custom the most hardened cases were kept till last. Those who had sailed as boys when Hawkins' fleet left Plymouth six and a half years before, and had no opportunity to learn the True Faith in their own country, puzzled Contreras on account of their insuperable ignorance. 'It is evident,' he reasoned, 'that these are Lutheran heretics and as such should be condemned and chastised, but in deciding the punishment much clemency and pity should be shown to them in view of their youth and the general order of the Queen Elizabeth and the training they received from their parents.' His assistant, the Licentiate Bonilla, went further and expressed a 'doubt if they have capacity to understand a trial by the Inquisition'.

In the circumstances they were allowed to make good their neglected upbringing by serving in monasteries for a period of years. During this time they would wear the sanbenito and receive religious instruction. Miles Philips was fortunate in this way and so were seven or eight of his contemporaries. Amongst them was Paul Hawkins, the young nephew of their captain, Richard Williams, and, perhaps the most pathetic of all the captives, William Lowe, a freckled, red-haired dwarf, who played the bass viol in Hawkins' orchestra, but was left behind when his master abandoned the *Jesus*.

Only one sailor was more fortunate at the hands of the Inquisition than these youths. He was Roldan Escalant, one of Captain Bland's men who managed to convince his interrogators that he was a good Catholic. To everyone's surprise he was unconditionally acquitted, on the grounds that he had been compelled against his will to accompany the Lutherans on their voyage. The others all suffered savage penalties. Most of them were condemned to one or two hundred lashes and thereafter to be transported back to Spain to serve in the galleys for a period of years. A few were sentenced to 300 lashes and ten years at the oar's end—a penance that they could scarcely hope to complete. All these men had been brought up as Catholics during the previous reign, and with the accession of Queen Elizabeth had consciously lapsed into the heresy of Protestantism. Their sins, therefore, required long and severe atonement.

All day the scrupulous, slow process dragged on, and dusk was falling when the last two men were called forward to hear their doom. One of them was Marin Cornu, a French barber who had been arrested in Yucatan and brought to Mexico to stand trial for heresy. The second was George Rively, an English sailor from the *Jesus of Lubeck*, described by one of his compatriots as 'tall of body, very fat, with an ugly face, bulging cheeks which appear to have an egg of flesh in each, hairless, beardless, and with a massive chin'. Miles Philips claimed there were others, but his memory was almost certainly at fault.

Both Rively and Cornu were considered to have committed crimes against the Faith too grave to be reconciled by earthly penance. They were 'Lutheran heretics, feigned and simulated confessant'. The Church extended her mercy toward their souls, and abandoned their bodies to the secular arm, 'begging and enjoining this branch very affectionately, as we have a right, to be benign and pious with them'.

The first *auto de fe* to be held in Mexico was over. The condemned, their dooms pronounced, were escorted back to prison. But the secular authorities, with less than usual concern for the sanctity of the Sabbath, or else impelled by the fervour of the crowd, proceeded immediately to carry out the inevitable sentence on the two men that the Holy Office had entrusted to them. No *quemadero*, or burning-place, existed in the city, but willing hands brought faggots and stakes to a nearby square, and in the failing light George Rively and his companion were shriven and prepared for death. The official certificate of execution records the rest. 'And then instantly on the day, month and year, the twenty-eighth day of February, one thousand five hundred and seventy four, the said Jorge Ribli, Englishman, was taken from the said platform and put upon a saddled beast, and his crime was announced by the voice of Francisco Galvez, public crier of this city, who proclaimed it loudly at intervals. Thus he was taken by Antonio Delgadillo, chief constable of this city, through the

S

street of San Francisco to the market-place of San Hipolito, and there made to dismount from the said beast, and was then tied by his hands and feet to a pole and garrotted by the neck until he died naturally. And when he was dead they set a great quantity of wood afire, and in the midst of it was burned the body of the said Jorge Ribli, Englishman, in such a way that it was converted to dust and ashes.'

The sanbenitos worn by the two men were not burnt with them, but were hung in the cathedral for all to see. Each coat was carefully marked with the name of its owner and the terse inscription, 'An obstinate, heretic Lutheran burnt'. As the years passed many others were placed nearby as mute witnesses to the augean task that the Holy Office undertook in establishing the purity of the Faith in a sinful world.

The morning after the *auto de fe* the inhabitants of Mexico City were entertained by a further spectacle. The prisoners who had been sentenced to a flogging—the majority of the accused—were paraded through the streets on horseback, stripped to the waist and securely bound. At the head of the procession walked public criers, drawing the crowds with their exhortations and inspiring them with zealous enthusiasm. There were many who urged the attendants to lay on with their long whips; but they needed no encouragement. While some counted the strokes aloud, others applied themselves vigorously to their task. Very soon the cracking and thudding of blows, and the uncontrolled cries and groans of the helpless prisoners, became almost drowned by the roar of the mob crying out for fiercer punishment, and reviling the sinners whose wickedness had been exposed. 'Strike,' they chanted, 'lay on those English heretics, Lutherans, enemies of God.'

Slowly the procession wound its way through the main thoroughfares of the city, pausing at appropriate places for more lashes to be administered, to the gratification of the vociferous, excited crowd. As the tally of stripes grew greater the prisoners sagged and swayed on their mounts. Some lost consciousness and were propped up so that the full number of strokes could be administered. The backs of all of them were scarlet with running blood.

When the punishment was completed they were dragged from their horses and returned to the cells, where Miles Philips and those others who had been fortunate enough to avoid the lash tended them as best they could. For many days they suffered almost unendurably. The skin was flayed from their backs, and the deep weals of the lash had left scars that would never disappear. There were no medicines or soothing ointments that could be applied. In the hot, foetid dungeon, wounds did not heal quickly or cleanly, and the slightest movement was agony. Yet most of the men survived the torment and infection, and, when the plate fleet came that autumn, were sufficiently cured to be marched to Vera Cruz for transportation to Spain and the remainder of their punishment.

Although these men, who rowed out their lives in the galleys of Spain, are lost to history, the fate of at least one of them continued to exercise his Queen. Innumerable petitions were filed on his behalf but to no avail. Noteworthy amongst these is the report by the Spaniard, Antonio de Guaras, of an interview he endured with Queen Elizabeth. 'During much of her time,' he records, 'she dwelt upon the constant complaints that were made by her subjects respecting the imprisonment of Englishmen in Spain by the Inquisition. She spoke about the matter rather warmly and off her guard, said, "I promise ye that my father would not have put up with it, and if the matter is not amended I shall be obliged to order the arrest of some of the King of Spain's subjects and treat them in the same way". She was very gracious afterwards and spoke about Collins of Gravesend, who was captured in the Indies in one of Hawkins' ships, and is now in prison in Spain; giving me the enclosed memorial about him. I said I would do my best for him.' But even the Queen's efforts were insufficient, and William Collins failed to regain his liberty.

Meanwhile, in Mexico, Miles Philips and his companions had been dispersed to various monasteries where, for their appointed terms, they were destined to wear the sanbenito and work without reward. They were also expected to receive instruction in, and become familiar with, the tenets of the Catholic Faith. Philips was sent to work at the house of the Company of Jesus, where he was treated with friendliness, despite the constant humiliation of his dress. Very soon he won sufficient trust to be given an outdoor job, and was put in charge of a gang of Indian labourers who were helping to build yet another church to adorn the city. He enjoyed the work, and took the trouble to learn the Mexican tongue. Before long he was able to converse with his workmen, and learned to respect them both for their passive virtues and for the undying hatred with which they regarded their masters, the Spaniards.

Philips was prepared to share their hostility, but to his surprise he found many individuals, even amongst the clerks with whom he lived, who secretly deplored the advent of the Inquisition. Though they could not voice their opposition they did their best to ease the lot of the wards of the Holy Office. Philips was given a room to himself and adequate clothing and food. He was also given sufficient instruction in the Faith to allow him to appeal successfully for his release after he had served three years. On May 7, 1577, his sanbenito was taken from him and hung in the cathedral with the comforting inscription, 'An heretic Lutheran reconciled', and he was allowed to take employment in the city as a free man.

During the time of his penance there had been a second *auto de fe* in Mexico. Most of Hawkins' men had been rounded up the year before, and the prisoners who were summoned to answer before the Tribunal in March 1575 were almost all Spaniards. But one seaman from the *Jesus*, John Martin, sometimes known as Cornelius the Irishman, had wandered so far that he could not be recalled in time for the earlier investigation. He had landed at Panuco and marched to Mexico under Anthony Goddard. As soon as he was able he made his way south, and eventually set up in business as a barber-surgeon at La Trinidad in Guatemala. Here he had married, and already had a child when the Holy Office demanded his return. He proved, on investigation, to be a most dangerous heretic, possibly because he was unable to conceal the fact that his father was sacristan at Cork Cathedral and his whole upbringing must, therefore, inevitably have been tainted with Lutheranism. He pleaded extreme youth, but the

Tribunal disbelieved him, and at the *auto de fe* he was handed over to the secular arm, strangled and burnt at the stake.

Miles Philips and the few young Englishmen who were left in Mexico followed his fate with pity and anguish, but they dared not express their feelings. Their own position was still perilous, as one of the boys, John Perrin, learnt to his cost. Bad behaviour at the monastery of San Agustin caused him to be tried afresh, and the more severe sentence of four years in the galleys was his reward.

Another of the boys, Thomas Ebren, died in the monastery of San Agustin before he had served his time. But the rest of them, now grown to manhood, were eventually set free and relieved of their sanbenitos. Their fates were various, and not all of them recorded. William Lowe was the first to be released. Because of his diminutive size he had been employed as a kitchen-boy. As soon as he was able he applied for permission to go to Spain, where, soon after his arrival, he is reported to have married. Paul Hawkins grew up to be a stout, slightly round-shouldered young man, fair and beardless. After his trial he had been kept in confinement owing to a dispute about his sentence. One night he and several companions dug their way through the wall of their prison, using an old horseshoe, and escaped. They were re-captured and Hawkins was sentenced to a hundred lashes. Chastened by this experience he became at length reconciled to his fate. After his release he married a rich half-caste and settled down with a comfortable jointure in Mexico.

He and his companions, immediately after their release, were encouraged to learn some craft or trade; and considerable pressure was exerted by the ever-watchful officers of the Inquisition to make them marry and thereby quench any lingering desires they might have to return to the land of their birth. Paul Hawkins and Richard Williams were fortunate in their wives, but several others who had no claim to gentility of birth were paired with negro women and retained in the service of the Holy Office.

Only Miles Philips was sufficiently determined to resist the matrimonial pressure of the Inquisitors. He was suspicious of their intentions and inwardly untouched by the indoctrination he had undergone. When the time came for him to choose a profession he declined the opportunity to work as an overseer at the mines, where he knew he could quickly become prosperous, because he feared that he might excite envy and again become the object of inquisitorial investigation. Instead, under the name of Miguel Perez, he bound himself apprentice to a half-breed silk-weaver in the Santa Catalina quarter of the city, and learnt this unexceptional craft for three years.

He had hoped to escape attention, but found himself constantly under surveillance. Familiars of the Holy Office engaged him in dangerous discussions, and once he was summoned before the Inquisitor who accused him of planning to escape. He denied the charge, and claimed that he could not marry while he was still apprenticed. Nonetheless he was warned not to leave the city of Mexico and, under pain of excommunication, never to venture near the coast. To all this Philips readily agreed, but his uneasiness increased.

Before Philips' apprenticeship was over, wild and incredible rumours began to spread through Mexico. An English fleet had been sighted in the South Seas and was marauding the defenceless and hitherto inviolate western seaboard. Then came reports of a landing in great strength at Acapulco, and an inland march destined to sack the city of Mexico and lay waste the treasure-houses of New Spain. For the first time the name of Francis Drake was heard in the streets. Imagination embroidered the sparse news that came from the coast, and panic began to grow amongst those who, though descended from the conquistadors, had grown accustomed to peace and prosperity. Womenfolk and children began to leave the city in an ever-increasing stream, and carriages laden with personal treasure filled the roads to the north.

In the face of such general confusion and fear the Viceroy was stirred from the seclusion to which by nature he inclined, and ordered a general muster to be made of all able-bodied men. The count revealed seven thousand Spanish householders, three thousand single men and twenty thousand half-castes. From this number a militia was hastily formed.

In order to learn something of the nature of his opponent Don Martin summoned Paul Hawkins and Miles Philips to appear before him, and enquired if they knew this Captain Drake, who was said to be a brother of John Hawkins. They replied, truthfully, that Hawkins had only one brother, William, who, on account of his age, was hardly likely to have come so far from his native Plymouth. The Viceroy then asked if they knew anyone by the name of Francis Drake. They said they did not; though had Don Martin taken the trouble to scan the *procesos* of the Inquisition, he could readily have discovered that they lied.

The defence of New Spain was scarcely under way when news came from Acapulco that the Englishmen had left. Most of the militia was disbanded, but eight hundred men were retained under arms and sent in four groups to the principal ports, partly to steady the nerves of the inhabitants, and partly to be at hand if Drake should make a second landing on the coast. In charge of the party that went to Acapulco itself was Doctor Robles Alcarde de Corte, and with him, by special permission of the Inquisition, travelled Miles Philips as interpreter.

Acapulco was as far distant from the capital as San Juan de Ulua, and the journey, along a rough, mountainous track, was quite as arduous. But Philips was travelling in comfort and enjoyed the change. His only disappointment was to find, when they reached the little port on the Pacific coast, that Drake had sailed fully a month before, and no news had been heard of him since.

Nevertheless Alcarde de Corte, in his determination to make a show of defiance, embarked his men on the only ships available, three unarmed and insignificant pinnaces, and set sail in pursuit of the English vessels. He assumed, wrongly, that Drake would have retreated southwards, and for three weeks he and his men coasted towards Panama, suffering not a little from seasickness, but failing to gain any news of their adversary. All the while they were at sea Miles Philips had great difficulty in concealing his excitement. He knew that Alcarde de Corte's little boats would be at the mercy of any English warship they chanced to encounter, and to be captured by his fellow-countrymen was a fate he most desired. Hopefully he strained his eyes to catch sight of a sail, but the horizon remained bare.

The three Spanish boats had reached a point off the coast south of Guatemala when they met several small craft of their own nation coming north from Panama. As they too had seen no sign of the enemy Alcarde de Corte was forced to assume that Drake was no longer lurking on the Pacific seaboard, but had, mysteriously, disappeared. He turned his ships about and laid a course for home. Only one of the two hundred on board was sorry to come ashore again at Acapulco.

Having done their duty and exposed themselves fruitlessly to great discomfort, neither Alcarde de Corte nor his fellow-citizens had any wish to linger on the coast. Their only thought was to go home. The day after they landed, therefore, they took horse and made their way back to the capital. The journey took nearly a fortnight to complete. As soon as he had returned Alcarde de Corte reported to the Viceroy, who felt confident that Drake was trapped. Either hunger or bad weather would certainly drive him ashore again. It was essential to be prepared to intercept him without delay. Miles Philips, as interpreter, was told to be ready to leave for the coast at an hour's notice, and again warned, this time by the Viceroy, that in no circumstances should he leave the city without permission.

That neither Philips nor the militia was recalled is not surprising. Drake had sailed north, further than Spanish rule extended, and did not return the way he came. More than a year passed before the citizens of Plymouth, one morning in September 1580, witnessed the return of the *Golden Hind* and learned of the circumnavigation of the world.

The excitement of the threatened invasion having died down, Philips was able to resume his interrupted apprenticeship. He had acquired skill in his craft, and although still bound to his master he was able to earn a little money for himself from various commissions and evening work. He was frugal in his spending, for he realized that any attempt he might make to escape would certainly cost money. As his savings grew he sewed the gold pesos into the lining of his doublet.

Not much more than a month after his return from Acapulco the longed-for opportunity arose. A group of Spanish merchants with whom Miles Philips' master was engaged in business, were on the point of departure for Amecameca, a settlement some sixty miles from Mexico that lay under the shadow of the two great volcanoes Popocatepetl and Ixtaccihuatl. It was needful that Philips' master, or some responsible person, should ride with the merchants, and inspect the hides and cochineal that were stored there before they were transported. As he could not go himself the master-weaver applied for permission for Philips to go on his behalf. Leave was granted, Miles Philips was mounted upon an excellent horse, and the party made their way into the mountains, following the main road in the direction of San Juan de Ulua.

They arrived safely and transacted their business at Amecameca over the space of several days. While he was there Philips learned from travellers who passed that the annual plate fleet had arrived at San Juan and would shortly depart for Spain. An opportunity presented itself that could hardly be expected to recur. Well mounted and riding hard Philips reckoned that he could reach the coast in three days. In speech he could pass for a Spaniard, and if he could take passage aboard one of the ships he would be at sea before the hue and cry caught up with him. The risks were great, and he very well knew the fate that would await him if the attempt failed. But without taking chances he could never hope to escape from Mexico. He did not hesitate.

At night, under a full moon, Miles Philips led the best of the horses from the stable, tied his small bundle of possessions to the saddle-bow, mounted and rode for the coast. More than two hundred miles of hard going lay before him, but he spared neither his horse nor himself. For two nights and two days he kept riding, forcing the pace and pausing only long enough to snatch an hour or two of sleep and rest his mount. He encountered no trouble on the road and arrived, exhausted and travel-stained, at the gates of Vera Cruz by nightfall on the second day. Here he purposed to rest and refresh himself for a day or two, before following the coast road to where the galleons of Spain lay moored, side by side, their bows overhanging the stony island of San Juan de Ulua.

Miles Philips had reason to congratulate himself on his escape, but not for long. He had been in Vera Cruz no more than half an hour, and had scarcely dismounted, when he found himself under arrest. It was, of course, a mistake: news of his flight had certainly not preceded him. But the situation was dangerous. The officers of the watch took him straightway to the Justices where, as always when an arrest is made, a crowd gathered. There was considerable excitement and everybody seemed to be talking at once, accusing him of running away, witnessing his capture, and expressing opinions, the drift of which Philips found it impossible to understand. At last the Justices called for silence, and from their interrogation Miles Philips at last realized that a well-born youth, who had run away from his home in Mexico, was indeed being sought, and that he had been mistaken for the truant. He denied that he was the gentleman's son in question, but, as he could not easily explain who in fact he was, his denial was not taken seriously. Until he could be properly identified it was decided to commit him to prison, and despite his protests he was taken from the Justices and marched between guards to the town gaol.

By this time a considerable crowd had assembled, amongst whom, by ill-chance, was a man who had known Philips in the days when he had worn the sanbenito in Mexico. He was of no standing—merely a poor man who had come with a wicker basket of hens to sell in the city—but he had always liked Philips, and now, recognizing him and understanding that he was the victim of mistaken arrest, thought to do him a good turn. Pushing himself to the front of the crowd he shouted out that they had caught the wrong person: the man they were taking to prison was in any case not even a Spaniard, he was an Englishman.

Philips had been anxious enough before, but this unexpected and misguided act of friendship dashed his last hopes. The Justices were recalled and attention centred on the innocent informer, whom they suspected of being an accomplice in the escape. They demanded the truth and threatened him with imprisonment too. But the poor man held to his story and added so many circumstantial details of his familiarity with Philips in Mexico, that the Justices turned again to their prisoner and pressed him for certain proof of his identity. It was impossible for Philips to deny any longer that he was indeed one of Hawkins' Englishmen, and his presence at Vera Cruz was sufficient evidence of his intentions. Not a little proud of their prowess in capturing so dangerous a fugitive, the guard hustled Miles Philips to gaol and consigned him, fettered by the legs, to the public cell.

For three weeks he remained in confinement, dejected, and ignored by his captors. During this time he struck up acquaintance with most of the felons who shared the cell, and even met some old acquaintances from Mexico who had been condemned to the galleys for various faults and were awaiting transport to Spain. From his fellow-prisoners he received unexpected friendship and occasional gifts of food to supplement the meagre and irregular official issue. To endure the rigours of prison life it was very necessary to have friends outside who could bribe the guard and pass gifts and information through the iron grille. One of the men who befriended Miles Philips had such a friend, and from him he learnt that as soon as the plate fleet had sailed, a convoy of waggons was due to leave for the capital, in one of which Philips would travel in order to stand trial in Mexico.

The next time Philips' new friend received a visit from outside, not only the welcome gifts of bread and wine were smuggled through the bars, but also two knives, strongly made, with files down the back edges. One of these priceless treasures the Spaniard kept himself; the other he offered to Philips. He asked two pesos for it, and the Englishman, whose money had not been detected and taken from him, gladly paid. Given time and opportunity he now had the means to free himself from his shackles, but at present the knife was best concealed. He hid it in the foot of his boot.

Three or four days later Philips was taken from prison and brought before the chief justice. He was told, what he already knew, of his impending journey. Evidently the authorities were determined to prevent him from escaping, for the fetters were removed from his feet and a new and stronger pair were forged, together with manacles for his hands and an iron collar for his neck. In this helpless condition Philips was placed, alone, in one of sixty waggons, most of which were laden with merchandise that had come with the *flota* from Spain.

All around him the Englishman could hear the bustle of preparation, as mules were harnessed and goods loaded and checked. Soon the procession moved off, the waggon in which Philips travelled leading the way. Creaking laboriously it jolted along the rutted track that led to the hills, drawing Miles Philips slowly back towards the city from which he had so hopefully fled.

When he was certain that the driver and the guard were occupied Philips began to strain at his new manacles in an attempt to free his hands. To his delight he was successful: they had been made too large, and allowed him, with some discomfort, to slip them on and off at will. He was thus able to retrieve the precious file from his boot, and start to work on the thick metal bolt that secured his ankles. The rasping of the file could hardly be heard when the waggon was in motion over rough ground, but great caution was needed if the mules unexpectedly halted, or if one of the guards who walked past from time to time paused to peer inside at the prisoner on his bed of straw. All the time that he was busy with his file Philips was tense and alert, ready in an instant to hide the incriminating tool and force the manacles back on to his wrists.

He worked as fast as he dared, and the cumbersome procession of waggons had only gone twenty miles inland and reached the foothills of the central plateau when he judged that he had filed the metal as deeply as he could without actually breaking the bolt. By good luck at this moment one of the wheels of the waggon in which he was travelling broke. While an Indian carpenter was being found to repair the damage all the other waggons in the convoy overtook them, and arrived first at a hostelry that lay a little further on at the foot of a steep hill. It was customary with loaded waggons to pause at this place, both for refreshment, and also to allow three or four teams of mules to be harnessed to a single waggon for a few miles where the gradient was steepest. When the waggon reached the top the mules were unhitched, and returned to the bottom of the hill to repeat the performance. Understandably this operation took time, and dusk was falling before the majority of the waggons had been hauled to the top. Miles Philips, whose waggon had now been mended, was last in the queue.

In fading light, with most of his escort several miles away, the time seemed opportune for Philips to make his escape. A few strokes of the file freed him from his leg-irons, and he regained freedom of movement. Carrying his fetters with him he slipped quietly over the tailboard of the waggon, and, choosing a moment when nobody was watching, ran into the woods that bordered the road. His escape was not observed, but he did not linger in the neighbourhood. Pausing only to hide his fetters in the undergrowth he pressed forward all night in the direction, as far as he could judge, that he wished to go.

The rising of the sun confirmed him on his course, and allowed him to take stock of his situation. He presented a strange picture as he strayed through the pathless woods. His trim suit of clothes was soiled and shabby from prison; during his blind flight through the undergrowth it had become torn as well. In his hands he carried two small cheeses and a few biscuits that he had providently saved, and round his neck was the iron collar from which he had not been able to free himself. His only plan was to make his way south-east, following the coast some way inland, so that he might put the greatest distance between himself and the authorities who would undoubtedly attempt to seek him out.

Philips had not walked far through the woods that morning when he saw smoke rising amongst the hills to the north. He judged that he would find an Indian encampment there, and made his way towards the fires intending to seek guidance and provisions. Before he reached the settlement he was intercepted by a band of Indians who were out hunting deer. Greeting them in their own language, he told them frankly of his escape from the Spaniards. As he rightly suspected they had no love for their conquerors. They welcomed Philips with enthusiasm, rejoicing at his good fortune and marvelling at his ability to speak their tongue. In view of their friendliness Philips asked them if they would file the collar from off his neck; this they eagerly did, and provided one of their number to act as a guide to the nearest Indian town where he could equip himself for his journey to the south. The town, Shalapa, was a day's march away. Philips was glad to reach it, for he was sickening with a fever, which laid him up for three days. During his illness he was treated with great kindness, and when he had recovered an Indian sold him a horse, which he was able to pay for by unstitching six pesos from his doublet.

As soon as he was fit to depart the Indians led Philips by forest tracks to a road leading to Guatamala and the south; then they parted from him. To travel on one of the main Spanish staging roads involved risks, but Philips felt less conspicuous now his iron collar was removed, and if he was to progress speedily and on horseback he had no choice but to risk an encounter with Spaniards. He felt sure, at least, that the search for him would not have spread so far afield.

By a strange freak of fortune he had not ridden seven miles when he overtook a solitary Franciscan whom, on greeting, he recognized as a friendly and sympathetic acquaintance from Mexico. After the first shock had passed Philips recollected that this friar had been more than usually outspoken in his condemnation of the methods of the Inquisition. He determined, therefore, to be open with him, and confessed that the reason for his journey was an attempt to escape from New Spain. He besought the friar to give him advice on how best to bring this about. Philip's confidence was not misplaced. The Franciscan never questioned the Englishman's motives, but, being familiar with the road, gave Philips much sound information about the safest manner of travelling. He also volunteered to keep Philips company for a few days.

The friar travelled slowly, calling at all the Indian settlements along the road, where he received food, and courteous treatment, and a contribution in the wooden bowl that he invariably passed round before his departure. Philips, although he felt a certain impatience, was content to loiter with his friend for three days; but when he indicated that he wished to ride on, the Franciscan gave him his blessing and pressed on him the entire sum he had received from begging since they had been together. It amounted to twenty pesos, and Philips accepted it gratefully. He knew that he would need money if ever he found a ship that would allow him to take passage back across the ocean sea.

Miles Philips was never afraid of riding hard and far. The road to Guatamala provided few comforts for the traveller or for his horse, and to ride alone was not without its dangers. But Philips was only prepared to recognize one danger—that of being recaptured by the Spanish authorities. Other incidents and perils must surely have beset him, though his narrative does not pause to record them. But it can be assumed that his ability to speak with the Indians kept him provisioned with maize-bread and fruit, and at times he must have paused to rest himself and his fast-tiring horse within the protection of their wayside villages.

The road led him to Guatamala on the Pacific coast—the wrong side of the isthmus to seek a ship returning to Europe. He remained there barely a week, then pressed forward on a less frequented, easterly track towards the Caribbean coast of what is now the Republic of Honduras. A week's trek through relatively populated country brought him to an Indian town where he learned that his route would lead through dense, deserted rainforests. Food was unobtainable, the track obscure and easy to lose, and no habitation would be encountered in ten or twelve days' journeying. Undaunted by the prospect Miles Philips hired two Indians to be his guides, bought hens, bread and a tinder-box, and set off, following the rivers as they descended from the highlands, weaving their way through sodden green abundance and towering trees down to the humid plain.

It was a nerve-racking journey, haunted with uncertainty by day and panic at night. Pumas and jaguars abounded in the thick cover, and many less dangerous beasts added unseen and imagined perils by noises which darkness magnified. At night the three men lit fires on which they cooked their meals, and kept them burning until dawn to protect themselves from the intrusion of wild beasts. During these hours, when sleep would not come, Philips spent his time calming his fearful horse, stoking the fires between which they lay encamped, and listening to 'heare the Lions roare, with Tygres, Ounces, and other beastes, and some of them we should see in the night, which had eyes shining like fire'.

Twelve days brought them clear of the great forests to within sight of the Caribbean. Philips paid off his guides and made his way alone to the small, unfortified harbour of Puerto Cabello. He entered unobtrusively and went straight to the waterfront where a number of small trading vessels were unloading their cargoes of canary wine. Striking up a conversation with the master of one he said, in reply to the seaman's enquiry, that he was a native of Granada and wished to go home. Could he pay his passage and sail back with him?

There were two awkward moments, first when the master revealed that he too came from Granada, and later when Philips was asked for a safe-conduct or testimonial to show that he was entitled to take passage. Because, as the Spaniard jokingly pointed out, you might be a debtor, or an escaped murderer. A little time and goodwill enabled Philips to gloss over this objection, and the Spaniard was persuaded to take the Englishman on board in consideration of sixty pesos for his fare.

Philips could barely conceal his delight. By selling his horse he managed to raise the necessary money and buy, besides, the necessary provisions for the voyage. Two days later they sailed, Havana being the first port of call.

The harbour of Havana, always a busy and well-garrisoned stronghold, was crowded with ships. Philips' arrival had coincided with the assembly of an armada, returning to Spain with treasure from the Indies. As always the fleet was short of men for the passage home and the press-gangs were busy, searching the town and all likely hideouts for suitable men to swell their complement. As soon as they discovered that Miles Philips was travelling as a passenger they signed him on and posted him to the flagship as a soldier. Before he went aboard Philips was obliged to provide himself with his own sword, arquebus, powder and shot.

The return journey to Spain was looked upon as particularly dangerous in the summer of 1581. The exiled pretender to the Portuguese throne, Don Antonio, held the Azores with a considerable fleet at his command, and threatened to intercept any Spanish vessels that passed nearby. The armada with which Philips sailed, a convoy of thirty-seven sail, was especially vulnerable as only two of the ships were sturdily armed, and all of them were deeply-laden and sluggish in their sailing. Don Pedro de Guzman, who commanded the Spanish vessels, had orders to give Don Antonio a wide berth. In consequence the voyage from Havana, though uneventful, was long. The fleet set sail on June 4th and sighted no land until September 10th, by which time they had almost arrived at San Lucar.

Until near the end Miles Philips had acquitted himself faultlessly as a Spaniard. But in some way—he never discovered exactly how—he must have betrayed himself. To his horror he chanced to overhear one of his fellow soldiers reporting to the Master that Philips was in fact an Englishman. He needed no second warning. While they were still at sea there was nothing he could do except cheerfully feign ignorance of the fact that his disguise had been penetrated. But when they had moored along-side the quay at San Lucar, and leave had been granted to the crew, Philips was among the first to ask to be allowed ashore. As he feared, permission was not granted. Instead the Master curtly informed him that he must stay with the ship as far as Seville. Knowing that this certainly entailed being handed over to the Inquisition when he arrived, Philips was determined to do no such thing. He made light of the prohibition and pretended to acquiesce with good grace; but secretly he made plans for yet another escape.

At night, when the Master was asleep and the duty watch nodding at their stations, Philips clambered down a rope that hung down over the stern and dropped into the ship's boat that was secured alongside. He cut the painter, pulled himself to the shore by the mooring lines, and scrambled on to Spanish soil without wetting his feet. The boat he allowed to drift away into the harbour; he himself set off on foot along the road to Seville.

It was a long walk, but Philips did not pause all night and kept going well into the morning. As soon as he had reached the city he knew he would have to lie low until the hunt, that would surely follow his escape, had died down. Sensibly, he determined that the best concealment was to take a job. Enquiry led him to the quarter where the weavers of silk carried on their trade, and his skill enabled him quickly to find employment. His new master was a weaver of taffetas, and Philips was installed in a large workroom

T

amongst fellow-journeymen, with whom the Englishman was soon on easy terms.

The shabbiness of his dress gave Philips an acceptable excuse for keeping indoors. He let it be known that he had had a run of bad luck, and needed to work hard in order to earn enough money to re-equip himself. From the gossip of his companions as they worked at their looms Philips heard the news of the city. One day, very soon after he arrived, one of the journeymen remarked that there was a hue and cry afoot for an Englishman who had escaped from the fleet.

'What,' enquired Philips with disarming boldness, 'a heretic Lutheran? I would to God that I could find him, for I should certainly give him up to the Holy Office.'

Three months passed before Philips felt confident enough to venture into the streets. He called for the wages he had earned and bought himself new clothes, but even then he was fearful of detection. News reached him, however, that some English merchant vessels had called at San Lucar, and the risk of a journey there seemed justified. He reached the port without difficulty, and as the ships were lying in the roads he hired a boat and rowed over to one of them.

The captain received him courteously and listened to Philips' story; but instead of welcoming him aboard with open arms, and rejoicing in the escape of a fellow-countryman, he asked to be excused from smuggling him back to England. It was too dangerous an undertaking he declared, and he would not meddle with it.

As a trader whose presence in Spanish ports depended on an untarnished reputation it was an understandable, though pusillanimous, attitude to take. To Philips it was a bitter blow. For thirteen years he had been taking risks and living in danger of his life, sustained throughout by the hope of returning home. Now that he was within sight of his goal a compatriot had denied him help. But there was no arguing with the decision. Heavy at heart Philips returned to his boat and rowed back to the unwelcome shore.

He could not return to Seville: he could not linger in San

Lucar. In both places the chance of detection was too great. Sooner or later, Philips knew, he would be challenged and caught. He decided to move down the coast to Puerto de Santa Maria, across the water from Cadiz. Here, he gathered from the sailors on the waterfront, there was a Spanish galley on its way to Majorca, which stood in need of soldiers.

Because he felt that more English ships were likely to call there, and the scrutiny would be less intense, Philips enlisted, and arrived at Palma during the last days of 1581. Two English ships rode in the harbour, laden with cargo and awaiting a wind. One was from London; the other, the *Landret*, was from the West Country. Philips chose to approach the latter, but this time he did not neglect the cloak of dissimulation that he had learnt to perfection over many years. He was, he told the English captain, a student who had been two years in Spain to learn the language. Now that his funds had run out he was anxious to return home.

The captain of the *Landret* agreed to convey him back, and Philips realized, without regret, that the last obstacle had been overcome. In February 1582 he stepped ashore at Poole, a free man, unburdened of the trepidations that had masked his life for so long.

Of all the men who were left behind in Mexico and whose fates have been recorded, Job Hortop endured most, but Miles Philips was the most indomitable for the perseverance he exercised in achieving liberty. The thirteen-year-old page-boy, who waited on Hawkins when he left Plymouth on his third slaving voyage, matured quickly into a self-reliant man. 'Advancement by diligence', his captain's motto, he justified by his own actions. Hawkins, who listened to his story soon after Philips' return, must have applauded the combination of caution and resolution that enabled the young man to retain his initiative of action despite overwhelming odds.

It is natural for a prisoner to strive for freedom. To some the opportunity never comes; but enough captives have, over the years, regained their liberty by nimbleness of body and wit, for legends to grow, particularly when national honour overrides the law. The escape of Miles Philips never swayed the destiny of nations, but it reflected a rift that made two ambitious countries irreconcilable—a mistrust of each others' laws. An individual like Philips, who evaded the ponderous machinery of Spanish justice, could be exalted in England, yet be a temporal and spiritual law-breaker in Spain.

The edge of conflict has long been dulled: the choice of emphasis now rests with the narrator. Miles Philips' achievement survives— an honourable monument to the human spirit acting under adversity.

CHAPTER 16

The Improbable Walk

T HE fate of the survivors from John Hawkins' third slaving voyage has been followed as faithfully as facts permit. The stories they have told are adventurous but credible. Except in certain unimportant details they are borne out whenever substantiation can be obtained from independent sources. But one group of men has not yet been accounted for; and here, in a limbo between fact and fancy, the reader must form his own judgment on the veracity of David Ingram, whose narrative, so vague and improbable that no one seriously believes it, nevertheless begins and ends with two irreconcilable events.

It will be recalled that, soon after enduring their first attack at the hands of the Chichimeca Indians, a number of the castaways, whom Anthony Goddard was leading down the coast from the beach where Hawkins had landed them, determined to strike north and seek freedom rather than captivity. A second Indian attack had undermined their resolutions, and all but two dozen retreated and rejoined Goddard's men. David Ingram, a sailor from Barking in Essex, was elected leader of the remnant and decided to press forward into the unexplored territories that separated them from their assumed objective, the River of May.

Eleven months later three ragged, but vigorous, individuals encountered a French sea-captain, whose ship the *Gargarine* had come to fish, and stayed to trade with the Indians. They asked for passage home, and M. Champaine, the captain, agreed to take them. The three men were Ingram and two of his companions, Richard Twide and Richard Browne. The place was Nova Scotia, barely a hundred and fifty miles below Cape Breton and at least three thousand miles overland from the River Panuco.

How, and indeed if, Ingram succeeded in making this fantastic journey through country that no European had ever visited before is a problem that it is probably no longer in our power to solve. He talked to Hawkins soon after his return, and was well rewarded by his old captain, but no details of the interview exist. Not until much later does notice seem to have been taken of his marvellous story. In the autumn of 1582 Ingram was summoned to appear before Sir Francis Walsingham and various other notables who interrogated him on certain aspects of his travels. His replies are on record, but, as will be seen, they throw very little light on the trip itself, and some of his assertions are palpably untrue.

Walsingham's committee was interested in obtaining facts, not about Ingram's journey, but about the eastern seaboard of North America along which he claimed to have travelled. Sir George Peckham, a sponsor and friend in court of Sir Humphrey Gilbert, was present at the enquiry—and Gilbert himself may have been there too. These men were enthusiasts, ambitious to plant the first English colony in the new world. Gilbert had obtained a grant, valid for six years, of all the lands he might discover and occupy in the northern parts of America. Most of the time had passed, and no voyage had taken place. Nothing had been achieved. A sense of urgency inspired those who still believed fervently in the project, and Gilbert was preparing a fleet to sail during the following summer.

All the questions that Ingram was asked were, therefore, relative to this one purpose. The future colonists needed to know what reception they might expect from the Indians, how nature might aid them in establishing their settlement, and whether gold or precious stones would reward their enterprise. They were not interested, as we are now, in the manner whereby Ingram and his two companions achieved their long and suspiciously swift overland trek, nor in the route they took.

Ingram was now forty years old, and recollecting events that he had experienced in his middle twenties. He was anxious to oblige his distinguished questioners, even to the point, we must regretfully assume, of embroidering and inventing the replies that would be most acceptable to his audience. The accuracy of what he said could not be checked: Browne had been killed on board the *Elizabeth* five years before, and Twide had died ashore in 1579. Ingram alone possessed the facts, and needed to fear no contradiction.

It is reasonable to believe that many intervening voyages and innumerable messdeck yarns had clouded his memory; and a certain pride might have prevented him from confessing ignorance of any matter that seemed of special concern to his interrogators. Certainly we may infer that he enjoyed the interview to the full. It was not often that an elderly seaman could offer such a pantomime before Her Majesty's Principal Secretary of State as Ingram, when demonstrating Indian customs. According to the dry, official record he could 'very (well) discribe there gesture, dauncinge, and songes'.

The mainland of America north of the Gulf retained its secrets long after Mexico had been thoroughly explored. The Spaniards had poor success in their attempts to open up the country. Rumours of gold and unicorns, of a people, tall as a man's arm, who came from the sea with sharp, stiff tails that encumbered them when they sat down, and many another strange story excited curiosity; but those who did travel in those unfriendly regions brought back no treasure, if they were lucky enough to return alive.

With wealth to be had in plenty within the boundaries of New Spain there was little incentive to look further. Only one rumour, more persistent and alluring than all the others, continued to draw men to the north. This concerned the seven, fabulously-rich cities of Cibola.

Where the story originated it is impossible to say, but the return of Alvar Nuñez Cabeza de Vaca from eight years of enforced wanderings across the continent gave impetus to the quest. The hardships endured by Vaca and the two men who survived with him are interesting to compare with the ease and speed of Ingram's much longer journey. Vaca had been cast ashore, forty years before Ingram, to the north of Tampico in the vicinity of Galveston. He and eighty companions wintered among the destitute, nomadic Indians who frequented the coastal plains. At first there was fruit and nuts and some seaweed that could be gathered, but as these meagre supplies failed starvation faced them. Fifteen Spaniards survived the first winter: they had practised cannibalism, and even dried human pemmican in their desperate attempts to keep alive.

In the spring they moved inland. Vaca, who had won the confidence of the Indians by his skill as a healer, made a precarious living for several years trading between the coastal tribes and the Indians who dwelt in the south-eastern part of what is now Texas. But although the distance was not enormous he was unable, until 1534, to make any effective attempt to escape from his thraldom. Then he struck westward with four companions. They travelled as itinerant medicine-men, passing from one mean pueblo to the next, glimpsing on their way the great herds of bison that roamed the plains, and hearing stories, that they can only partly have understood, of the turquoise-and-gold-encrusted streets of Cibola and Quivira.

Vaca and two companions reached the most northerly of the Spanish settlements on the west coast of Mexico in 1536. The tales they told, far from deterring the adventurous, precipitated a wave of exploration amongst men hungry for treasure and priests eager for unconverted souls.

Before following the legend of the seven cities further, it is worth pausing to consider certain similarities and points of difference between the epic journeys of Vaca and Ingram. Although they both started in destitute circumstances from the Gulf Coast, the course they pursued was quite divergent. Vaca crossed the continent westward, following roughly the thirtieth degree of latitude; Ingram, we must assume, kept within touch of the eastern seaboard. Ingram had by far the longer journey, yet he accomplished it, according to his statement, in eleven months, never pausing for more than a day or two at any one place. Vaca was six years in the wilderness, for much of the time incapable of progress, either on account of his physical condition or because of the passive restraints put upon him by the Indians among whom he dwelt.

Both men admit that the tribes they encountered were friendly, and neither they, nor their companions, were molested by Indians who had never seen white men before. The casualties that Ingram's party suffered in the first few days were at the hands of Indians who were already roused to hostility by the Spaniards. The reason that Ingram gave to Miles Philips for the fact that only two companions arrived with him at Cape Breton was that the others, though fallen by the wayside, were 'yet alive, and married in the said countrey, at Cibola'. Although we may well be sceptical of this pleasing explanation, there is no hint of violence or foul play, far less of a cannibalistic reduction in numbers, to be read in Ingram's account of his travels. Indeed, if he had met with circumstances in any way comparable to Vaca's grim sojourn on the coast he would have had neither the time nor the physical endurance to travel so swiftly to the north-east. Ingram must, however, have passed very close to the scene of Vaca's winter encampment near Galveston Bay, but he mentions no shortage of food at any point on his journey. Indeed he encouraged his questioners to rely upon the natural resources of the country—though here, and throughout the interrogation, the emphasis seems to lie upon the latter part of his travels, within the area where Gilbert proposed to plant his settlement.

The rumour of the seven cities is mentioned by both travellers, but it seems likely that in Ingram's case it was inserted as an afterthought. By the time he came to tell his tale Cibola had become an accepted part of the mythology of the New World. To many Englishmen it had merged with the legend of Madoc, the Welsh prince who sailed to a western land in 1170 with a band of his compatriots. Ingram was quite positive that the Great Auks, that he had heard called Penguins, derived their name from the Welsh words for 'white head'. He persuaded Sir George Peckham that this, and several similar etymologies, should be ascribed to the Cambrian colonists of four centuries before. It was generally expected that their descendants would eventually be discovered, and in what more likely place than the American Avalon called Cibola?

The first European who claimed to have seen the seven cities was Friar Marcos; but his travels, we now know, took him nowhere near the pueblo centre in the land of the Zunis that bore the enchanted name. In 1540 Coronado did indeed track the legend to its source, and found 'a little, crowded village' on the plateau be-

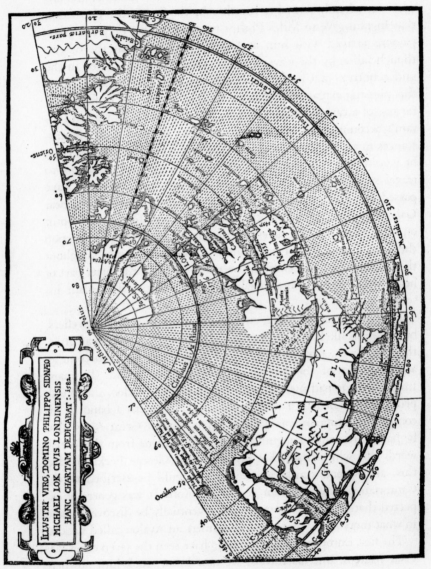

Michael Lok's map of the North Atlantic in 1582

tween the Little Colorado and the Rio Grande. But the myth was now too strongly rooted to be destroyed. The great wilderness of land that stretched to the north of Mexico needed a rich focus for ambitious eyes. 'In the city called Cebola,' Jean Alfonse declared only three years later, 'the houses are all covered with gold and silver. These lands are attached to Tartary, and I think that they form the outer limit of Asia.'

Thirty years past, and Cibola was still as elusive and desirable as ever. Henry Hawks reported to Hakluyt that 'the Spanyards have notice of seven cities which old men of the Indians shew them should lie towards the northwest from Mexico. They have used and use dayly much diligence in seeking of them, but they cannot find any one of them. They say that the witchcraft of the Indians is such, that when they come by these townes they cast a mist upon them, so that they cannot see them.' Even as late as 1622 the Professor of Astronomy at Oxford declared his belief in the rich, populous cities of Cibola and Quivira. The legend persisted, because men wanted to think it true.

Throughout the sixteenth century the map of North America remained a capricious and hazy exercise of the cartographer's fancy. The Spaniards comprehended the main outline of the continent, but they were careful not to share their knowledge. Michael Lok's English map shows they were successful in their secrecy. But within the coastal framework even the Spaniards were unsure. A freakish web of waterways is often shown, lacing the land; and even the Mississippi—Pineda's River of the Holy Spirit—was long considered to flow from the Pacific.

Two major Spanish expeditions had attempted to unravel the secrets of the northern lands. Coronado led an armed band through the weary labyrinths of the western plains in an unprofitable search for gold. De Soto, at about the same time, wandered for four years through the watershed of the Mississippi on a dogged quest that only ended with his death.

So unsuccessful were these two undertakings that very little more had been explored when Ingram began his long walk thirty years later. The Spaniards were disillusioned by the poverty of the settlements and the uncultured, nomadic state of the inhabitants.

Compared to the wealth and civic dignity of the Aztecs, the Indians of the pueblo and the plains were indeed a primitive race. But Ingram endowed them with a dignity and a degree of material wealth that can only be regarded as fanciful. In all his wanderings de Soto found no township more extensive than Ocali, which, he reckoned, contained six hundred houses. Ingram reports half a dozen towns of very considerable size, including (though the comparison of names, imperfectly recollected and transcribed, is a hopeless guessing-game) 'Ochala a great Toune a myle longe'. The largest of all the habitations on Ingram's list, 'Balma a Ritche Cyttie a mile and a halfe longe', detained him for a week, and implies a degree of civilization that we know did not exist in these regions.

In his description of the Indians and their culture Ingram seems far more accurate and credible, though we must discount the rubies 'sixe ynches longe and twoe ynches broade' worn by the local Kings, the 'great abundunce of Pearle' that was to be found 'in every Cottage', and the 'Bracelettes, . . . great plates of goulde . . . and Chaynes of great Pearle' with which the natives were said to adorn themselves. These attractions were most likely invented for the encouragement of future colonists.

With less incredulity we learn from Ingram that the rule of each Indian King extended for about a hundred miles, that they were at constant war with their neighbours, and within their territories they exercised despotic and absolute power. Ingram told his examiners in some detail the ceremonial that was necessary in order to approach any such chieftain and obtain an audience. He also described the feathered headdresses by which the most favoured of the tribe might be distinguished.

Ingram's descriptions are so generalized that little distinction is drawn between the variations of appearance, custom and speech that we now know existed amongst the various tribes. In the southern regions, he points out, 'they goe all naked', whereas in the colder regions to the north 'they are clothed with beastes skynnes, the heare syde beinge next to there bodyes in wynter'; but for the rest 'the people commonlye are of good favor feture and shape of bodye, of growthe aboute five foote highe, somewhat thicke, with there faces and skynnes of colloure like an Ollive and towarde the Northe somewhat Tawnye, but some of them are paynted with dyvers colloures, they are very swyfte of foote, the heare of there heades is shaven in sundrye places and the reste of there heddes is traced'. [Tattoed?]

It is not an anthropologist's description, but Ingram manages to portray with considerable accuracy the general appearance of the American Indian. Few of his contemporaries could have done better. There are not a few similar instances where Ingram's sober recollections bear all the stamps of observation at first hand.

Yet is it creditable that in eleven months he should have walked at least three thousand miles through an unknown land? It is extremely doubtful, but just possible. La Salle's classic march, from the Illinois to the St Lawrence in two months in 1680, shows how quickly an intrepid man could travel. But let us first examine a few alternative explanations.

Other than walking, the only means of transport between Rio Panuco and Cape Breton was by sea. It is just possible that Ingram and his companions encountered a ship at some point on the coast and took passage. But why did they go only to Cape Breton, which was not a final destination for any craft, and why should Ingram wish to hide the fact so many years later? Alternatively, like Henry May who was shipwrecked on Bermuda in 1594, did Ingram's party build themselves a boat and sail it, as May intended to sail [how?] his, towards Newfoundland? Again the unnecessary secretiveness forms an obvious objection.

Turning to Captain Champaine and his ship the *Gargarine*, we have only Ingram's evidence for their presence on the Grand Banks in the autumn of 1569. If Ingram had missed a year from his calculations he must have done so consciously and for no apparent reason. He claims to have reached England, by way of the *Gargarine's* home port Le Havre, in 1569, and such a statement could reasonably have been checked by his interrogators. Ingram volunteered the additional fact that several of the French crew of the *Gargarine* were 'yet lyvinge . . . uppon the Coaste of ffraunce as he thincketh, for he did speake with some of them within these three yeares'. Evidently Ingram did not fear any embarrassing disclosures from this quarter.

However much we may distrust the evidence, we are faced with no reasonable alternative. There was a beginning and, eleven months later, an ending to the story; only Ingram himself knew how much truth lay in between.

A reasonable objective for Ingram's party, when it set out in the first place, was Laudonnière's settlement on the River of May. Ingram indicated that he went there and took four months on that part of the journey. This would be unbelievably good time; for a half-circle of the Gulf Coast, interrupted by extensive swamps and massive estuaries, would need to be negotiated, and the neck of Florida traversed, in order to arrive at the ransacked site of Laudonnière's colony. The English party seem to have possessed neither compass nor astrolabe, and even with such aids could scarcely have hoped to locate this one small place so swiftly. Besides Ingram never mentions Laudonnière, nor the settlement, nor any surprise or disappointment at finding it deserted and in ruins.

It seems more likely that, having reached approximately the correct latitude and misidentified some river on the Gulf as the River of May, Ingram's men struck north, following, perhaps, the course of the Alabama River, and never touched the Florida peninsula at all. The estuaries of some of the great rivers that flow sluggishly into the Gulf might have been those that Ingram reports as being up to ten miles across and which his men crossed in canoes and boats. Perhaps the Mississippi itself was that one 'soe large that they colde scarce crosse the same in XXIIII howers'.

We can imagine, if we wish, Ingram and his companions trudging steadily north, passing from one tribe to the next, always being received with the courtesy and curiosity of a simple people. Very soon they learnt the customs that it was needful to observe. A white flag waved from a distance indicated peaceful intent; a little nearer and they would lift up both hands, kissing the backs as a token of friendship. If a messenger came to them from an Indian chief carrying an emblem like a horse's tail they knew he could be trusted, and would follow wherever he led, until they came to a cluster of huts, 'made rounde like dove howses'. Here they were assured of hospitality and food, although they had nothing to offer in return. The Indians regarded only a few domestic possessions as private property; all else was free to give and free to take. The Englishmen must have been thankful for this tolerant attitude, and wasted little time loitering or providing for themselves.

If indeed they had so clear a motive, the reason that drove them north with such determination was the knowledge that the numerous fishing boats that frequented the Grand Banks, and occasionally anchored off the coast, were summer visitors. If they delayed, all the ships might have returned, and winter in those bleak lands would offer them little chance of survival. In the event the three Englishmen were only just in time.

Despite the speed at which they travelled Ingram was able to observe numerous small incidents that impressed themselves upon his mind, and were diligently recorded at his subsequent questioning. He watched Indian craftsmen whittling and carving wooden and bone figures with their crude iron knives. He saw fires kindled by rubbing dry sticks together; and listened to their musicians beating drums and playing upon a peculiar hollow cane instrument that 'they smighte uppon there thighes and one of there handes, makinge a pleasunte kynde of sownde'.

Ingram was also present when war parties set out to do battle, perhaps against their professed enemies the Cannibals (who 'have teethe like dogges teethe'), or else against some other tribe. He saw them march, two or three abreast, accompanied by the music of horn trumpets and drums. The warriors were armed with hide shields, throwing spears, and, of course, bows and arrows. To Ingram the latter did not appear to be very dangerous weapons, although he indicates that they were often poisoned. For hand-to-hand encounters Ingram alleges that the Indians carried crude iron broad-swords.

An armed attack against peaceful colonists did not seem, from Ingram's experience, to be likely. He dwells at greater length, and with evident enthusiasm, on the natural paradise that awaited the first-comers to those fortunate shores. The vegetation of tropical and temperate lands are mingled in a benign hotch-potch. Frequently one wonders if Ingram was suitably rewarded by Sir Humphrey Gilbert for the deceptively favourable picture he had painted. The greatest fertility of soil and the greenest grass, he said, was to be found around the River of May; elsewhere the pasture tended to be burnt up in high summer. But even in these parts 'the countrye is good and most delycate havinge greate playnes as large and as fayer in many places as maye be sene, beinge as playne as a boarde'. Evidently Ingram had glimpsed the prairies—the first Englishman to do so—and marvelled at the smooth, level horizons that stretched around him. On these great plains roamed herds of bison, and Ingram (as we shall see) describes these beasts, having, perhaps, observed them at a distance as in Coronado's vivid report, with the sky visible between their legs, 'like smooth-trunked pines whose tops were joined'.

In other parts Ingram describes great forests of trees. Many of the varieties that he mentions—date palms, lignum vitae, guavas, and plantains for example—could only be found in the tropics, and most probably were memories of Caribbean lands. His lengthy description of the many virtues and uses of the palm-tree would have proved of little use to the prospective colonists, who would have searched equally in vain for bananas, the fruit of which Ingram likens to a pudding, and 'which is moste exelent meate Rawe'. Yet had they landed in Virginia they would have found 'the highest and reddest Cedars of the world' and 'the tree that beareth the rine of blacke Sinamon' exactly as Ingram had reported, and as Amadas and Barlow confirmed a few years later.

Had he directed his course further south Gilbert and his party might well have tasted the Indian corn that Ingram describes, and even found the wild grapes that grew, according to his report, 'as bigge as a mans Thombe'. In fact, by landing at Newfoundland, Gilbert can have profited very little from Ingram's advice. Only one plant that Ingram describes did Gilbert actually find when he went ashore at St John's. Here, in a little garden, he was moved by finding that 'Nature it selfe without art . . . confusedly hath brought foorth roses abundantly, wilde, but odoriferous, and to sense very comfortable'.

The temperate lowlands choked with ungrazed grass, and the parklands on the rolling foothills of the Appalachians, were not destined to be settled by Sir Humphrey Gilbert's men. He and most of his company were drowned on their ill-fated venture; and

Ingram had been discredited, when, years later, others came and claimed the glory of discovery for themselves.

Amongst the verifiable facts that Ingram reported about his journey, the wild beasts that he claimed to have seen furnish the most conflicting evidence of authenticity in his narrative. There can be no doubt about his description of bison. So vivid is the picture he draws of these beasts that it would seem incredible that he was repeating a twice-told tale. He refers to them as Buffes, and describes them as 'Beastes as bigge as twoe Oxen in lengthe almost twentye foote havinge longe eares like a bludde hownde, with long heares aboute there eares, there hornes be Crooked like Rames hornes, ther eyes blacke, there heares longe, blacke, roughe and hagged as a Goate'. Likewise there is little reason to doubt his description of various sorts of deer, wild sheep, wolves, foxes, 'Beares boathe blacke and white', hares, rabbits and even 'Uunces', which were presumably lynxes or some other member of the cat tribe. Ingram's passing reference to horses is suspect, but perhaps a forgivable slip of the tongue. During eleven months' walking through the length of America an observant traveller might have seen all these animals, or at least inspected their pelts at some Indian village on the way.

But there are three animals mentioned by Ingram that make even the most tolerant reader pause. The first is, perhaps, the most explicable. It is described as 'a Monstruous Beaste twyse as bigge as a Horse and in every proportyon like unto a Horse bothe in mayne, hoofe, heare, and neighinge, savinge yt was small towards the hinder partes like a Greyhounde: these Beastes have twoe teethe or hornes of a foote longe growinge streight furthe of there nostrelles, they are naturall Enimyes to the horse'. In all respects save one this is a perfect description of a moose, which Ingram may well have seen during the latter part of his travels. As with the bison Ingram is the first Englishman to describe this animal. It is most unlikely that he was passing on someone else's description, and in any case it must have been from a different source, as, to the best of our knowledge, no one European had ever seen both animals before. The snag is the 'twoe teethe or hornes' that emerge from the animal's nose. Possibly there is a confused recollection of the spreading antlers of the bull-moose. Certainly it mars an otherwise impressively accurate description.

The second strange beast is not so easy to identify. According to Ingram it was 'bigger then a Beare. Yt had nether heade nor necke, his eyes and mouthe weare in his brest. this Beaste is verye ouglie to beholde and Cowardlie of kynde, yt bearethe a very fyne skynne like a Ratte, full of sylver heare'. It can only be suggested that Ingram saw a pelt and not the living creature, and failed to realize that it was a sea, and not a land, animal. If this is granted the description corresponds very tolerably with a walrus or a sea-lion. If we assume the former a further interesting point emerges. Ingram's walrus lacks one distinctive feature. Ingram's moose has exactly that one feature too much. 'Twoe teethe or hornes of a foote longe growinge streight furthe of (its) nostrelles' would suit a walrus but scarcely any other animal. Is it possible that in telling or recording the story the tusks were transposed?

Thus far Ingram may be considered to have emerged relatively unscathed as an observer of natural history. He made one statement, however, so outwardly untrue that it has from time to time been taken as evidence that he fabricated his whole story. According to his interlocutors Ingram 'did alsoe see in that Countrye . . . Eliphantes'. It is well known that the elephant is not, and never has been, indigenous in America. Why should Ingram depart from his usual scrupulousness and include elephants in his list, not as hearsay but as observed fact? One solution has been suggested: improbable, yet so exciting that it deserves at least to be recorded.

We know from archaeological evidence that in pre-historical times mammoths roamed freely throughout North America. Their bones have been unearthed in many places, but they were thought to have died out long before man became articulate. From recently-acquired knowledge of the Maya civilization in Southern Mexico we now know that the hairy elephant not only lived on into recorded time, but was used as a draught-beast in Yucatan and Guatemala. No one knows when or why they became extinct. Is it possible that they lingered on, known only to the Indians who hunted them, into the sixteenth century; and that David Ingram stumbled unknowingly upon a living remnant of these ancient beasts?

One man who might not have been surprised by the suggestion is Thomas Jefferson. In 1800, when he was President of the United States, he received a delegation of Indian chiefs from remote and unexplored areas. He questioned them about the game that could be hunted in their territories, and received descriptions of many animals, one of which accurately corresponded to an elephant. Yet how could these unlettered and unimaginative men have invented such a beast?

What Ingram and, three centuries later, the Indian chiefs actually saw will always remain a mystery. As exploration pushes back the boundaries of the unknown many strange beasts are discovered. Even in this century reports of living mammoths have come out of the waste lands of Siberia. If by chance the great-tusked hairy elephant, with which our ancestors did battle, should prove to have survived in some remote corner of the globe, Ingram's story may not appear so fantastic as it does today.

Anything they can do we can do better!

Many of the birds that Ingram saw on his travels are faithfully recorded. In the Caribbean area he observed 'abundunce of Russett Parrettes but very fewe grene', and flamingoes he not only saw but ate. Turkeys, which Ingram in common with many of his contemporaries mistook for guinea-fowl, were often to be found in the Indian settlements, and they also furnished a welcome article of diet. Off the coast and further north we have already heard that colonies of great auks were to be found. Already the sailors who came to the Grand Banks were slaughtering them in thousands, a process that continued without mercy until the breed became extinct.

But Ingram would not be true to style if he did not furnish the earnest investigator of later years with a bird that defies all identification. No living creature corresponds to its size or features. It can only be suggested that in his contacts with Indian tribes Ingram might have heard tell, and seen representations, of the thunder-bird, and mistaken the myth for reality. It was, says Ingram 'a very straunge Birde thrise as bigge as an Eagle, very bewtyfull to behoulde, his feathers are more oryente then a Peacockes feathers, his eyes are as glistringe as any Hawkes eyes, but as great as a mans eyes, his heade and thighe as bigge as a mans heade and thighe. Yt hath a Creste or tufte of feathers of sundrye colloures on the toppe

or a totempole.

of the heade like a lapwinge, hanginge backwardes, his beak and Tallentes in proportyon like unto an Eagle, but very huge and lardge.'

Many of the inducements that persuaded Christian countries to send colonists to heathen lands were material and self-interested; but a prime cause, sincerely believed by Catholics and Protestants alike, was the glory that would ensue from bringing the doctrine of salvation through Christ to those who lacked the Faith. It was, therefore, with scrupulous attention that Walsingham and his committee in London inquired of Ingram concerning the religion practised by the Indian tribes through which he had passed.

Their worship was, he reported, entirely pagan. They honoured the sun, moon and stars, but stood in great awe of a most tangible devil called Collochio. It is not clear whether this familiar spirit, which appeared in the likeness of a black dog or calf, was observed generally or only in one locality. The latter seems likely, and was probably the disguise of a particular medicine-man whom they encountered. Ingram, Twide and Browne had entered the hut of a poor Indian, and in the gloom of the interior found themselves face to face with this singular apparition. Both parties seem to have been equally startled. Browne cried out 'There is the Devil' and blessed himself in the name of the Trinity; but Twide very vehemently declared 'I defy thee and all thy works'. To their gratification Collochio 'shrancke away in a stelinge manner furthe of the doers', and disappeared.

Collochio was also to be found, reports Ingram, at executions and ritual burials. Despite their open sexuality and the multiplicity of their wives, Ingram singled out adultery as an offence for which the Indians required the death of both parties. But in such instances, unlike occasions when death was natural, a living friend was not expected to accompany the dead man on his lonely journey into the other world.

The last question put to Ingram concerning the nature of the Indians was obviously designed to help the future colonists in their initial attempts to make contact with the coastal tribes. He had already explained how barter should be conducted; now he was asked to recollect whatever knowledge he had acquired of Indian

speech. His contribution was sadly inadequate to the most modest
needs. *Grando*, he said, was a word of general salutation. The rest
of his vocabulary consisted of five substantives—King, Lord, Bread,
the Sun, and the Private Parts. A strangely basic speech for so enterprising a traveller.

As an afterthought Ingram added two disjointed statements to
his narrative. One of these concerned the 'Islande called Corrasan'
—presumably Curaçao—where five or six thousand tractable Indians were governed in their labours by a single negro slave. This
assertion, put forth to demonstrate the docile nature of the Indians
once they had been conquered, sounds most unlikely, particularly
when Ingram adds that there was often no Christian within one or
two hundred miles—a situation that certainly did not apply on
Curaçao.

The second avouchment is even more curious, and would seem
to have been drawn from him by leading questions. It concerns the
latter part of Ingram's journey. Travelling northward he claimed
to have 'founde the mayne Sea uppon the northe syde of Ameryca,
and travayled in the sighte therof the space of twoe whole dayes,
where the people signifyed unto him that they had seene Shippes
on that Coaste'. Ingram goes on to say that the inhabitants had
drawn unmistakable pictures of sailing ships upon the sand, and
that this fact, corresponding to Coronado's experience in seeing a
Chinese ship off the north-west coast of America, was indubitable
proof of the existence of the straits of Anian and the long-sought
north-west passage.

With our present geographical knowledge it seems incredible
that during the first two centuries of American exploration the
continent was assumed to accommodate a navigable waterway linking the Atlantic with the Pacific Oceans. Despite the failure of one
expedition after another, faith in the existence of such a desirable
short cut to the riches of the east persisted. The straits were named
before they were discovered, and many men no less intelligent
than Sir Humphrey Gilbert eagerly used hearsay as arguments of
established fact. If we are inclined to believe Ingram we shall
assume that his wanderings took him along the banks of the St
Lawrence, or even to one of the Great Lakes. The interpretation

drawn from his report belongs to the committee who questioned him, some of whom were enthusiasts and wanted to hear confirmed that which they already believed in their hearts.

While Ingram and his two companions were making their way through these northerly regions they must have felt a coolness in the night air, and been aware that the onslaught of winter was not far off. How they proposed to live through those bitter months Ingram does not disclose. The Indians who had proved so hospitable to passing travellers might have been less kindly disposed towards three winter-bound, helpless white men who lacked all necessary means of survival.

Fortunately Ingram's party were not put to this extreme test. Word reached them, through their Indian friends, that other white men had landed on the coast nearby and were endeavouring to conduct trade. Without delay Ingram, Twide and Browne set off to find them. They saw the *Gargarine* lying off-shore, and several of her boats were beached close to the river's mouth. The Englishmen quickly made themselves known to the captain, who promised to give them passage back to France. They could offer no money for their fare, but as some return Ingram offered to help the Frenchman with his traffic ashore. So, with M. Champaine and several of his ship's company, Ingram returned to the village of Baryniathe, twenty miles inland, where he was able to persuade the Indians to barter many fine furs, a quantity of silver ore, and some red leaves that were thought to be useful as dye-stuffs, in return for various trifles of manufactured ware.

Of the return voyage Ingram has nothing to report, but before the winter was past the three Englishmen had come safely to Le Havre, and taken passage across the Channel to their homeland. Apart from his brief appearance at Sir Francis Walsingham's committee of investigation, Ingram was never heard of again.

Until greater knowledge of the terrain—or of the man—was acquired, Ingram's narrative seems to have been accepted as a truthful account. In particular, Sir George Peckham's persuasive discourse on planting, quotes Ingram frequently and with approval. Hakluyt, in 1589, considered a transcript of Ingram's evidence valuable enough to reproduce in his own book.

But something seems to have occurred within the next decade that caused Hakluyt to omit Ingram's narrative from the revised edition of 1599. It is impossible to estimate how damaging the evidence against him was. Perhaps the death of Hawkins in 1595 brought to light from amongst his private papers some record of Ingram's unreliability, or perhaps a general sense of uneasiness led Hakluyt to make the excision. But this is all speculation.

Those who came afterwards drew their own conclusions. Samuel Purchas in 1625, referring to 'some incredibilities of (Ingram's) reports', set the tone that has prevailed ever since. He may have been right, though he does not substantiate the moral judgment with which he dismisses the entire narrative. Undoubtedly, as Purchas says, the reward of lying is, not to be believed in truths; yet to the curious historian there seems to be sufficient basis of veracity to make some effort at disentanglement worth while. The skeins will always be somewhat enmeshed, but they do not seem to be confused by deliberate untruths. Over-willingness to please, a capricious memory for past experiences, and an incomplete comprehension of events are equally damaging to truth, and of these failings Ingram is abundantly guilty. Had he been lying he would surely have made up a more breath-taking and logical story; and there was no need for him to acquire such a mass of detailed information about the North American Continent: more, probably, than any other one Englishman at that time possessed.

Another prime culprit in the obfuscation of Ingram's tale was the committee that interrogated him. They wanted facts for colonists: they did not attempt to obtain an orderly or consecutive narrative. Ingram answered their specific questions, so the gaps he left were not necessarily of his own choosing. Confusions of time and place are more a sign of unmethodical interlocutors than of wilful obscurity on the part of the narrator. At times too there is a strong impression that the committee persisted with certain points until Ingram's replies could be said to justify their own preconceptions.

It is an irritating and inconclusive ending, but one that Hawkins might have regarded as a curiously appropriate grace-note to an adventure that had failed. The relation of David Ingram's wanderings was the last, frayed thread in a rope of circumstance that had bound 400 men and boys together in Plymouth harbour one October morning, touched three continents, passed over countless miles of ocean in calm and storm, and returned, shorn of grandeur, to its starting place.

For the most part it had been an orderly undertaking, as Hawkins would have wished it to be, for he was himself an orderly man. But when his grasp was loosened, and the enterprise he had controlled disintegrated, the history of a great fleet dwindled into microcosms.

To a chronicler of the voyage it is no less relevant to trace the fate of particular seamen than it has been to establish the actions of a fleet that, while it existed, protected their anonymity. The raw material of all history is the experience of the individual. The fabric of armies, fleets or nations comprises an interwoven pattern of human action. From all these individual strands a corporate will may emerge—strong, yet synthetic; dominant, but coloured by its parts. The task of a biographer is to balance the history of events against the history of individuals.

But all too often the corrosion of time intervenes. It does not need 400 years to find evidence engulfed and truth blurred. The farther we stretch back into the past the more significant become the casualties. Soon the history of individuals becomes so precious that we cherish fragments, and bulk out the surviving legends or artefacts with our imagination. The bare bones of events last longer, although they too have their span.

The story of John Hawkins' third slaving voyage seems to have been preserved by marvellous good fortune with a wealth of detail and well-founded fact. But, at the close, it is salutary to be reminded by the travels of David Ingram that much remains unsaid. The sea does not hold for long the wake of passing ships.

SELECT BIBLIOGRAPHY

The Africa Pilot, Part I (10th ed., London, 1942).

Allison, R. S., *Sea Diseases* (London, 1943).

Arber, E. (ed.), *An English Garner*, Vol. 3 (*Voyages and Travels, Vol. 1*) (London, 1903).

Blake, J. W., *European Beginnings in West Africa 1454-1578* (London, 1937).

Brebner, J. B., *The Explorers of North America 1492-1806* (London, 1933).

Burns, Sir Alan, *History of the British West Indies* (London, 1954).

Conway, G. R. G. (ed.), *An Englishman and the Mexican Inquisition 1556-1560* (Mexico, 1927).

Conway, G. R. G. (ed.), *The Rare Travailes of Job Hortop, Being a Facsimile Reprint of the First Edition* (Mexico, 1928).

Corbett, Sir J. S., *Drake and the Tudor Navy* (2 Vols., London, 1898-9).

Hakluyt, R., *The Principal Navigations, Voyages, Traffiques and Discoveries of the English Nation* (8 Vols., London, 1927). Vol. 6 contains Philips' and Hortop's Narratives: Vol. 7 contains Hawkins' Narrative.

Jewitt, L., *A History of Plymouth* (London and Plymouth, 1873).

Lea, H. C., *The Inquisition in the Spanish Dependencies* (New York, 1908).

The Mariner's Mirror, Vol. 22, pp. 324-45, Professor Michael Lewis, 'The Guns of the *Jesus of Lubeck*' (Cambridge, July 1936).

The Mariner's Mirror, Vol. 23, pp. 295-315, Professor Michael Lewis, 'Fresh Light on San Juan de Ulua' (Cambridge, July 1937).

Markham, C. R. (ed.), *The Hawkins' Voyages* (London, The Hakluyt Society, 1878).

Masefield, J., *On the Spanish Main* (London, 1906).

Nuttall, Z., (ed), *New Light on Drake* (London, The Hakluyt Society, 1914).

313

Prescott, W. H., *History of the Conquest of Mexico* (Ed. J. F. Kirk, London, 1886).

Wendt, H., *I Looked for Adam* (London, 1955), pp. 539-47.

The West Indies Pilot, Vol. I (10th ed., London, 1941).

The West Indies Pilot, Vol. II (9th ed., London, 1946).

Weston, P. C. J. (ed.), *Documents Connected with the History of South Carolina* (London, 1856). Contains Ingram's Narrative.

Williamson, J. A., *Hawkins of Plymouth* (London, 1949).

Williamson, J. A., *Sir John Hawkins: The Times and the Man* (Oxford, 1927).

Wright, I. A., *Spanish Documents Concerning English Voyages to the Caribbean 1527-1568* (London, The Hakluyt Society, 1929).

Unpublished transcripts and translations of Inquisition and other documents relating to Hawkins' crew are contained in the *Conway Papers* held at the University Library, Cambridge, *Mss Add* 7229-66.

INDEX

Acapulco, 278–80
Alas, Martin de las, 158–60
Alexander VI, Pope, 18
Alva, Duke of, 33
Amecameca, 281
Anahuac, Valley of, *see* Mexico City
Angel, The, 25, 60–1, 69, 73–4, 82, 84–6, 92–3, 96, 138, 140, 204, 215
Anian, Straits of, 309
Arawaks, 121
Armada, The Great, 229, 261
Asuncion, La, *see* Margarita
Auto de Fe, 258–9, 268–74, 276–7; *see also* Inquisition
Azores, 28, 38, 44, 161, 228, 255, 288

Baeshe, Edward, 23
Baker, Thomas, 240
Barbary Coast, 42, 71–5
Barrett, Robert, 26, 50–1; on African coast, 83, 85–90, 97–100; in W. Indies, 125, 134–6, 145, 149; at San Juan de Ulua, 175–6, 191–3, 198; in captivity, 217, 240, 248–9, 251, 253–60
Bastidas, Rodrigo de, 154
Bernaldez, Alonzo, 128
Bijouga Islands, 83, 90, 92, 94
Bland, Captain, 79, 161, 207, 272
Bolton, Thomas, 24
Bonilla, The Licentiate, 272
Bontemps, Captain, 140
Borburata, 128–38, 142
Boronel, Edward, 224
Bourgogne, Alphonse de, *see* Wachen
Browne, Richard, 293, 295, 308, 310
Bustamante, Francisco de, 173, 177, 179, 189, 198

Cacheo, 84–8; C. River, 84–90, 95
Caldeira, Gaspar, *see* Homem
Calousa River, 92–3, 96
Campeche, 167–8, 176
Canary Islands, 38, 42, 54, 60–1
Cape Blanco, 70, 73–5, 80
Cape Breton, 293, 297
Cape Canaveral, 254, 256
Cape de la Vela, 141
Cape Palmas, 42–3, 94
Cape Roxo, 81–3
Cape San Antonio, 162
Cape Verde, 76, 78–9, 83; C.V. Islands, 18, 38, 42
Carabajal, Luis de, 237–8
Caracas, 131
Caribs, 121–3
Cartagena, 156–60
Castellanos, Miguel de, 129, 138–49, 151–2
Castros, King of, 96–101, 105, 107–8
Cateau-Cambresis, Treaty of, 161
Catwater, The, 24, 28, 44
Cecil, Sir William, 19, 21, 23, 33–6, 39, 46, 227, 252
Chamberlain, John, 193
Champaine, M., 293, 310
Chaymas, 123
Chichimecas, 232–5, 240, 293
Cibola, 37, 230, 295–7
Coche, 123
Collier, James, 234
Collins, William, 249, 260, 265, 268, 275
Columbus, Christopher, 119
Conga, 97–100, 102, 104, 108
Contreras, Moya de, 264–5, 268, 271–2
Cornish, John, 232

Cornu, Marin, 273
Coro, Santa Ana de, 130-1, 136-8
Coronado, Francisco Vasquez de, 297, 299, 304, 309
Corte, Robles Alcalde de, 279-80
Cortes, Hernando, 170, 244
Cuautitlan, 241
Cuba, 153, 161-3, 264
Cubagua, 123
Curaçao, 136-8, 140, 219, 309

Delgadillo, Antonio, 172, 175-6, 178-83, 185, 198, 202, 214-15, 269, 273
Dominica, 118-22
Drake, Francis, 25-7, 45, 80, 87, 138, 140-1, 203, 207, 212, 226-7, 229, 259, 261, 268, 278-80
Ducket, Sir Lionel, 20
Dudley, Edward, 27, 63-8, 76-8, 83, 87-8, 114, 118

Ebren, Thomas, 277
Elizabeth, Queen, 17, 19, 21-3, 26, 33-6, 39-40, 62, 67, 130, 246, 253, 275
Elmina, 28, 37-8, 43, 94
Enriquez, Martin, 172, 177-86, 189-92, 197-8, 200-1, 212, 214-17, 245-8, 250, 263-5, 271, 278-80
Escalant, Roldan, 272

Farenton, John, 249
Fenner, George, 40, 43-4
Feria, Duke of, 252
Fitzwilliam, George, 23, 34-6, 53, 63-4, 183, 246, 251-3
Flores de Valdes, Diego, 254-6
Florida, 163-5, 233, 302; F. Channel, 153, 162, 164, 222, 227, 254

Galveston Bay, 295, 297
Gambia, The, 79
Garrard, Sir William, 20

Garret, John, 28
Gilbert, Sir Humphrey, 294, 297, 303-4, 309
Gilbert, John, 259
Goddard, Anthony, 220-1, 231-8, 245-6, 251, 253, 293
Gold Coast, 28, 43
Golfo de Triste, 137
Gomera, 54, 69
Gonson, Benjamin, 20
Grace of God, The, 79-80, 87, 161, 204, 206-7, 215, 219, 221, 233
Guadaloupe, 241-2
Guadalquivir, River, 153, 251, 257
Guaiquerias, 123
Guatamala, 276, 280, 286-7, 306
Guinea, Coast of, 18-19, 21, 23, 26-7, 37-8, 43, 93, 108, 119, 259
Guzman, Pedro de, 289

Hampton, John, 28, 207, 220-1
Havana, 254, 288
Hawkins, John, plans voyage, 17, 20-8, 38, 41-5; at Plymouth, 29-36, 46-8; departs, 49-51; at sea, 53-60, 111-15; at Canary Is., 61-9; off African coast, 73-83, 89-92, 94-7, 100-1, 103-9; at Dominica, 122; at Borburata, 130-4, 136-8; at Margarita, 124-9; at Rio de la Hacha, 139-52; at Santa Marta, 153-6; at Cartagena, 157-61; in Gulf of Mexico, 163-9; at San Juan de Ulua, 171, 174-7, 179-80, 183, 186-7, 189, 191-3; during battle, 194-7, 203-10; sails home, 217-27; tries to free prisoners, 229-30, 252-3, 259; experiences from pervious voyages, 40, 44-6, 117, 123, 233; mentioned, 9-12, 261, 291, 294, 311-12
Hawkins, Katherine, 48
Hawkins, Paul, 210, 265, 272, 277-9
Hawkins, Richard, 48

Hawkins, William (junior), 10, 22, 24, 48, 227
Hawkins, William (senior), 38, 94
Holy Office, *see* Inquisition
Homem, André, 17–20, 22, 28, 34, 237
Hooper, John, 234
Hortop, Job, 86, 91, 135, 156, 168, 240, 245–6, 249, 254–62, 291

Ilcombe, John, 31
Ingram, David, 11, 234, 293–312
Inquisition, The, 257–8, 260, 263–8, 275–9; *see also* Auto de fe

Jalapa, 184, 217
Jalofs, 76
Jefferson, Thomas, 307
Jesus of Lubeck, The, 17, 21–8, 35; at Plymouth, 29–31, 44; sails, 49, 51; at sea, 53–61, 110–11, 114, 116–17; at Canary Is., 65, 68–9; off African coast, 71, 74, 79, 81, 92; in W. Indies, 127, 129, 136–8, 149–50, 155, 160–1, 163–4, 167–8; at San Juan de Ulua, 174–7, 179, 183, 185, 187, 192–3, 195–7, 199, 203–7, 209–11, 213–15; mentioned, 219, 245, 260
Judith, The, 25, 61, 69, 73–4, 82, 87, 92, 96, 138, 140, 203, 206–7, 209, 211–12, 227–8

Laudonnière, Renè de, 233, 302
Lee, John, 248
Letters of Marque, 39, 73, 79
Lok, Michael, 40, 299
Los Islands, 95
Lovell, John, 25, 40, 128, 138, 140–1
Lowe, William, 272, 277
Luis, Antonio, 17–20, 22, 28, 34, 237
Luxan, Francisco de, 177–81, 190, 197, 199, 202, 213–14, 246

Madeira, 19, 61
Magdalena, River, 157
Maldonado, Francisco, 167–8, 176
Marcana, Martin de, 173, 176
Marcos, Friar, 297
Margarita, 123–7, 129, 139, 156
Martin, John, 248, 276
Mary Stuart, Queen of Scots, 253
Mary Tudor, Queen, 38, 40, 252
May, River of, 233, 293, 302, 304
Mendoza, Juan de, 227–8
Metztitlan, 240
Mexico City, 176, 217, 238, 241–9, 263–78, 282–3
Minion, The, 22, 24–5, 27–8; at Plymouth, 30, 44; at sea, 55, 111; in W. Indies, 136, 138, 150, 159, 168; at San Juan de Ulua, 174, 176, 185, 187, 191, 193–7, 199, 204, 206–7, 209–11; sails home, 213, 217–29
Mississippi, River, 299, 302
Monluc, Peyrot de, 19
Montezuma, 170, 242, 244

Orango Channel, 92
Orlando, William de, 246
Orizaba, 172, 178, 203

Pachuca, 241, 249
Panuco, River, 220, 223, 231, 233, 235–7, 293
Peckham, Sir George, 294, 297, 310
Perrin, John, 277
Philip II, King, 19, 32, 125, 127–8, 130, 144–5, 149, 250, 252–3, 284
Philips, Miles, 240, 245, 247–8, 265–7, 272–3, 275–92
Piracy, 38–41, 124, 126, 133, 139, 152, 161; *see also* Privateering
Planes, Captain, *see* Bland
Plymouth, 22, 24, 29, 33–4, 42, 45, 47, 50, 53, 227, 253, 280; P. Sound, 32, 46, 50; P. Hoe, 30, 49

Ponce de Leon, Diego, 130–3, 136
Ponte, Pedro and Nicolas de, 62
Pontevedra, 224–5
Portugal, Overseas territories of, 37–
40, 42–4, 94; see also Barbary Coast,
Gold Coast, Guinea, Senegal
Privateering, 19, 38–40, 43, 79–80;
see also Letters of Marque
Puerta de Santa Maria, 291
Puerto Cabello (Honduras), 288
Puerto Cabello (Venezuela), 130

Quivira, 296, 299

Raunce, James, 24–5
Ribero, Miguel, 26
Ridolfi Plot, 252–3
Rio de la Hacha, 128, 138–47, 149,
151–3
Rively, George, 249, 267–8, 273–4
Ruiz de Vallejo, Diego, 133–4

Sacina, King, 97, 101, 106
St Nicholas' Island, 29–30, 50
San Domingo, River, see Cacheo River
San Juan de Ulua, battle at, 11, 194–
211, 228–9, 236; port of, 33, 167–
93, 212–16, 218, 223, 226, 264,
281
San Lucar, 256–7, 261, 289–90
Santa Cruz, see Tenerife
Santa Marta, 153–6
Santo Domingo, 153, 168
Sao Thomé, 38
Sao Jorge da Mina, see Elmina
Sapies, 95
Senegal, Coast of, 18, 37–8, 42–3;
River, 42, 75–6
Sestos, River, 42
Setecama, King, 97, 101, 106
Seville, 128, 230, 246, 249, 251–3,
255–60, 289–90
Sheri Bangi, 102, 108
Sheri, King, see Sierra Leone, King of

Ships (mentioned in text); Castle of
Comfort, 43–4; Dudley, 261; Eliza-
beth, 295; Gargarine, 293, 301, 310;
Golden Hind, 280; John Baptist, 28;
Landret, 291; Merlin, 27; Paul, 38;
Primrose, 117; see also Jesus of Lubeck,
Minion, Judith, William and John,
Swallow, Angel, Grace of God
Sierra Leone, 42, 91–2, 94–7; King
of, 96–102, 105, 107–8
Silva, Guzman de, 23, 32–3
Slave trade, 18, 21, 23, 36–8, 42–3,
94–5, 127–8, 130–4, 141–56
Soria, Hernando de, 261
Soto, Hernando de, 299–300
Sumbas, 38
Sussex, Earl of, 261–2
Swallow, The, 25, 48, 55, 87, 196,
214–15
Sweeting, Robert, 247, 266

Tagarrin, see Sierra Leone
Tampico, San Luis de, 233–4, 236–8
Tecoantepec, 216
Tenerife, 54, 60–2, 68–9
Texcoco, 246–9, 266
Texeda, Antonio, see Goddard
Tillert, Morgan, 268
Tipton, Hugh, 251–2, 257
Turren, Jean, 31
Twide, Richard, 293, 295, 308, 310

Ubilla, Juan de, 178, 181–2, 190,
193, 197, 199–201, 213–16

Vaca, Alvar Nunez Cabeza de, 295–6
Valencia, 130–1, 134–6; Bishop of,
132–3, 136, 138
Velasco de Varre, Juan de, 253–6
Vera Cruz, 170–1, 173, 183–4, 186,
215–16, 275, 281–3
Vigo, 226
Villanueva, Agustin de, 168, 177,
192–3, 213–14

Wachen, Baron de, 29–34

Walsingham, Sir Francis, 294–5, 308, 310

William and John, The, 24, 89, 164, 227–8

Williams, Richard, 267, 272, 277

Windward Islands, 119

Winter, William, 20, 22, 40

Yebra, Pedro de, 184, 198

Yhoma, King, *see* Castros, King of

Yucatan, 166, 273, 306; Y. Channel, 162

Zambulo, King, 92, 94

Zegri, Luis, 184, 189, 197

GEORGE ALLEN & UNWIN LTD
London: 40 Museum Steeet, W.C.1

Auckland: 24 Wyndham Street
Bombay: 15 Graham Road, Ballard Estate, Bombay 1
Calcutta: 17 Chittaranjan Avenue, Calcutta 13
Cape Town: 109 Long Street
Karachi: Metherson's Estate, Wood Street, Karachi 2
Mexico: Villalongin 32-10, Piso Mexico 5, D.F.
New Delhi: 13-14 Ajmeri Gate Extension, New Delhi 1
Sao Paulo: Avenida 9 de Julho 1138-Ap. 51
Singapore, South East Asia and the Far East: 36c Pinsep Street
Sydney N.S.W.: Bradbury House, 55 York Street
Toronto: 91 Wellington Street West

A table of those who returned home,
& who were captured.   400
                    Total.   10
        the ten hostages
    prisoners on the Island & from the "Jesus"²¹ 83
    those who went ashore voluntarily
                        (philips)   11 q
                        (Hortop)   96.
                                        c. 145

killed   by   Indians   3
                Northern party   10?
                Souther   "   1
                N. party who retd.

    the   northern party who contd.   25-30
                retd home   3
arrived   at   Mexico   64?

retod t

put to death by Inquisition   3
    sent back to Spain   28
    died soon afterward   1

    retd home   1 philips